SONG OF SOLOMON

PASSION, PURITY, AND THE GLORY OF CHRIST

The Proclaim Commentary Series

THE PROCLAIM COMMENTARY SERIES

SONG OF SOLOMON

PASSION, PURITY, AND THE GLORY OF CHRIST

OLD TESTAMENT
VOLUME 22

MATTHEW STEVEN BLACK

PROCLAIM
PUBLISHERS

WENATCHEE, WASHINGTON

Song of Solomon: Passion, Purity, and the Glory of Christ
(The Proclaim Commentary Series)
Copyright © 2018 by Matthew Black
ISBN: 978-1-954858-12-1 (Print Book)
        978-1-954858-13-8 (eBook)

Proclaim Publications
PO Box 2082 Wenatchee, WA 98807
proclaimpublishers.com

Cover art: *My Beloved Has Gone Down to His Garden*
by John Melhuish Strudwick (1888)

Notes: (1) Ancient quotations have been at times changed to the ESV as well as some archaic language updated, and additional phrases added for clarification. At times verse references (non-existent until recent times) have been interspersed as well to guide the modern reader. (2) We have done our best to be careful in footnoting. Due to the nature of the sermonic material, various items are quoted freely, and may not have proper footnoting. If any great error is noticed, please contact the publisher, and it will be remedied in whatever way is available to us.

First Printing, January 2018
Manufactured in the United States of America

Dedicated to my sweet wife, Jill Marie. I will forever thank the Lord for joining our paths together. What a joy to be fulfilling this mystery of marriage together. To Jesus be all the glory!

CONTENTS

INTRODUCTION

The Song of Songs, which is Solomon's.
SONG 1:1

The study of the Song of Solomon is enriching for any child of God. Like any portion of Scripture, we must not interpret it through our modern context. In order to understand this particular book of the Bible, we must consider a very popular way of communicating in the ancient world: the love poem.

THE GENRE

God more often speaks to us through narrative in the sixty-six books of the Bible than through propositional truth. While poetry in the Bible is common, the love poem genre is quite sparse in holy Scripture. Because of the nature of this genre, it draws us in. Who doesn't like a love story? This love story has many plot turns with fascinating character development. Our journey begins in the Old Testament book of the Song of Solomon. This is a love song that was sung by the ancient Hebrews. We are told that we are to sing "psalms, and hymns and spiritual songs" (Eph 5:19; *cf* Col 3:16). Solomon's love poem would be a "spiritual song." More precisely, the Song of Solomon is a messianic love poem that points us to Someone greater than Solomon: the true King of all kings, David's greater Son, the Lord Jesus Christ.[1]

THE AUTHOR

Many references to Solomon throughout the book confirm the claim of 1:1 that Solomon wrote this book (*cf* 1:4-5, 12; 3:7, 9, 11; 6:12;

---

[1] James M. Hamilton, Jr. "The Messianic Music of the Song of Songs: A Non-Allegorical Interpretation" Westminster Theological Journal, Vol 68 (2006), 331-45.

7:5; 8:11-12; 1 Kgs 4:33). There is considerable similarity between vocabulary and syntax between Song of Songs and Ecclesiastes which was also by Solomon. The book speaks of royal luxury and abundance which Solomon would have enjoyed (1:12, 13; 3:6, 9) as well as imported goods such as cosmetic powders, silver, gold, purple, ivory, and beryl, his expensive carriage (3:7-10), his royal chariots (6:12). The geographical references favor a date prior to 930 B.C.

Archer writes, "The author mentions quite indiscriminately localities to be found in both the Northern and Southern Kingdoms: Engedi, Hermon, Carmel, Lebanon, Heshbon, and Jerusalem. These are spoken of as if they all belonged to the same political realm. Note that Tirzah is mentioned as a city of particular glory and beauty, and that too in the same breath with Jerusalem itself (6:4). If this had been written after the time when Tirzah was chosen as the earliest capital of the Northern Kingdom in rejection of the authority of the dynasty of David, it is scarcely conceivable that it would have been referred to in such favorable terms. On the other hand, it is highly significant that Samaria, the city founded by Omri sometime between 885 and 874, is never mentioned in the Song of Solomon."[2] Judging from internal evidence, then, the author was totally unaware of any division of the Hebrew monarchy into North and South.

Solomon reigned between 971 and 931 B.C. How could Solomon, who had 700 wives and 300 concubines (1 Kgs 11:3), be the same faithful lover this book presents? He could be if he became polygamous after the events in this book took place. That seems a more likely explanation than that he was polygamous when these events occurred but just omitted reference to his other loves. Solomon likely wrote the book before he became polygamous. We do not know how old Solomon was when he married the second time. Deer writes, "Some wonder how Solomon could be the author of a book that extols faithfulness in marriage when he was so unfaithful, having 700 wives and 300 concubines (1 Kings 11:3). Perhaps the answer is that the 'beloved' in the Song whom he married was his first wife. If so, then the book may have been written

---

[2] Gleason L. Archer, Jr. *A Survey of Old Testament Introduction* (Chicago: Moody Publishers, 2007), 499.

soon after his marriage, before he fell into the sin of polygamy."[3] The history recorded in Kings and Chronicles is not in strict chronological order. The Shulamite farm girl who lived among the tribe of Dan was obviously not Pharaoh's daughter in view of references in the book (1 Kgs 3:1; cf Song 4:8). There does seem to be Scriptural evidence that King Solomon was married to a girl from the tribe of Dan before he began the pagan tradition of political marriages.[4] It seems that this is the context of this love poem.

WHY STUDY THE SONG OF SONGS?

There are many reasons that the child of God should study the Song of Songs. First, this love poem, interpreted rightly, both historically and typologically is an amazing guide for those entering marriage as to how to honor God in the marriage covenant especially in light of the relationship of Christ and the Church that marriage represents. This love poem points us to the messianic King who pursues and rescues his worn, weary and downtrodden bride. Solomon is seemingly infinitely rich. his bride is destitute and poor. The messianic imagery of David's son is unmistakable. Images of the garden paradise restored are joyously presented in prose and poetry (cf 4:12, 15, 16; 5:1; 6:2, 11; 8:13). The messianic hope of Jesus is the primary reason to study this God-breathed poem. If any secondary reasons (i.e., success in courtship and marriage, a healthy and godly view of sex, proper roles in marriage) are elevated above the prime reason, the book quickly is stripped of its majesty with a message that is trite, earthly, and temporal. If the book is read correctly with redemptive lenses on, only then in its proper context in Israel's messianic hope can the message of the Song be timeless and transformative.

Second, though success in marriage is not the primary message of this book, the Song celebrates marital intimacy enjoyed as God's good gift, designed by him. What is unique about this love poem is the discretion and modesty that envelopes the language of the sacred love relationship in marriage. The Song of Songs elevates physical love with

---

[3] Jack S Deere, *Song of Songs*. In *The Bible Knowledge Commentary: An Exposition of the Scriptures*, Vol 1, John F. Walvoord, Roy B. Zuck, eds. (Wheaton, IL: Victor Books, 1985), 1010.

[4] For a more in-depth study of the Shulamite farm girl and who she is in Scripture, read chapter one's examination of the characters of the Song of Solomon.

dynamics of care and tenderness, associated with the depths of transparency, intensity, and delight between husband and wife. When read,
one quickly recognizes the God-designed, benevolent, and powerful in-
strument of sexual intimacy within marriage. This explains Hebrews
13:4, which declares the marriage bed (sexual relations in marriage) is
to be held sacred and honored by all. And yet, there is a mystery and
metaphor to the language of this divine love poem. The aim is not to
sully the sacred Scriptures with unlawful or ungodly images in our
minds. Instead, this God-breathed message is a powerful word from
God to his people to delight in his institution of marriage and guard its
sanctity through purity and holiness both within and outside of marriage.

Third, the Song of Songs is countercultural. Though the main message of the Song is messianic, its underlying structure as a marital love
poem powerfully promotes the purity of marital love and relations as
something to be enjoyed and guarded strictly within the institution of
marriage as defined by God. Marriage then is covenantal, monogamous, and heterosexual. Any other definition of marriage will destroy
a society. This is particularly relevant in the present day, when society
is attempting to redefine marriage, sexuality and even gender identity.
Again, this is not in any way a primary focus of the Song but the assumed presupposition and culture of ancient Israel.

Fourth, it attacks today's resurgence of neo-paganism, which declares the spiritual as good and the physical as evil. When God made
man - male and female - and the marriage covenant, he declared that
both the spiritual and physical are "good." The fall brought death to
both. Therefore, redemption renews both. We are not only born again
spiritually, but we are also renewed so that our bodies become "temples
of the Holy Spirit" anticipating the new body, the new heavens and new
earth. This includes God's good gift of sexual intimacy within marriage
as renewed and by grace properly enjoyed. Any other use of sexuality is
idolatry and is destructive.

Finally, and perhaps surprisingly, the Song of Solomon is a proper
instructor for those preparing for marriage. The first half of this love
poem is directed toward single people and how the ancient Israelites
approached courtship, betrothal, and marriage. If approached carefully, the Song of Solomon can be utilized as a guide for young people
to guard their purity and not to "stir up love before its time" (2:7; 3:5;

8:4). Again, without the New Testament instruction that marriage is a type – a "mystery" that illustrates Christ's love for the church, then the reading of the Song of Solomon would be reduced to that of a self-help book for marriage. This poem is anything but that. It is a messianic revelation through marriage of Christ's love for his bride.

METHOD OF INTERPRETATION

While one must refrain from allegorizing the text in order to promote spiritual meaning, it is valid to see how Christ is being presented in biblical typology. Ephesians 5, while defining the marriage relationship between man and woman, also declares that the marriage covenant is a proper way to understand the relationship between Christ and his Bride, the church. The beloved Puritan John Flavel describes the Song of Solomon as, "A crystal stream of pure spiritual love, gliding sweetly between two pleasant banks – Christ and the Church."[5] While allegory abuses Scripture by introducing what is not there, typology rightly uses pictures, illustrations, and dramas revealed to us by God in order to point us to Christ. For example, Jesus is our divine Israel, and as Hosea says God called Israel out of Egypt in the crossing of the Red Sea, so Matthew tells us that Jesus is God's ultimate promised Son, Israel, who is also called out of Egypt when fleeing from Herod (Hos 11:1; Mt 2:15). The messianic types in Scripture point us to our Savior Jesus Christ. It is then entirely proper to exalt the Lord Jesus Christ in this romantic love poem which points to the ultimate love story between Christ and his Bride, the Church. R.C. Sproul helps bring clarity to the difference between allegory and typology.

> Paul describes his interpretive work in Galatians 4:21–31 with the same Greek word from which we get the English term allegory (v. 24), but he does not embrace fanciful allegories. Instead, he uses typological interpretation, which, John Calvin writes, is consistent with "the true and literal meaning" of the original text. Typology is based on the fact that God works in recurring patterns throughout history and says that a past event or person can prefigure or serve as a type of a future person or event. In the antitype, a future person or event more fully expresses the truth of what came before. For example, consider the relation of

---

[5] John Flavel. *The Whole Works of Mr. John Flavel*, Vol 1 (Glasgow: John Orr, 1754), 205.

the exodus to the work of Jesus. God's rescue of His people from Egyptian bondage typifies the greater salvation from slavery to sin and death He accomplished in Christ. The latter work is consistent with the meaning of the first — in both instances the Almighty Himself rescues a helpless people. But His work also has a fuller meaning, for while people can return to physical slavery, he whom the Son sets free is free indeed, never to be enslaved to evil again (Jn 8:36).[6]

John Calvin comments: "The true meaning of Scripture is the natural and obvious meaning; and let us embrace and abide by it resolutely. Let us not only neglect as doubtful, but boldly set aside as deadly corruptions, those pretended expositions, which lead us astray from the natural meaning."[7]

A typological interpretation of the Song of Solomon is appropriate because of the genre of the poem. Poetry lends itself to typology and not literalism. The nature of this particular poem points back to Eden and what was lost when Adam and Eve plunged the human race into sin. The way Eve named her sons reveals she was waiting for the messianic promise of Genesis 3:15 (the woman's seed would crush the serpent's head) to be fulfilled immediately. She is waiting for Paradise to be restored. Here in the Song of Solomon, you have the ideal messianic figure restoring Edenic qualities using the relationship of marriage. As James Hamilton so beautifully put it, "the Song of Songs is in the canon because it was written from a messianic perspective in order to nourish a messianic hope. This messianic hope is rooted in the soil of the promise that the seed of the woman will crush the head of the seed of the serpent, watered by the expectation of a king from the seed of Abraham via Judah, and fertilized by anticipations of an eschatological return to the Garden of Eden."[8] In the person of Solomon, we have the messianic hope of Israel rescuing a powerless farm girl. Though some would leave the interpretation of this love poem there, I believe it is proper to apply

---

[6] R.C. Sproul. "Typology Verses Allegory." *Daily Devotional*, Ligonier Ministries, 12 October 2017, http://www.ligonier.org/learn/devotionals/typology-versus-allegory/

[7] John Calvin. *Commentary on the Epistles of Paul to the Galatians and Ephesians* (Edinburgh: Calvin Translation Society, 1854), 136

[8] James Hamilton, "The Messianic Music of the Song of Songs" (WTJ), 333. (Note: Hamilton does not agree with the typological interpretation of Song of Songs. Yet I believe his conclusions lead to a typological view.)

the New Testament's indication that marriage is a type (Eph 5:32) and to climb the heights of how marriage points us to a higher and eternal love story: the marriage between Christ and his church. We should interpret this poem in light of the ultimate type that we find in John's Apocalypse.

> Then I heard what seemed to be the voice of a great multitude, like the roar of many waters and like the sound of mighty peals of thunder, crying out, "Hallelujah! For the Lord our God the Almighty reigns. Let us rejoice and exult and give him the glory, for the marriage of the Lamb has come, and his Bride has made herself ready; it was granted her to clothe herself with fine linen, bright and pure"—for the fine linen is the righteous deeds of the saints. And the angel said to me, "Write this: Blessed are those who are invited to the marriage supper of the Lamb." And he said to me, "These are the true words of God." —Revelation 19:6-9

SOURCES

This commentary is devotional and practical in nature. I have purposely drawn from the most beloved commentaries and sermons of the Song of Songs from throughout church history. My goal is not primarily to be critical in approach to the text, but to stir up the affections of the Christian with the text of Solomon's Song. Several of the earliest sources, including fathers of the church and even some of the Reformers, have taken an allegorical view. Though I do quote from them, I have tried to mine the portions of their commentaries which were more typological than allegorical.

A WARNING

A word should be said about the modern manner of interpreting this sacred love poem as a sex manual. Many have attempted this in our modern day and have done great violence to the text. John MacArthur has said that this type of popular interpretation is in essence the "wraping" of the Song of Solomon. The cherished Puritan, Richard Sibbes, gives us a similar warning from his time so long ago, yet so relevant for today.

> RICHARD SIBBES (1577-1635), "There are divers things in this song that a corrupt heart, unto which all things are defiled, may

take offence; but 'to the pure all things are pure,' Titus 1:15. Such a sinful abuse of this heavenly book is far from the intention of the Holy Ghost in it, which is by stooping low to us, to take advantage to raise us higher unto him, that by taking advantage of the sweetest passage of our life, marriage, and the most delightful affection, love, in the sweetest manner of expression, by a song, he might carry up the soul to things of a heavenly nature." [9]

This love poem is meant to be interpreted with great discretion and modesty, though not prudishness. In other words, the ancient Israelites were not afraid to talk about marital relations, but neither were they given to licentiousness. They deeply honored the marriage union and spoke of it with gentle, tender, modest words. This book ought to be handled in the same way.

Matthew Henry, the great puritan theologian, described this book as "an *Epithalamium*, or nuptial song, wherein, by the expressions of love between a bridegroom and his bride, are set forth and illustrated the mutual affections that pass between God and a distinguished remnant of mankind."[10] Marriage is not a part of the eternal state but while in this age is a living illustration of Christ's love for his bride, the church. When interpreted through this lens, the Song of Solomon has some of the most exalted language of adoration and worship to our beloved and exalted Bridegroom, Jesus Christ.

---

[9] Richard Sibbes. *The Love of Christ* (Panama, PA: GLH Publishing, 2015), Kindle Locations 107-111.

[10] Matthew Henry. *Commentary on the Whole Bible* (Peabody: Hendrickson, 1994), 1056.

1 | SONG 1:1-4

WHAT SHOULD ATTRACT YOU TO A POTENTIAL MATE?

Your name is oil poured out; therefore virgins love you.
SONG 1:3

God made marriage, he made our bodies, and he has direction for us all. And we will be supremely blessed if we heed what God says about how a person ought to approach marriage. There is an attack on the family directed to both singles and married people. The best way to secure yourself or your family from harm is to take shelter under the Word of God.

When you are looking for a mate, remember that this is a person you are going to spend your entire life with. The vows are still "Till death do we part" not "Till my desire changes do we part." We are committed together until death as Christian people because marriage is a picture of Christ and the church (Eph 5:22-33).

As Christians, we want to look for a mate that we can serve God with – someone that we can raise godly children with (as Malachi 2:15 says, we are to raise up a "godly seed"). Thankfully we have the Bible, and we ought to follow its wisdom in finding a godly mate. The truth is, it is not easy. The world is not on our side. The world thinks that purity is no big deal and passion should always be fulfilled immediately. The most popular philosophy of the day is "instant gratification." The world does not want you to be pure until you are married. The world says, "You need to test drive your potential marriage – you need to live together." The world is not on the side of marital fidelity. Those without Christ are not on the side of growing old together. The world has established a breathtakingly destructive pattern.

THE DANGERS OF MODERN DATING

We have an awful process in our country that is really nothing more than preparation for divorce. Most of what is called "dating" should really be called "destruction" because it ends in disaster and the forfeiting of one's purity. Young people in this activity are encouraged to hang out together and perhaps "go steady" or be boyfriend and girlfriend. They are often left alone; they give away their purity, and they are scarred morally as a result. There is a cycle that prepares a young person to not want commitment – to be afraid of commitment and marriage. They want to give up easily. The world establishes this pattern very early on in our children.

Have you ever seen the scribbling testimonies of love on a tree or a wall that said something like "Joey *hearts* Sally"? I remember as a young person, this was something around the 5th or 6th grade that occurred on a weekly basis. A boy would become infatuated with a girl, and the word would get out that "Joey likes Sally." Word would get to Sally, and Joey would write a note to Sally: "Will you be my girlfriend? Circle YES or NO." If the girl circled "yes," they would be a couple. This is what goes on in the fifth grade. That juvenile relationship might last a day or a week or maybe a month, but eventually Sally and Joey "break up" and move on to other juvenile "romances." Now this all sounds cute, but it gets much more serious in high school, and it prepares our young people for disaster when they get married. Sadly, by the time they get married, they have had plenty of preparation and training for divorce.

One novel idea practiced in many cultures is to have the parents arrange the marriage. You would be surprised that arranged marriages are far more successful than those built on dating. Often people from other cultures who have arranged marriages are baffled by the stupidity of our "dating" system in America. They cannot believe the practice of a young person choosing who they are going to marry based merely on superficial feelings and the very limited insight I have into a potential mate.

I read about one such visitor to America who asked, "Why do these young people think they can make a wise choice about marriage when they've never been married? Why do they think they are able to choose their own mates when they don't even know who they are themselves, much less who they will become? Why don't they trust their parents, who understand something about marriage and know that beauty is deceitful and charm is vain?"[11] This is why in our western context, dating and courtship can be a blessing if there is accountability, especially if parents or godly role models are carefully involved.

For this book, to see the joy of godly companionship on the road to marriage, we must not begin from our own limited perspective. Instead, we are going all the way back in time and interview a married man and his wife as they give us inspired biblical advice as to what to look for in a potential mate. In this song, there are certain characters that give advice about passion, purity, and fidelity.

THE CHARACTERS OF SOLOMON'S SONG (1:1)

King Solomon

The first and most distinguished character we meet is the famous King Solomon. He is the illustrious son of David and Bathsheba and of course the king of Israel during her golden age. As the author of this song, Solomon is one of the main speakers. He gives us the first verse:

Song of Solomon 1:1 | The song of songs, which is Solomon's.

This is a folk song composed by Solomon that begins with his wife testifying of her unique journey of how she as an impoverished peasant farm girl marries a great king. We might also add that this love song is highly distinguished as the only ballad to be inspired by the Holy Spirit. Therefore, this is really the authoritative standard on passion, purity and marital faithfulness.

So why should Solomon, who in later years was not known for marital fidelity, write this book? It is a fair deduction to believe Solomon wrote this book before he strayed. The fact that God brought him back

---

[11] Tom Nelson. *The Book of Romance* (Nashville: Thomas Nelson Publishers, 1998), 2.

by the end of his life, as we see in the book of Ecclesiastes, demonstrates God's grace and should give all of us hope.

The Shulamite Farm Girl

Of course, there is another character we meet in this love song: the Shulamite farm girl who becomes King Solomon's bride and queen. It is quite intriguing that her actual name is never mentioned. Solomon's song is about the love he shares with a peasant girl who becomes his princess. The first biblical record we have of Solomon marrying is to a pagan, Pharaoh's daughter as part of a political alliance (2 Chron 8:11).

Yet, it seems that the Song of Solomon is set in a time well before that—a song written to Solomon's first wife and first love, a young and beautiful Shulamite girl from the tribe of Dan. She has become known throughout the ages as "the peasant princess." The record of the Chronicles is not always in chronological order. King Solomon was likely already married before he began the pagan practice of political marriage. It could be the Shulamite is Naamah the Ammonitess, Solomon's first wife; the mother of Rehoboam (1 Kings 14:21) who was born one year before Solomon became king, which probably occurred around age twenty. Thus she would be his first love. It's possible that Solomon met her through one of his father's mighty men, Zelek the Ammonite who might have lived in the rural Ammonite town of Shulah.

This girl was not someone who should have been on the radar of a great king. The Shulamite girl was so poor that her brothers made her a shepherdess—"they made me keeper of the vineyards" (1:6). This was not a flattering vocation for a girl. Not much was on her side. She was impoverished and without striking natural beauty. Yet Solomon loved her and wrote this letter as the standard for marital love in the Bible.

Though there is great joy in matrimony, marriage was not created mainly for our happiness, but for God's glory. Ultimate happiness comes from giving our lives away, not to each other, though that is important. Ultimately happiness comes by each one of us giving him or herself to God. God created marriage as a picture to tell the story of his love for his bride. Marriage is an expression of God's love for people who don't deserve it. The Apostle Paul says in Ephesians 5:32-33, "This mystery [of marriage] is profound, and I am saying that it refers to Christ and the church. So, let each one of you love his wife as himself, and let the wife see that she respects her husband." Everything about Solomon seeking a poor peasant farm girl to marry is meant to tell the greatest love story ever told. This is the story of how God can love the most unworthy people. God takes impoverished sinners and pursues them. He overcomes them with his relentless love.

The Virgin Daughters of Jerusalem

The virgin daughters of Jerusalem appear many times in this love poem. They serve as a point of comparison to the Shulamite bride. These daughters are maidens—unmarried women—and we learn in chapter 6 that Solomon's bride surpasses all other maidens. So not only do they provide an entourage, they also showcase the bride as the best of the best. This group of maidens ("virgins," 1:3) appear throughout this love poem.[12] They are addressed only by the Shulamite farm girl, usually with some sort of exhortation or request. Some interpreters see them as the female members of the wedding party, others as members of the royal court. The text itself gives no clear indication of their identity except their association with the city of Jerusalem. The women then might be those who display the refined characteristics of the city girls of Jerusalem as opposed to the very "backwoodsy" disposition of the farm girl Solomon is displaying.[13]

THE MESSAGE OF SOLOMON'S SONG

Reflecting the Highest Love

The message of Song of Solomon is that it is God's will for married believers to have a full and happy marriage, which ultimately reflects God's love for his people. God created marital love to be spiritual at its very root. Married people can only be happy as they give their lives away for each other and pursue one another as God has pursued us. That is most successfully done when each is in a committed relationship with Christ. Without a focus on Christ, a marriage can degenerate into war. In so many ways, marriage is simply a measuring stick of one's relationship with God. If the marriage is filled with conflict, it is likely one's walk with God has grown lukewarm. This is not true in every case, since Jesus promised conflict because of the Kingdom. But often a tense marriage can point to one or both spouses not wanting to give

---

[12] For example, see 2:7; 3:5, 10ff; 5:8, 16; and 8:4.

[13] G. Lloyd Carr. *The Song of Solomon (TOTC)*. (Downers Grove, IL: Intervarsity Press, 2009), 84-85.

their lives away for each other. Marriage should be a picture of Christ lavishing love on his bride.

Song of Solomon is not only a love song about godly marriage—it ultimately points to a far greater love—the love Jesus Christ has for his church. We must always remember that marriage is a temporary institution which will be ended by death and whose purpose is to tell us of God's everlasting love for his people. The "Prince of Preachers," said this about the Song of Songs:

> CHARLES HADDON SPURGEON (1834-1892), "This Book stands like the tree of life in the midst of the garden, and no man shall ever be able to pluck its fruit, and eat thereof, until first he has been brought by Christ past the sword of the cherubim, and led to rejoice in the love which hath delivered him from death. The Song of Solomon is only to be comprehended by the people whose standing is within the veil. The outer-court worshippers, and even those who only enter the court of the priests, think the Book a very strange one; but they who come very near to Christ can often see in this Song of Solomon the only expression which their love to their Lord desires."[14]

What we are going to see in the first section (1:1-7) is two married people reflecting on what it was that attracted them to each other. Of course, this is a love song, but it is filled with wisdom for both single and married people. It teaches us how to deal with our passions in a godly way. Here we learn to walk in purity while single and to be faithful in marriage.

WHAT KIND OF PERSON SHOULD I BE ATTRACTED TO? (1:2-4)

As we enter the first chapter, we must remember that this is a married woman remembering the days leading up to her wedding day. She's going to talk about what attracted her to Solomon.

Physical Attraction

The initial level of attraction mentioned is physical attraction. Immediately we notice the first words from Solomon's bride would have to be the words of a married woman. The Jews would have forbidden

---

[14] Charles Spurgeon. *Metropolitan Tabernacle Pulpit,* Vol 42, Sermon 2469, "The Incomparable Bridegroom and His Bride" (London: Passmore & Alabaster, 1896), 285.

any and all sensual contact outside of the context of marriage, recognizing that such contact would inevitably lead to intimacy. Solomon's bride gushes with deep affection reflecting on her love for her husband:

Song of Solomon 1:2 | Let him kiss me with the kisses of his mouth! For your love is better than wine.

Such a strong expression of intimacy to begin this love poem is typical in this genre of poetry. She is obviously using soliloquy, which is expressing one's thoughts to oneself. This is especially used in poetry to discover what is in the heart of the speaker. As the beginning scene of this love story commences, it is likely the voice of the bride, later in her marriage, telling her love story. "Let me tell you about his love, about his kisses!" Here is a married woman looking back and testifying to what we all know about physical attraction. She now has her husband, and his kisses are sweet. Now she is saying: "Let me take you back to the story of how our love began."

Love is powerful. There is a powerful jolt of electricity that God designed with physical touch. There is a physical urge in most of us that is reserved only for marriage. This kind of love is worth the wait. Physical love is like electricity – it can be very helpful, but it must be harnessed, or it will destroy! I remember the first time I held my wife Jill's hand. We were on the Farris Wheel at the annual carnival in Oak Forest, Illinois. About half way up she told me she was afraid of heights. She grabbed my hand and asked if I would sing "Amazing Grace." She was not aware, but as the adrenaline of fear was coursing through her veins, my heart was pounding with joy! I do not remember if my version of "Amazing Grace" was in tune or not, but I'll never forget the electricity of her innocent grasp of my hand.

We do have a level of passion and attraction in our hearts that is not wrong, but it must be very guarded. Solomon's Shulamite bride reflects on her struggle with attraction before she was married: "I adjure you, O daughters of Jerusalem... that you not stir up or awaken love until it pleases" (2:7). How easy it is for us to stir up the emotional and physical fires of love prematurely.

Sexual Love is Exalted in Marriage

The sad thing is that the world paints this kind of sexual love as the ultimate goal of love for those who are not married. That is tragic. Solomon's pure Jewish bride says that sexual love in marriage is "better than wine." It is holy intoxication. It is a godly ravishing in the marital union which God invented. Sexual love in marriage expressed in God's time and in God's way is truly heavenly and holy. It is something to be esteemed. It is sacred and pure – precious and priceless. It is not something that we should ever say is "dirty." It is holy and it should be carefully guarded and reserved for marriage. What Solomon and his pure Shulamite bride symbolize is also expressed by the writer of Hebrew: "Let marriage be held in honor among all, and let the marriage bed be undefiled, for God will judge the sexually immoral and adulterous" (Heb 13:4).

Sexual Love is Destructive Outside of Marriage

Sexual intimacy in marriage is pure, but if you remove the marriage covenant from the equation, all sexual activity (including that which occurs only in the imagination) is nothing but fornication, a serious sin that is especially defiling and shameful—so much so that merely talking about it inappropriately is a disgrace according to Ephesians 5:12.[15] This is why the words about marital intimacy in the Song of Solomon are shrouded and hidden and mysterious. God uses words that are purposely metaphorical to guard the sacredness of marriage. This physical desire must be harnessed by holiness, not as dirty, but as eminently and gloriously pure, sacred, God-given, and precious – reserved for marriage alone. Of course, we must never establish a marriage on romance alone. That would be a recipe for disaster. On the other hand, physical desire for one's spouse is designed by God to be intoxicating. Love that is reserved for marriage will make a person light-headed. God says to the husband concerning his wife: "be intoxicated always in her love" (Pro 5:19). Sexual love in marriage is exhilarating. This is why it is extremely dangerous if that is all you have.

Sadly, many people rush to marriage only on the fumes of romance. It is like putting lighter fluid on a fire. There is a great explosion of fire at first, but then the fire quickly dies out and gets very cold. There is

---

[15] See John MacArthur. *The Rape of the Song of Solomon.* Blog archive. Challies.com.

nothing of substance to make that fire burn. In our day, couples too often rush into marriage on passion alone. Soon after marriage, after the romantic vapors evaporate, what is left are two very flawed and selfish people. We have to build on something greater than mere physical attraction. We must build it on the "kisses" of God's Word – when God fills our hearts with excitement as the joy of truth electrifies our soul. St. Ambrose, speaking of this verse, had much to say.

> AMBROSE (333-397), "Therefore such a soul also desires many kisses of the Word, so that she may be enlightened with the light of the knowledge of God. For this is the kiss of the Word, I mean the light of holy knowledge. God the Word kisses us, when he enlightens our heart... It is with the kiss that lovers cleave to each other and gain possession of the sweetness of grace that is within, so to speak. Through such a kiss the soul cleaves to God the Word... She sought the kiss, God the Word poured himself into her wholly... that is, his teachings and the laws of the wisdom that is within, and was fragrant with the sweet fragrance of his ointments. Captive to these, the soul is saying that the enjoyment of the knowledge of God is richer than the joy of any bodily pleasure."[16]

Jesus is Better than Sex, Wine, or Any Earthly Pleasure

Truly, as we consider the biblical mystery of marriage, only in Christ can we find a perfectly satisfying love that is "better than wine" (1:2). It must also be said, that since only Jesus is a perfect Savior with a perfect love that satisfies and intoxicates far more than wine or any human love, then we must not think that a spouse can be depended upon for lasting and satisfying love. No spouse, besides Jesus, can be your Savior. A person who is needy (and there is usually one in every marriage) can depend too much on a spouse for emotional, social, and sexual satisfaction. Sex is not a Savior, only Jesus is. Jesus is better than sex, wine, or any love or pleasure on this earth. Spurgeon's words are especially insightful:

---

[16] St. Ambrose. *Letter 62, To His Sister.* In *Fathers of the Church: A New Translation*, Vol 26 (Washington, D.C: Catholic University of America Press, 1947-2013), 390.

CHARLES HADDON SPURGEON (1834-1892), "Wine in the Bible is frequently used as the symbol of joy; so certainly, Christ's love is better than wine. Whatever joy there may be in the world's love (and it would be folly to deny that there is some sort of joy which even the basest of men know), yet the love of Christ is far superior to it. Human joy derived from earthly sources is a muddy, dirty pool, at which men would not drink did they know there was a stream sweeter, cooler, and far more refreshing. The love of Jesus brings a joy that is fit for angels, a joy that we shall have continued to us even in heaven itself, a joy which makes earth like to heaven; it is therefore far better than wine."[17]

Do not misunderstand. Every spouse should build a lasting and satisfying friendship in marriage that is socially, emotionally, intellectually, and sexually stimulating. But this is not what makes a marriage. True and godly love is far more than companionship. Love can take place even if one spouse is incapacitated. We are called to love one another in marriage "for better, for worse, for richer, for poorer, in sickness and in health, 'till death do we part." This means that if an accident occurs or a disease takes hold of a partner's body and physical relations were rendered impossible or social interaction was limited, that the marriage would still be intact. The vows are still in effect, until death parts that couple. Therefore, though we are usually initially attracted physically to someone, that it is not the most important aspect that ought to attract a person to a mate.

Social Attraction

Another aspect of attraction mentioned in Solomon's song is social attraction. I have heard girls say, "He's such a hunk!" My first question is "a hunk of what?" What is this guy made of? What you ought to be looking for, single girls, is a man that is made of godly character. Young men as well need to remember that physical attraction in a woman can be very misleading. "Charm is deceptive, and beauty is fleeting; but a woman who fears the LORD is to be praised" (Pro 31:30, NIV). Dads and moms, you need to teach your children what to look for in a mate. Listen how the peasant girl begins:

---

[17] Spurgeon. *Pulpit,* Vol 42, Sermon 2459, "Better than Wine" (1896), 157.

Song of Solomon 1:3a | your anointing oils are fragrant.

Orderliness ought to attract us. The Shulamite says, I like your "anointing oils." She is saying, "I like his cologne." The first thing she notices is that the king is well put together. He is well groomed. Solomon took care of himself.

In Solomon's day, men rarely bathed. They used scented oils and ointments—kind of like cologne. These oils kept their skin from drying out in the dry Middle Eastern climate. Often the superficial outward things like being well groomed and clean first grab our attention. I can remember in college we would get intercollegiate letters (from the various dormitories on campus), and no matter who it was from, every letter smelled like perfume!

By Solomon's time, the Hebrews had adopted the Egyptian practice of applying fragrance not only on themselves during a feast but also on their guests (cf Psa 133:2). Hosts placed small cones of perfumed ointment on the foreheads of their guests, whose body heat gradually melted the ointment, which then trickled down their faces onto their clothing, producing a pleasant aroma.[18]

You can tell when love begins to awaken in young people. The kid who used to hate baths is now taking showers twice a day! They are constantly brushing their teeth and swishing with mouthwash. Orderliness is important, but what really impressed the Shulamite girl was something much more important than his outward togetherness.

Spiritual Attraction

We ought to seek a mate that has given themselves to God. What should we look for that would clue us into to a person's spiritual vitality? A person's heart for God is what ought to be considered most when seeking a potential mate.

Character

Godly character ought to attract us. The young woman exclaims:

Song of Solomon 1:3b | your name is oil poured out.

A person's name in Israel was equal to the person's character. Solomon's cleanliness goes far beyond how he kept the outside. His godly

---

[18] J. D. Douglas, ed., *The New Bible Dictionary* (Grand Rapids, MI: Eerdmans, 1962), 906.

character is pleasing and above reproach. There is nothing in Solomon's character at this time that "smells bad." His reputation is like "oil poured out."

This oil is referring to the most purified oil there is. It is the first pressing of the oil—this was the oil that "was used in the lampstand that burned day and night in the Temple. The first pressing of any olive harvest went for Temple use only… it was designated solely for the worship of the Lord. Purified oil, therefore, was the best, but even beyond the best, it was the best given to God."[19]

The hidden person of the heart is far more important than the external beauty a person may have. Peter encouraged Christian women in the way of prioritizing inner beauty over outer beauty and wrote: "Do not let your adorning be external— the braiding of hair and the putting on of gold jewelry, or the clothing you wear— but let your adorning be the hidden person of the heart with the imperishable beauty of a gentle and quiet spirit, which in God's sight is very precious" (1 Pt 3:3-4).[20]

JOHN NEWTON (1725-1807), "Before my conversion, I knew nothing about the fear of God. I never had a hearty desire to keep his commandments, till I began to know a little of Christ. I was starving, and he fed me. I was sick, and he visited me. He healed me with his name, like ointment poured forth. These oils were more frequent in use and many of more costly composition in the ancient world than common amongst us today. Some were healing, to be applied to wound and bruises and putrefying sores. Now the sinner when he is awakened and comes to himself, finds himself like the man (Lk 10) stripped and wounded and half dead. Jesus like the good Samaritan comes with an eye of pity, to pour in the ointment of his name. This is the only cure for the wounds of sin. Many can witness to this. How when they began to feel their misery and see their danger, they made use of many means but found them all physicians of no value… But this ointment made them whole. Other ointments were gentle and reviving. The believing soul is subject to fainting – it has but little strength and meets many discouragements – but is relieved from time to time by the good aroma of this ointment. The name

---

[19] Nelson. *Romance*, 4-5.
[20] Matt Chandler. *The Mingling of Souls: God's Design for Love, Marriage, Sex, and Redemption* (Elgin, IL: David C. Cook), 33.

of Christ refreshes the soul with new strength under the remains of sin in us, namely, the assaults of Satan and the troubles of life. Ointments were also used in feasts (Lk 7:46). Hence Psalm 23:5, "he anoints my head with oil"). And the name of Jesus is a precious banquet to the believing soul. This fills him as with marrow and fatness – this puts an honor and a beauty upon him - therefore we remember his love more than wine (Song 1:4). Precious ointments as well have an aroma, a perfumed smell, which distinguishes the person that bears them. So this ointment of the name of Jesus, when poured into a believer's heart, makes him smell as a field which the Lord has blessed. It is this anointing of grace and holiness which we have received from our beloved which makes us known to each other and distinguishes us from the world."[21]

A Potential Mate May or May Not Have a Godly Past

The person you spend the rest of your life with ought to have a godly name and blameless reputation. This does not mean that a person has had a perfect upbringing or a spotless past. For instance, I was raised in a non-believing home and was very tainted by the world before I knew Christ. Sadly, I gave away my virginity as an unsaved, worldly teenager. When I trusted Christ, the Lord cleansed me and restored my dignity. He made me a new creation. When I sought the girl who was to be my wife, I felt so unworthy. She was raised in a devout Christian home, but I was a new believer with a blemished past. She was a virgin with a blameless life, a gentle heart, and a godly character. I came to realize that because Christ had washed my sins away that I really had a new beginning. It is true the Apostle Paul declares that the "sexually immoral" person will not enter the Kingdom of God. But then he says: "and such were some of you. But you were washed, you were sanctified, you were justified in the name of the Lord Jesus Christ and by the Spirit of our God" (1 Cor 6:9-11). That immoral person I was had been crucified with Christ. My old life was dead, and my new life had begun. I was a new creation (2 Cor 5:17). Once I was born again, by the

---

[21] John Newton. "Your Name, Like Ointment Poured Forth." Sermon, preached March 3, 1765 from Song of Solomon 1:3. Accessed 10 October 2017 from johnnewton.org (The John Newton Project). Transcribed by Marylynn Rouse from John Newton's sermon notebook at the Cowper and Newton Museum.

grace of God I maintained a blameless reputation. The fragrance of Christ attracted my future wife. I was not bound by my past sins. Because I was radically committed to following Christ, that special girl who I am now married to would one day say: "your name is oil poured out" (1:3). God is able to "give a crown of beauty for ashes" and "festive praise instead of despair" (Isa 61:3).

It should also be noted that in order to attract a godly mate, you must first live up to your proposed standards. If you want a chaste spouse, then you must be chaste. If you want a spouse with a heart for God, then you must first have a heart for God. You will inevitably attract someone of like character. David said, "I am a companion of all who fear you, of those who keep your precepts" (Psa 119:63). We might say in today's language: "Birds of a feather flock together."

Chastity

Chastity ought to attract us. Godly young women were attracted to Solomon because of his godly spirit and character.

Song of Solomon 1:3c | Therefore virgins love you.

Young women of marriable age loved Solomon. They respected him. The chaste women of Solomon's court felt safe with Solomon. Why? Solomon had the reputation with others of having a pure, godly, and chaste lifestyle. He apparently treated women with dignity and respect. He kept himself pure. This was well known. He was chaste and careful with the opposite gender. The unmarried girls felt respected by him. He had a reputation of godliness and purity.

Are you chaste? If you are a flirt around the opposite gender, you will attract a person who is flirtatious and careless as well. Ladies, if you flirt, you are prostituting yourself and will attract the wrong kind of man. Men, if this is your practice, you are not protecting and respecting God's daughters. When considering a lifelong mate, ask yourself: Do I have the reputation as a chaste, godly person? Am I attracted first and foremost to the physical, or is this person's beauty more than "skin deep"? Is their godliness the primary reason for my attraction? Would I be proud to bring this person home to meet Mom and Dad, Grandma and Grandpa, aunts and uncles?

Real chastity flows from a converted heart. Self-control is a fruit of the Holy Spirit (Gal 5:20-21). It should be concluded then that all who are true believers love Christ above all others. All believers are like the virgins of Jerusalem – they love the king. In a higher way, all born again people have Jesus as their highest love. So said Augustine, bishop of Hippo, North Africa:

> AUGUSTINE (354-430), "The Song of Solomon sings a sort of spiritual rapture experienced by holy souls contemplating the marital relationship between Christ the King and his queen-city, the church. But it is a rapture veiled in allegory to make us yearn for it more ardently and rejoice in the unveiling as the bride-groom comes into view—the bridegroom to whom the canticle sings, 'The righteous love you,' and the hearkening bride replies, 'Your name is like oil poured out' and 'There is love in your de-lights.'"[22]

Chivalry

Chivalry ought to attract a young woman. What is "chivalry?" The future queen says to Solomon:

Song of Solomon 1:4a | Draw me after you; let us run.

Chivalry is when the man takes the lead. A young man sets the tone for his future marriage by being a man of character and responsibility, unafraid to take the lead. He "draws" the woman after him by his un-compromised heart. He demonstrates trustworthiness. He is a gentle-man. He opens the car door. He esteems her with his words. He treats her gently. He draws her in the right way.

Ladies, if a man wants to put you into a compromising situation, then he is not a leader but a coward. A godly man will always lead you to safe places. He will insist that you never be alone. If you suddenly come on to him, he will warn you. He will be a man that protects and guards the purity of the any young woman around him. It is that kind of man that every young woman wants to "run" with. **Let us run,** says the Shulamite. By the way, women ought not to put themselves forward. A godly woman will wait for a godly man to draw her after him. A man is made to lead, and a woman is made to respond. A godly

---

[22] Augustine of Hippo. *The City of God*. In ed. P. Schaff, trans. M. Dods. *St. Augustin's City of God and Christian Doctrine*, Vol. 2, (Buffalo, NY: Christian Literature Company, 1887), 357.

man will take the lead and always steer away from compromising situations.

We might add that a chivalrous man will be one who is able to provide for his potential wife. If a man does not have a job and a means to support himself, a bride, and future children, then he ought not to be considering marriage. A man that has the fragrance of Christ will draw a godly woman after him. She should follow her suitor as her suitor follows Christ. St. Augustine said we ought also to "run with Christ."

> AUGUSTINE (354-430), "'Draw me after you; let us run,' said the bride. Christ, as Solomon, had a sweet ointment that makes us run after him. Christ came and gave forth a sweet smell that filled the world. Whence was that fragrance? From heaven. Follow then toward heaven. Lift up your thoughts, your love and your hope, that it may not rot upon the earth. 'For wherever your treasure is, there will be your heart also.'"[23]

Luther tells us that the farm girl is forceful in her words. She is filled with life with Solomon around. She does not want to simply walk, but to run.

> MARTIN LUTHER (1483-1546), "This is emphatic. She does not say 'let us walk' but 'let us run.' 'If you breathe your Spirit upon me, then I shall be glad to perform the task of prince, teacher, husband, pupil, etc. Unless you inspire, no one will accomplish anything, no matter how great his zeal and care." [24]

Jerome, a contemporary of Augustine who helped translate the Greek into the Latin Vulgate, was especially touched by the thought of Christ, who is the fragrant ointment from heaven. It is the aroma of Christ that brings us to life and enlivens us to "run" after him.

> JEROME (347-420), "There also—the Lord himself is my witness—when I had shed copious tears and had strained my eyes toward heaven, I sometimes felt myself among angelic hosts and

---

[23] Augustine of Hippo. *Expositions on the Book of Psalms*. In ed. P. Schaff, trans. A. C. Coxe, *Saint Augustin: Expositions on the Book of Psalms*, Vol 8 (New York: Christian Literature Company, 1888), 452.

[24] Martin Luther. *Luther's Works*, Vol. 15. *Ecclesiastes, Song of Solomon, and the Last Words of David* (St. Louis: Concordia Publishing House, 1971), 198.

for joy and gladness sang, 'Because of the sweet smell of your good ointments, we will run after you.'"[25]

Young men and women need to be attracted to those who are attracted to Christ. That leads us to the last thing that the Shulamite names that attracts her.

Self-Control

A person with self-control ought to be attractive to us. Solomon was of such blameless character that he took the lead in his courtship of his pure Jewish bride. There is a need for self-control. Notice that the desire for marriage is strong.

Song of Solomon 1:4b | The king has brought me into his chambers.

The bride is looking back from her wedding day with no regrets! The sacred day did arrive for the Shulamite. But they kept pure until that day. Solomon protected her. He was a man of blameless reputation. He never put her in any compromising situations. Here is a married woman reflecting on her courtship and what attracted her to Solomon – The king waited until the wedding day to bring her into his chambers.

To single men and ladies, what is reserved for marriage is so precious that you must carefully guard it. Some men will say, "Well I love her!" Single men, if you want to express your love, then you protect her, and never treat her like a prostitute. We must never act as if we are married if we are not married. Be careful not awaken that overcoming romantic love until you are married. You ought never to put yourself in a situation where you are alone with your potential mate.

Notice Solomon's future bride speaks of marital love as a place that is hidden and secret: the "chambers." Intimacy is reserved for marriage. Marital love is sacred and should be mysterious. It should be something shared only between a man and the wife that he has covenanted to be with whether they are poor or rich, whether they are sick or in good health. They are together until death parts them! This is why

---

[25] Jerome. *Homilies on the Psalms*. In *Fathers of the Church: A New Translation*, Vol 57 (Washington, D.C: Catholic University of America Press, 1947-2013), 54.

we ought to be offended when marital intimacy is prostituted on television commercials and on internet ads. We ought to be incensed and infuriated! If we men are truly men at all, we will guard our homes from this refuse. We will guard our own eyes from that which trashes the most sacred love between two people.

Do not misunderstand. The couple who is engaged should look forward to marital intimacy. God designed sex. The Israelites of old did not have a prudish view of the physical union. They looked forward to it is something beautiful. And because of this great respect for intimacy, they took every measure to guard themselves from wasting the gift God gave to them to give to each other. We need men and ladies who have this kind of character. Where is this man of character? Every lady who is interested in marriage ought to want a man like this. Every mother ought to diligently teach her son to be a man like this.

In speaking of the delights of intimacy in marriage, let us not forget that even the most exalted love between man and wife cannot in any way compare to the love and satisfaction we have in the Lord who says, "I have loved you, my people, with an everlasting love. With unfailing love I have drawn you to myself" (Jer 31:3, NLT). The King of kings brings us into the chambers of his salvation. He must do it, for in ourselves we would never come to him. Christ said, "No one can come to me unless the Father who sent me draws him" (Jn 6:44), and "I told you that no one can come to me unless it is granted him by the Father" (Jn 6:65).

> JAMES DURHAM (1622–1658): "'He drew me and brought me into his chambers.' Here we may see that Christ is easily intreated. He draws us. 'Before they call, I will answer' (Isa 65:24). Believers should expect answers to prayer and bless Christ for them. The bride acknowledges Solomon had brought her into his chambers. She magnifies and commends the mercy of this marriage all the more. It's the greater honor that not only is she there, but that the King himself (like the Prodigal's father) met her, and took her in. So, Christ's community of believers are given mercy without price, and sinners may boldly approach his throne of grace and not despair of access. She attributes their relationship squarely to him ('he drew me'), that she may be always mindful of his grace, whereby she stands and enjoys these

privileges. She remains continually humble under them as having none of these high privileges from herself. It is remarkable
under the reality and realization of this fair gale of flowing love,
to be steady and humble. It's rare to be full of this new wine of
love and be able to walk straight."[26]

True and eternal intimacy is found in Christ. Marriage is just a
weak reflection of the much deeper intimacy we have in the new birth.

> ORIGEN (185-254), "To the person who comes to Christ, or to
> the soul that cleaves to the Word of God... Christ's chamber is
> the storehouse of the Word of God into which he brings his
> church and the soul thus cleaving to him."[27]

The chamber of Christ is powerful to take in his bride, no matter
who the opposition is. God's love through the Word is so powerful that
it turned the world upside down in the sixteenth century, so is the testimony of the most prominent Reformer.

> MARTIN LUTHER (1483-1546), "I will preach the Word, teach
> it, write it, but I will constrain no one by force, for faith must
> come freely without compulsion. Take myself as an example. I
> opposed indulgences and all the papists, but never with force. I
> simply taught, preached, and wrote God's Word; otherwise I did
> nothing. And while I slept (Mark 4:26–29), or drank Wittenberg
> beer with my friends Philip and Amsdorf, the Word so greatly
> weakened the papacy that no prince or emperor ever inflicted
> such losses upon it. I did nothing; the Word did everything. Had
> I desired to foment trouble, I could have brought great bloodshed
> upon Germany; indeed, I could have started such a game that
> even the emperor would not have been safe. But what would it
> have been? Mere fool's play. I did nothing; I let the Word do its
> work." [28]

Listen to the godly daughters of Jerusalem:

---

[26] James Durham. *Clavis Cantici: An Exposition of the Song of Solomon* (Glasgow:
David Niven, 1788), 81.

[27] Origen. *Commentary on the Song of Songs*. In trans. R.P. Lawson. *Ancient
Christian Writers: The Works of the Fathers in Translation*, Vol 26 (Mahwah, N.J.:
Paulist Press, 1946), 84.

[28] Martin Luther. ed. Eric Lund. *Documents from the History of Lutheranism*,
1517-1750 (Minneapolis: Fortress Press, 2001), 38.

Song of Solomon 1:4c | We will exult and rejoice in you; we will extol your love more than wine; rightly do they love you.

A man like this is one in a thousand. Men – married or single – be a true man that protects that which is sacred. Be a man who honors what God honors. Do not contribute to the decadence of our culture. Keep sacred that which God calls sacred. If you do that you will be highly honored by women in general. They will point to you and "exult and rejoice in you." They will rightly respect you.

Marriage must not be based merely on those human attributes that fade. Good looks and outward togetherness may initially attract us to a potential mate, but those things will fade over time or may be taken away in an instant through a sudden change in health or an accident. The Christian who seeks marriage must seek someone who is following hard after the only Savior. No spouse can compare to the true Spouse, Jesus Christ whose love is better and more than the very best wine.

> CHARLES HADDON SPURGEON (1834-1892), "Higher, far, is your joy than ever came to them that have made merry at earthly feasts! More delightful, more intense, more real, more true are your hallowed ecstasies than anything that wine or wealth can ever bring! …We remember the love which Jesus bore in his heart right up into glory at the right hand of the Father—that love which is still as great as when he hung on Calvary to redeem us unto himself. The wonderful part of all this to me is that it should be the love of such a one as Christ is. That ever so divine a person should set his love on us is very wonderful. I can understand my mother's love. I can understand my child's love. I can understand my wife's love, but I cannot understand Christ's love. Oh, brothers and sisters, we are nothings, we are nobodies! Yet this glorious Everybody, this All in All, did actually set his love upon us! Suppose that all the holy angels had loved us, and that all God's redeemed had loved us? All put together, it would be only so many grains of dust that would not turn the scale! But Christ's love is a mountain, no, more than all the mountains in the universe! I know of nothing to be compared with it."[29]

---

[29] Spurgeon. *Pulpit,* Vol 42, Sermon 2461, "Rejoicing and Remembering" (1896), 181.

Conclusion

Perhaps you are thinking about marriage. The first question you ought to ask yourself about your potential mate is: Is this person born again? Do they truly have a walk with Jesus Christ? Does this person love Christ above the best things that are in this world? Has this person grown in the faith? Do they have a reputation about being bold and courageous about the things of God? Is God more important in this person's life than any human relationship? The heart of a spiritually dynamic believer in Christ ought to be what is most attractive to you as you consider choosing a potential mate.

2 | SONG 1:5-7

WHEN ARE YOU READY TO MARRY?

Why should I be like one who veils herself [as a prostitute]
beside the flocks of your companions?
SONG 1:7

When are you ready to marry? What age should a young person marry? How do I know I am ready? Is there a certain time frame I should be following? More important than time frame, the one considering marriage should be a person of godly character.

You are ready to marry when you are the kind of person that you ought to be. You need to come into marriage with godly character, ready to work hard. Marriage exists for the glory of God and not merely for our happiness. Joy and happiness come when you are submitted to God whether you are married or single. If you cannot be happy and content in Christ as a single person, then no human being will ever make you content. So many people rush into marriage thinking it will make them happy and solve all their problems. That is a recipe for disaster. To be married takes tremendous work and sacrifice on the parts of both spouses.

WHEN YOU KNOW WHAT IS MOST IMPORTANT (1:5)

You are ready to be married when you are concerned about what is most important. Your focus must not be to mind fulfillment in marriage, but to realize you are "complete in Christ" (Col 2:10).

Inner Beauty Matters

You are ready for Christian marriage when you are not beguiled by superficial and shallow attractiveness. This Shulamite is no princess. We find out that she's grown up on a farm. She's not so concerned about superficial beauty. She ponders true beauty:

Song of Solomon 1:5-6 | I am very dark, but lovely, O daughters of Jerusalem, like the tents of Kedar, like the curtains of Solomon. Do not gaze at me because I am dark, because the sun has looked upon me. My mother's sons were angry with me; they made me keeper of the vineyards, but my own vineyard I have not kept!

In this section of Solomon's song, we should consider the messianic implications. The farm girl doubts her appearance. This is in contrast to Adam and Eve before the fall in the Garden of Eden when they were "naked and unashamed." There is a great level of self-doubt in the human condition. Courtship in all its forms and traditions throughout history and cultures pictures the sweet drawing of the Spirit of God in the voice of Jesus who says, "Come to me all you who labor and are burdened down, and I will give you rest" (Mt 11:28). We find this farm girl working the vineyard, not prepared for a kingly courtship. Nonetheless, she is soon thrust into it. This unlikely courtship is reminiscent of the surprise of salvation when the sinner begins to hear God's voice in his Word, for "faith comes by hearing and hearing by the Word of Christ" (Rom 10:17). She is "**very dark but lovely**" – lovely because she is made in the image of God but worn down in her body.

The Importance of Inner Beauty

Solomon's future queen was not socially attractive. She's from a broken and poor family. We first notice she addresses the "daughters of Jerusalem"–the single, eligible ladies in Solomon's royal court. She was not from the royal city. The Shulamite is from the tribe of Dan in Lower Galilee—she's from the wrong side of the tracks. There is always that desire to compare. But she does not gain her value from her family or hometown. Her father is not named, but her brothers have put her to work. Many commentators believe the father has either left the family or has died. What hope does this girl have of marrying?

The godly Shulamite girl is from a poor Jewish family in the tribe of Dan and does not have the pampered beauty of the urban women of the upper class. She is a working-class peasant girl. She is not a princess. Her skin is dark not only because of natural beauty but also because of the sun-tan that comes from working so many grueling hours in the fields. She says:

Song of Solomon 1:5a | I am very dark, but lovely, O daughters of Jerusalem.

She was dark and radiantly beautiful, but she was also "weathered." She was sun-tanned. Though she was beautiful, she had a very low standing on the social totem pole.

The Shulamite girl in our passage is looked down upon not because of her skin but because of her low social standing. Her face was dark and sun-tanned, and she had blisters on her hands. Everybody knows farm girls don't marry kings. Some Jewish people have darker skin. They are not European but Semitic. Most of the royalty in the world at this time in history were brown skinned people. In fact, many Africans in this girl's day were royal and dignified and respected. We think of the famous Queen of Sheba (from the area that is no present-day Yemen). The social standing of the Shulamite may have been a turn off, but she is a brown-skinned and beautiful woman, and more than that, we find out she is she is spiritually attractive! Inner beauty mattered to this farm girl.

The Model of Inner Beauty

You may not realize it, but Solomon's pursuit is really telling a wonderful part of God's love story for us. The Bible says no one comes to God unless they are "drawn" and pursued by God the Father (Jn 6:44). The peasant princess is an ancient picture of the church being pursued by her Groomsman, our Lord Jesus Christ. There was a day when Solomon met the peasant girl, and he deemed her a very special young lady. He began to show his love to her, and he began to pursue her.

The King and the farm girl have a love story that points to Christ's love for his bride. God is pursing poor sinners to be in his kingdom. He wants us to surrender to him. He's done everything for us to come to him. He's given us great gifts as a Bridegroom pursuing his bride. He's given us life, a body, the sunshine and rain, our family and friends. But most of all, God has given us his own Son. He has pursued his people. He wants each of us to be part of the people that make up the Bride for his Son. Solomon's pursuit of the farm girl, while impressive, is nothing compared to God's pursuit of each one of us. Many have observed this comparison through the history of the church.

> MATTHEW HENRY (1662-1714): "The church is sometimes dark with persecution, but lovely in patience, constancy, and comfort, and nevertheless attractive in the eyes of Christ, dark in the account of men, but *lovely* in God's esteem, *dark* in some that are a scandal to her, *but lovely* in others that are sincere and are an honor to her. True believers are *dark* in themselves, *but lovely* in Christ, with the comeliness that he puts upon them, *dark* out-wardly, for *the world knows them not*, but *all glorious within* (Psa 45:13)."[30]

> AMBROSE (333-397): "'I am dark and lovely, O daughters of Jerusalem.' Dark through sin, lovely through grace; dark by nat-ural condition, lovely through redemption, or certainly, dark with the dust of her labors. So the church is dark while fighting but lovely when she is crowned with the ornaments of victory when Christ returns."[31]

The Modesty of Inner Beauty

Song of Solomon 1:5b | I am very dark, but lovely... like the tents of Kedar.

The material that makes up the Bedouin tent is the same as the sackcloth of Bible days. It must be remembered that this oriental sack-cloth is a material made of prickly, coarse goat's hair which could pro-tect the one sheltered from the fiercest onslaught of the elements and also provided a place of great privacy and discretion.[32]

---

[30] Matthew Henry. *Commentary,* 1058.

[31] Ambrose of Milan. *Three Books of St. Ambrose on the Holy Spirit.* In eds. P. Schaff & H. Wace, trans. H. de Romestin, E. de Romestin, & H. T. F. Duckworth. *St. Ambrose: Select Works and Letters,* Vol 10 (New York: Christian Literature Com-pany, 1896), 129.

[32] John D. Whiting, "Bedouin Life in Bible Lands," The National Geographic Magazine, January 1937, 64-65. See also pp. 68-69 for photographs of goat's hair tents.

The Shulamite was a woman who protected that which was on the inside. She guarded her character and her purity. She was like the tents of Kedar – beautifully fashioned yet not flashy. She was instead practical. The tents of the Bedouin shepherds of Kedar are blackened by exposure to the elements and are strong enough to endure the desert climate.[33] So the Shulamite shepherd girl is not dainty and fragile like the ladies at Solomon's royal court. Instead we see her modesty and discretion woven with her dark features as "lovely" like the famous tents of the Bedouin shepherds of Kedar.

The tents of Kedar were designed more for protection than presentation. Our peasant princess is good looking but not at all pampered or in with all the fads of the day. She's out of touch with what's "in" because she's been working in the field. The tents of Kedar were beautiful sprawling cloth enclosed gazebos that functioned as a shelter of protection for the Bedouin shepherds and their family. These tents were places of security and covering—they took the wear and tear to protect what was in the inside.

The Shulamite was willing to take the wear and tear on the outside to protect that which was most important on the inside. These tents soaked up the heat and provided cover for the family and the belongings. It was a place of comfort and rest.

Jonathan Edwards was struck at her comparison to the tent, like the Tabernacle where the presence of the Lord was manifested.

> JONATHAN EDWARDS (1703-1758): "That the spouse in this song is compared to a tent, and to the curtains of the tabernacle and temple, is an evidence that this song is no ordinary love song, and that by the spouse is not meant any particular woman, but a society, even that holy society, the church of God. It is common in the writings of the Old Testament to represent the church of God by a tent, or tents, and a house and temple, but never a particular person (cf. Isa 54:2; Zech 12:7; Isa 33:20; Lam 2:4, 6; Isa 1:8). And the tabernacle and temple were known types of the church, and the curtains of both had palm-trees embroidered on them, which are abundantly made use of to represent the church. The church of God is called a house, in places too many

---

[33] D. A. Garrett. *Proverbs, Ecclesiastes, Song of Songs*, Vol. 14 (Nashville: Broadman & Holman Publishers, 1993), 386.

to be mentioned. The church used to be called the temple of the Lord, as appears by Jeremiah 7:4. The church is represented by the temple, as is evident by Zechariah 4:2-9."[34]

The Mystery of Inner Beauty

Like Solomon's curtains, this farm girl was a woman who was also mysterious and modest, **"like the curtains of Solomon"** (1:5c).

The curtains of Solomon were dark, but you never knew what was happening on the inside. There was mystery and modesty. You are ready to be married when you know not to blab all your problems to the world. When you can be quiet and take your problems to the Lord. A lady is ready to be married when she can be like the curtains of Solomon and have some shamefacedness and modesty and mystery about her. There is something attractive about a girl who is content with herself. She is not chasing after the guys. She is secure and spiritual and happy, wanting to reflect the character of her just and merciful God.

Some ladies are tempted to chase after superficial fads so that they can get noticed. That is a dangerous road to follow. Even if it worked, what kind of guy would she get? It would be a guy that's going to be superficial spiritually, who will break her heart in the end. If the totality of a woman is merely make up, cool clothes, and a good hair style, then she is not ready for marriage. If she has to flirt with a guy to get him to notice her, she is not ready for marriage.

What are you on the inside? Are you godly? When's the last time you prayed for an hour? When's the last time you read the Bible from cover to cover? When was the last time you had answered prayer? You are not ready to marry if your standard for living comes from your peers. You have to be able to stand on your own on the Lord's side.

We don't know what the woman of Proverbs 31 looked like, but we read: "Charm is deceptive, and beauty is fading, but a woman who fears the LORD is to be praised" (Pro 31:30). True beauty is far more than skin deep. A woman's beauty comes from her modesty and mystery as she fears the Lord.

---

[34] Jonathan Edwards. *Notes on Scripture*, in *Works*, Vol 15, 359.

WHEN YOU ARE CAREFUL TO SERVE GOD (1:6)

You are ready to be married when you are careful to serve God where you are. So many people serve themselves and put on rose colored glasses thinking that Mr. Right or Miss Perfect is going to make them happy. If you are looking for someone to make you happy, you are not ready to marry. The Shulamite farm girl had a tough life, but she was faithfully serving God where she was.

Responsibility Matters

Song of Solomon 1:6 | Do not gaze at me because I am dark, because the sun has looked upon me. My mother's sons were angry with me; they made me keeper of the vineyards, but my own vineyard I have not kept!

What the Shulamite is saying here is that she does not have the time to tend to her own attractiveness. Unlike Queen Esther, she hasn't been getting her twelve-month beauty treatments—her skin softened with oil of myrrh for six months, and then spices and ointments for another six months (Est 2:12). She has a working-class complexion, *and* her hair is undone, *and* her attire is unattractive. She has been on her feet all day pruning vines or picking grapes, shooing away sneaky foxes. And when she gets off her shift, she calls it a day. No time for a manicure and pedicure, and certainly no time to powder her sunburnt cheeks.[35]

On the surface, we would all say, she does not compare to the women of the royal court. She's only a farm girl. She's a peasant, not a princess. But this girl was content to be single. She wasn't looking to marry Solomon. Though her life was rough, she was faithfully serving God where she was. The Shulamite's brothers might have been angry and mean to her, but God used that situation in her life to make her a hardworking young lady learning to submit to God even in a difficult and perhaps tragic situation.

This farm girl was not looking to be married. It seems she didn't have time to even think about those things. She was faithful to God. At first glance, it seems serving God did not help her cause. Her faithfulness to her Lord on the farm did not make her more eligible, but instead

---

[35] D. S. O'Donnell. *The Song of Solomon: An Invitation to Intimacy*, ed. R. K. Hughes (Wheaton, IL: Crossway, 2012), 43-44.

it seemed she was less marryable. She was submissive to authority, even in times of great stress. She did what she was told to the neglect of her own eligibility for marriage. She did not have an ideal family situation. When she speaks of her "**mother's sons**" (1:6), she's talking about her stepbrothers. We don't know why they were angry with her. Nothing is indicated that she did anything wrong. This is just her lot in life. She has no idea that one day she is going to be a princess. She just kept her eyes on God and trusted God. That's what we all need to do. She's looking back and saying, "I wasn't fretting about being single. I'm content to serve God right where I am."

You may not have an ideal family situation. Understand that God is not hindered by these things. God is in charge of finding you a mate if he wants you to be married. God sent Solomon one day to look out at his fields, and he noticed a humble lady that was distinguished from the women of his royal court. As he got to know her, he put aside all the superficial stuff and saw a girl who wanted to serve God. A man is attracted to a woman who is not afraid to work.

Do you have a servant's heart? Until your highest goal in life is to please God and serve him with all your heart, you are not ready to be married. One of the church fathers of the Middle Ages said this Shulamite girl is like the church because though she neglected her outward appearance, there was no neglect to her soul.

> BERNARD OF CLAIRVAUX (1090-1153): "Though the outward may be neglected, there can be no question of the abundance of the inner life where the apostles are the branches, the Lord is the vine, and his Father is the vine dresser. Planted in faith, the true Christian has his roots grounded in love, dug in with the hoe of discipline, fertilized with penitential tears, and watered with the words of preachers. Though the outward veneer may be dry and cracked, the inward life abounds with the spiritual wine of Christ that inspires joy rather than debauchery, wine full of the pleasure that is never licentious. This is the wine that gladdens the Christian's heart, even if their outward form is neglected by worldly standards. Their sorrow has the flavor of grace, the relish of pardon, the delight of reconciliation, the wholesomeness

of returning innocence, the gratification of a peaceful conscience."[36]

The Shulamite girl neglected her outward beauty while growing to
be abundant in godly character. She was focused on the well-being of
her family. She didn't have the money or the time to be worldly wise
with fashion. She says of her brothers, **"they made me keeper of the
vineyards, but my own vineyard I have not kept"** (1:6). She was
willing to put off marriage for the livelihood of her family. They needed
to eat. She gave of herself. If you think investing in outward beauty
alone is the road to a good marriage, you would do well to put off getting married. You need to adorn yourself with a humble servant's heart
that loves Christ. That's what makes for a lasting marriage.

Single men, if all you are attracted to is the outside, you are in for
a very rocky marriage. Single ladies, are you willing to trust God to send
the right man along if that is God's will for you? Do you see that God
wants to make you the woman that you ought to be so that if you get
married, you'll have the marriage God wants you to have?

Regeneration Matters

When we come to know the love of Christ, we are changed from the
inside out. Theologians call this regeneration. God takes away our heart
of stone, and gives us a tender heart of flesh (Eze 36:25-27). We may
be scorched by sin, but we are lovely to Christ. He has set his love upon
you and me.

Sometimes the scorch of sin discourages us, but we need to understand that Christ does not see his bride as the peasant and servant girl
she is now, but as the princess she will become. You are beautiful in
Christ's eyes. How about you? Does inner beauty matter to you? Have
you been born again? Have you come to know the love of Christ on the
inside, or are you more concerned about what you look like on the outside?

WHEN YOU ARE CAUTIOUS ABOUT THE SANCTITY OF MARRIAGE (1:7)

You are ready to be married when you are cautious about the sanctity of marriage. You don't have to give away your purity in order to get
a potential mate.

---

[36] Bernard of Clairvaux. *Commentary on the Song of Solomon*, "Sermon 30: Mystical Vineyards and the Prudence of the Flesh."

Purity Matters

The Shulamite looks back to her first conversation with King Solomon when she said:

Song of Solomon 1:7 | Tell me, you whom my soul loves, where you pasture your flock, where you make it lie down at noon; for why should I be like one who veils herself beside the flocks of your companions?

In Solomon's day, a veiled woman who would appear in midday was a prostitute. The Shulamite says, "I will not practice the immorality of a prostitute to get a man." Single ladies should have the same attitude: "I will not sacrifice my chastity and my purity for a man." The Shulamite girl had convictions. She's willing to wait. She wants to spend time with Solomon, but she wants to go about it in a legitimate way. We are to "make no provision for the flesh, to gratify its desires" (Rom 13:14).

If at any time you feel like you must set aside your biblical, godly convictions to win the attention of someone, then you need to put on the brakes. The right person for you if you are a Christian, is someone who is going to push you toward God, not away from Him. You should aspire to marry someone who is going to challenge you spiritually and is willing to tell you goodbye if you go the wrong way. If you are looking for a spouse, you should be looking for someone in whom Christ dwells. You see Jesus in them. As the farm girl was attracted to King Solomon tending his sheep, so a young lady should be interested in a man who loves the Shepherd of shepherds, Jesus.

> AUGUSTINE (354-430): "With good reason the future queen speaks to Solomon, shepherd of shepherds. So, Christ draws his beloved, his bride, his fair one to speak, for she is by him made fair. Before by sin deformed, she is beautiful afterward through pardon and grace. He draws her in love and ardor after him to ask him, 'Where do you feed?' Observe how the transport of this spiritual love is here animated. Far better love have they who have tasted of the delight and sweetness of divine love. They bear

this properly who love Christ. For in them, and of them, does the church sing this in the Song of Songs."[37]

Believers should seek marriage only with those who love the divine Bridegroom. If a Christian is to marry, they should marry the one who knows where Christ feeds his flock.

What You Wear Matters

Purity extends from the heart to every part of us, including what we wear. What you wear matters. Paul tells us that "women should adorn themselves in respectable apparel, with modesty and self-control, not with braided hair and gold or pearls or costly attire, but with what is proper for women who profess godliness—with good works" (1 Tim 2:9-10). Listen to the Shulamite.

Song of Solomon 1:7b | Why should I be like one who veils herself beside the flocks of your companions?

If you are a lady, I ask you: are you concerned that your apparel communicate the modesty and respectability of godliness and not the questionable morals of the world? It is quite difficult to buy clothes as a Christian woman these days because so much of what the world pushes is meant to accentuate your form. A single Christian lady should want to wear clothing that accentuates her face, not her body. She should want the man she marries to love her for a beauty that is more than skin deep.

WHEN YOU ARE CONTENT TO BE SINGLE

Song of Solomon 2:7; cf 3:5 | I adjure you, O daughters of Jerusalem, by the gazelles or the does of the field, that you not stir up or awaken love until it pleases.

The daughters of Jerusalem are the elite class of women in the royal court. The Shulamite girl never was jealous of her peers who had money and popularity in the royal court. She was content being single. She wasn't looking for Solomon. You might ask, if she doesn't have the money or the friends of the ladies in the royal court, then how can she

---

[37] Augustine of Hippo. *Sermon 88.6, Song of Solomon.* P. Schaff et al., eds. *A Select Library of the Nicene and Post-Nicene Fathers of the Christian Church,* Vol 6. (Peabody, MA: Hendrickson, 1994), 524.

compete? She wasn't competing. She was content to be single. She likely had desire for all the delights of marriage as most young people do. But she was careful not to awaken that desire.

Awakening romantic love too soon will quench the burning fire you have for Christ. The explosive and erotic feelings reserved for marriage cannot be overcome by a single person with no place to fulfill those desires. Instead of stirring up romantic love while you are single, stir up your love for Christ. Don't let anything put out the flame of affection for Christ.

> THEODORET OF CYRUS (393-466): "Do not allow love for God in you to slumber: stir it up and inflame it and pour the memory of God's kindnesses like oil on it lest it be said of us also, 'They fell into a deep sleep, and found nothing' (Psa 76:5). In other words, if you do not proclaim day in day out his salvation and recall the marvels he worked, and instead you forget his kindnesses, love will be extinguished and die, as it were. We must, on the contrary, continually rekindle our love for God. We must stir it up and lift the flame it on high."[38]

The Story of Jim and Elisabeth Elliot

I think of Jim and Elisabeth Elliot. Both loved each other. Both desired marriage. Both gave up marriage for missionary work. They did not want romantic love to quench their mission to expand the Kingdom of God. They met near a cemetery. As they told each other of their love, and that they would sacrifice that love for the cause of Christ, the shadow of a cross from one of the gravestones came between them. Elisabeth Elliot describes the scene in her book *Passion and Purity*:

> Jim and I walked to a cemetery and sat down on a stone slab. He spoke of a story he had read in his Bible study that morning—the story of Abraham's offering up Isaac. 'So I put you on the altar,' he said. Slowly we became aware that the moon, which had risen behind us, was casting the shadow of a stone cross on the slab

---

[38] Theodoret of Cyrus. *Commentary on the Song of Songs*. In Pauline Allen, et al., eds. *Early Christian Studies*, Vol 2 (Strathfield, Australia: St. Paul's Publications, 2001), 58.

between us. We were silent for a very long time, pondering this undeniable sign.[39]

Not only did Jim and Elisabeth Elliot put the Lord first, they actually put off getting married for quite a while for the advancement of the Kingdom of God in Ecuador. Yet this separation did not last forever. It was there on the mission field of Ecuador where they would one day get married.

You are not married until you are married. You may have whims of love as a single person, but you must not awaken it until you say "I do." This is the discipline of contentment in singleness. Like Adam, when God formed a woman out of his side, you must be "asleep in the will of God" and content serving God in your singleness. It is not wise to put your mind on the physical desires marriage until the right time.

Conclusion

What kind of foundation do you want for your marriage? Have you ever gone camping? Have you ever started a fire with twigs and lighter fluid that burned brightly and then quickly burned out? You know that in order to have a fire that lasts, you have to have some good strong mature lumber. In the same way, unless you are spiritually mature, you are headed for disaster. Unless the person you are interested is spiritually mature, you are looking at starting a long-term relationship with someone who has the short-term spiritual flair of lighter fluid. If you are considering a potential mate, you want someone with strong, godly character who loves the Lord and stirs up the spiritual embers in their heart.

---

[39] Elisabeth Elliot. *Passion and Purity, 2nd edition* (Downers Grove, IL: Revell, 2013) 61.

3 | SONG 1:7–2:7
DATING WITH A PURPOSE

I adjure you, O daughters of Jerusalem, by the gazelles or the does of the field, that you not stir up or awaken love until it pleases.
SONG 2:7

I know you are wondering, what is the pathway to marriage? What is the proper way to pursue that special someone and get to know them? For thousands of years there has been a time of getting to know one another, a time of courtship. Courtship is defined by the Miriam-Webster Dictionary as "the activities that occur when people are developing a romantic relationship that could lead to marriage or the period of time when such activities occur." What should a godly girl or a godly young man expect in courtship? Perhaps you are a parent asking the same question. Then you've come to the right place.

Courtship (or as we like to call it "dating with a purpose") is all about building trust. You want to find out if this is the person you can trust to care for you, to build a family together, to serve God together. How can you find out if the person is trustworthy? From this passage of Scripture, we are going to find that courtship rests on four pillars. It allows you to see if a person's character is wobbly or untrustworthy. If the relationship begins to wobble and fall as you put up these four pillars, you know it's not the right person for you to marry. How you begin courtship is quite important. Let's look at our first pillar.

PILLAR 1: DISCOVERY (1:7)

The first pillar you need to begin a courtship is *discovery*. Before a courtship begins, there needs to be safe places where the young man and young woman can talk and get to know each other as friends. In the Song of Solomon, remember we have a man and a woman looking back from their wedding day, telling us now about their courtship. Looking back from her wedding day, she says:

Song of Solomon 1:7 | Tell me, you whom my soul loves, where you pasture your flock, where you make it lie down at noon; for why should I be like one who veils herself beside the flocks of your companions?

What should we think about this strong language of love? Isn't she coming on strong? She tells the story with strong words towards Solomon, but most commentators agree that this is part soliloquy, that is, this is the sentiment of her heart, not exactly what she said to Solomon. Ladies, it wouldn't be appropriate to speak this way to someone you are just getting to know. But she was feeling this way. She had observed King Solomon. She saw that he was godly, a leader, someone any godly girl would desire.

Why is Solomon called a shepherd here? I thought he was a king. There is no problem in viewing Solomon as a shepherd since he owned many flocks (Ecc 2:7). This is like a pet name for Solomon after they are married. He is Israel's monarch. This "shepherd" imagery is common to the Near Eastern ancient love poetry. This is appropriate for the queen on her wedding day to reflect, and call King Solomon, her "shepherd." Solomon is very likely touring the countryside and inspecting his vineyards and catches the eye of the Shulamite.

In Song 1:7, the first thing we see are three commitments in discovering who that special person is that God may have for you to marry: visibility, accountability, and purity. By committing to never being alone with someone of the opposite gender until you are married, you will always have these three safeguards to provide a strong, safe foundation for discovering who you might marry. Again, let us remember, you are *not married* until you are married.

Visibility

The first commitment in discovering who you might court, is visibility. The Shulamite farm girl asks where Solomon might be so they can meet in a public place.

Song of Solomon 1:7a | Tell me... where you pasture your flock, where you make it lie down at noon?

She is asking where she can find him at a time when the sheep would be resting and not demanding the shepherd's complete attention. She wants to meet this young king. She wants to make sure there are plenty of other shepherds present so that she does nothing that is inappropriate. She is concerned about modesty and purity.

It is delightful and important for a girl to get to know a possible suitor, but there should always be visibility if you are with a person of the opposite gender that you are not married to. Preferably, you should be seen by people who share the same godly convictions you have. In a courtship relationship, or a friendship with a person of the opposite gender, this should, if possible, be the girl's parents and family.

Accountability

The second commitment in discovering who you might court, is accountability. This farm girl is coming at noon in the middle of the day when many people would be around, in broad view of the public eye. In Israel, "the oppressive heat of the middle of the day drives people and animals to rest in shady places."[40] "In the heat of the midday shepherds would lead their flocks under shady trees near a stream."[41] There was nothing questionable about this. There was a group of shepherds and others present, which means there was accountability.

As you consider the possibility of courtship, you need to meet anyone of the opposite gender in the broad daylight, so to speak. People with the same standards as you ought to be around. You ought always

---

[40] Carr. *The Song of Solomon*, 87.
[41] J.E. Smith, *The Wisdom Literature and Psalms* (Joplin, MO: College Press Pub. Co., 1996), Song 1:5-7.

meet with the right kind of people around, people who will hold you accountable.

Purity

The third commitment to have when you court someone is purity. We see from this peasant girl, that she made sure nothing questionable would be going on. Without accountability and visibility, she could be accused of being a harlot. She asks,

Song of Solomon 1:7b | Why should I be like one who veils herself beside the flocks of your companions?

She doesn't want to be like the prostitutes that would veil themselves and catch a shepherd all alone.

Just as discovery is important to courtship, let us remember that part of worshipping Christ is the constant discovery of his love. "In your presence is fullness of joy and at your right hand there are pleasures forevermore" (Psa 16:11). It was Augustine who said in the first few lines of his magnum opus, Confessions, "You have made us for yourself, and our hearts are restless until they rest in you."[42]

PILLAR 2: FRIENDSHIP (1:8-9)

The second pillar you need to begin a courtship is friendship. This is a time to get to know one another with proper accountability.

Protecting the Woman's Honor

The man is to take the lead by protecting the woman's honor. He thinks the world of her. He wants to honor her. He calls her, "O most beautiful among women," the one distinguished for beauty among all women. These are his inner thoughts being revealed in this love poem, so we know what is going on in his heart, not necessarily what would have been said (another example of soliloquy). This would have been entirely inappropriate to speak this way upon first meeting. He is a gentleman, and he wants to protect her modesty and insists that she come properly in public. He is teasing her a bit and says:

---

[42] Augustine of Hippo. *Confessions* (Oxford, UK: Oxford University Press, 2009), 3.

Song of Solomon 1:8 | If you do not know, O most beautiful among women, follow in the tracks of the flock, and pasture your young goats beside the shepherds' tents.

In other words, everyone would know where Solomon would be. All the shepherds would be with Solomon if he was visiting their fields. Nevertheless, she asked because it would be improper for her to have any hint of immodesty. Solomon protected the Shulamite's integrity and demonstrated a proper way to interact between eligible young men and women. Solomon initiates the relationship. She wonders where King Solomon might be, but he extends a personal invitation to kindle this special friendship. She sought him because he first made himself known to her.

So it is with Christ – "we love him because he first loved us" (1 Jn 4:19, KJV). Once we know where Christ is, we seek to follow him wherever he goes. In human romantic love, we will climb any mountain, cross any sea, and travel any distance to develop that special relationship. How much more do we need to know where we can meet Christ. He is our true friend, the friend of us sinners.

> BERNARD OF CLAIRVAUX (1090-1153): "O good Jesus, because of your friendship I am covered with the fullness of your light. While my spirit is fervent, graciously tell me where you pasture your flock, and give me unbounded joy in your presence. Serenely lovable above all others, tell me, where will you lead your flock to graze, where will you rest it at noon? Indeed, Moses of old, took advantage of the familiar friendship that had developed between him and God, and that holy man so longed for the great favor of seeing him that he said to God: 'If I have found favor in your sight, show yourself to me' (Exo 33:13). So let us seek our familiar Friend and find the pasture where we may meet him."[43]

Prizing the Woman as a Person

The man is to take the lead by prizing the woman as a person. As you begin a courtship, you need to develop a strong friendship in a non-romantic way. It is so interesting to read this God-breathed love poem, because this is one of the greatest, richest, most powerful kings ever to

---

[43] Bernard of Clairvaux. *Commentary on the Song of Solomon*, "Sermon 3: The Kiss of the Lord's Feet, Hands, and Mouth."

live, and he is absolutely stunned by the peasant Shulamite farm girl. He calls her a mare among Pharaoh's chariots, which is the highest of compliments. Imagine Solomon's young majestic voice paying this country girl a complement:

Song of Solomon 1:9 | I compare you, my love, to a mare among Pharaoh's chariots.

In ancient times, chariots would never be pulled by mares. "Stallions, not mares, were used to pull chariots in antiquity. A mare, therefore, among the chariots might very well start a chaotic experience."[44] To Solomon, she was as beautiful and sought after as if she were the only woman in a world full of men. He was attracted to her for all the right reasons. She was not like any other woman. The mare often would be white and represented grace, beauty and nobility. So the Shulamite girl was godly. She was pure. She was graceful – like "**a mare among Pharaoh's chariots.**"

> JOHN GILL (1697-1771): "Christ's church and people are compared to 'a mare among Pharaoh's chariots' for their strength, majesty, and comeliness; they are strong in Christ, and in his grace, and of an undaunted courage in bearing hardships, reproaches, and persecutions for his sake, and in fighting the Lord's battles; and are stately and majestic, especially a company of them in Gospel order, (Song 6:4) ; and are very comely and beautiful in their trappings, clothed with the righteousness of Christ, and the graces of his Spirit; and to a 'company' of them, a collection of goodly ones, as Egyptian ones, reckoned the best; and those in Pharaoh's chariot best of all; choice, costly, well fed, and well taken care of; and not wild and loose, but coupled and joined together in a chariot, all drawing one way. Christ's church and people are a choice and select company, distinguished from others by the grace of God; cost a great price, the blood of Christ; are well fed with the finest of the wheat; and are under the care both of angels and Gospel ministers."[45]

---

[44] John F. Walvoord, Roy B. Zuck, eds. *The Bible Knowledge Commentary: An Exposition of the Scriptures*, Vol 1 (Wheaton, IL: Victor Books, 1985), 1013.

[45] John Gill. *An Exposition of the book of Solomon's Song*, Vol 1 (Edinburgh: Thomas Turnbull, 1805), 94.

Single young lady, can you be described as that mare among Pharaoh's chariots? Are you a woman of high character? Are you maturing in inner beauty and grace? Are you able to have a brotherly friendship with a man that is discreet and not flirtatious? Do you have self-control and dignity? Are you able to kindle a friendship with a man without getting your hopes up or allowing yourself to dream too far into the future? What a joy this godly pursuit can be.

Those of us who are married men need to continually rekindle godly pursuit in our marriages. Remember when you were courting your wife, and you were willing to listen to Opera with her? You'd go to the store, and actually it didn't matter, you were happy to go anywhere with her. You prized her. You prized what she prized because she prized it. And that woman felt loved. You talked to her. She felt like she was one in a million. She needs to feel that way today and each day thereafter.

Husbands are called to love their wives and treasure them in the most exalted way possible, as Christ loved the church. Paul says, "Husbands, love your wives, as Christ loved the church and gave himself up for her" (Eph 5:25). That which a man begins in courtship, he is to continue in marriage. Some of you men know how to communicate love to your wife. You did it when you were courting. It's not that we don't know how. Married men need to ask God for grace to rekindle the godly pursuit of their wives anew.

In courtship, it is important to get to know the other person. Married men are told: "live with your wives in an understanding way, showing honor to the woman as the weaker vessel, since they are heirs with you of the grace of life, so that your prayers may not be hindered" (1 Pet 3:7). If you are a young man pursing an eligible and godly young woman, start getting to know this exceptional girl. Find out about her walk with the Lord. Listen to her. Make her feel treasured and prized as a special friend, because that's what you'll be doing in a marriage relationship. As you begin a courtship, you need to develop a strong friendship in a non-romantic way.

PILLAR 3: COMMITMENT (1:10-16A)

The third pillar you need to begin a courtship is commitment. The courtship is founded upon careful commitment to the principles of godly living. There are a flood of emotions that accompany the possibility of courtship. These emotions are expressed, but they are checked and balanced with great caution and commitment in honoring God and putting Christ first.

Commitment principle #1: Be responsible

Spending time with that special someone is for long-term goals, not short-term pleasure. Be responsible. You enter into courtship with marriage in mind. It may be way down the road, but courting is dating a person with the purpose of finding a mate. Why is this? Because marriage means commitment. Worldly dating is dangerous because its purpose is often temporary pleasure or companionship without any meaningful goal in mind. In the world's version of dating, a person wants all of the pleasure of love with none of the work, none of the vows, none of the sacrifice. This generation wants intimacy without obligations. Courtship works, because it brings in accountability and purity with two people who love the Lord but *do not trust themselves*. They learn to trust each other, because they are two people who care more about each other's good than their own momentary pleasure.

Having marriage in mind does not mean that things need to get serious immediately in courtship. In fact, it's important that there is not that kind of pressure, otherwise it would be hard to get to know each other. It's good to get to know people in group settings where there is no pressure. And even once you begin courting that special someone, remember the first goal is to be friends and to get to know each other. With that in mind, when a man and a woman see the Lord possibly leading their paths together, it is something to take very seriously.

Solomon pursued this farm girl with marriage in mind. Solomon pictures this peasant girl as his Bride and his Queen. He's not looking for superficial pleasure from her. He's looking for commitment. He honors her with honorable words:

Song of Solomon 1:10 | Your cheeks are lovely with ornaments,
    your neck with strings of jewels.

"It was a centuries-old fashion in the East for a woman to wear a cord of gold around her forehead... which hung down over her checks...

Neck chains or necklaces were made of gold or other metal, or consisted of strings of pearls, corals, or precious stones."[46]

It seems that he was imagining her wearing this jewelry, because in the next verse, the daughters volunteer to make these for her. She is poor. She is likely adorned with no jewelry. Her chief attraction is her grace and purity. She is an unlikely candidate for a king. Yet in pursuing a woman, Solomon wasn't looking for mere social interaction, it is clear he had major, lifetime commitment in mind. And so, the daughters of Jerusalem, the elite women in Solomon's court, volunteer to make the peasant girl her royal jewelry.

Song of Solomon 1:11 | We will make for you ornaments of gold, studded with silver.

This is a gesture of commitment from the heart of the king.

> JOHN GILL (1697-1771): "The church has her golden chain of redemption, her pearl necklace; which are either the graces of the Spirit, so linked together, that where there is one there are all; and which consists of those links, or pearls: faith, hope, love, repentance, humility, patience, self-denial, contentment in every state, spiritual knowledge, longsuffering, or forbearance; sincerity goes through them all. With them come the spiritual blessings of the covenant of grace, with which the church and all the saints are blessed in Christ at once, and with one and all; and which golden chain of salvation, one link of which cannot be broken, is excellently described by the apostle, 'And those whom he predestined he also called, and those whom he called he also justified, and those whom he justified he also glorified' (Rom 8:30)."[47]

What a beautiful picture of Christ and the church. We were poor, and Christ has made us rich. We were servants to our sin, but Christ has freed us, not to be a mere servant, but to be his bride. We were unkempt in our unrighteousness, and Christ has adorned us with his righteousness. He takes us seriously. He laid down his life for you and

---

[46] H. J. Chadwick & J. M. Freeman. *Manners & Customs of the Bible, revised edition* (North Brunswick, NJ: Bridge-Logos Publishers, 1998), 344.

[47] John Gill. *Solomon's Song,* Vol 1, 98.

me! Marriage, as a picture of Christ and his church, should be approached with sobriety and commitment.

Commitment principle #2: Be picky

You must carefully understand a person's character before you can commit to them. Solomon had the character to make his intentions known to this poor farm girl. He had beautiful jewelry made for her – **"ornaments of gold, studded with silver"** (1:11). Be picky. Don't necessarily go for the first person that you are attracted to. Do some research on this person. Get to know them in many different situations – in groups, at church, at a public event. There may be many opportunities, but identify the godly characteristics you want in a mate. Be that person first. Then don't settle or cut corners when it comes to the character of the person you might be interested in. This goes without saying, but everything leading up to this point showed that both Solomon and the Shulamite were mature, godly people who were ready to marry because they had a strong commitment to God and to purity and accountability. She compared his name to the oil that was "poured out" in worship of the Lord at the Tabernacle (1:3).

Commitment principle #3: Be patient

The joy of intimacy is the reward of commitment. Be patient. Guard your heart. Don't act like you are married if you are not married. In other words, marital intimacy is the reward of those who wait until they are committed through a marriage vow before God.

Remember Uzzah who touched the Ark of the Covenant (2 Sam 6:1-7; cf 1 Chron 13:9-12) when he shouldn't have? What did God do to him? God killed him. Why? Because he was not the one committed to carrying the Ark. The Ark was so sacred, you had to be a priest to touch it. And it had to be a specific family of priests. Why? It shows the sacredness of the Ark. It is only to be touched by those who commit their entire lives and livelihood to protecting and caring for the Ark. In the same way, only a man who has committed his life to protecting and caring for a woman before God and witnesses, may touch that woman. The joy of intimacy is the reward of commitment.

Intimacy without commitment contradicts what the Bible teaches about love. Instead of being selfless, it's selfish. Instead of looking out for the ongoing good of the other person, it's focused on the needs of the moment. Instead of cherishing the person as a brother or sister in

Christ, the person becomes an object to fulfill your desires. Look at how Solomon and the Shulamite girl dealt with passion. It is beautiful. They have very real passions, but they keep them under control.

You must be careful to guard the rush of emotions that accompany the possibility of courtship. It is natural to think highly of someone you are interested in. Both the peasant girl and the king think of each other when they are away. The affection seems to be out of this world!

When referring to this passage, Spurgeon said, the Song of Solomon was "one of the most heavenly portions of God's Word." Consider the words of the Shulamite farm girl.

Song of Solomon 1:12 | While the king was on his couch, my nard gave forth its fragrance.

The language here seems a bit shocking to the Western mind, but it really is not to the Eastern thinker. We must be careful not to make that which is pure and innocent to be worldly and sensual. To the pure all things are pure. She is speaking of that which is closest to her heart. These are the thoughts of her heart.

It was common for a woman to wear a pouch of perfumed spices and flowers around her neck. Whenever she smelled it, she thought of Solomon. The "nard" is simply a very expensive perfume from near the Himalayan mountains in India. By referring to Solomon as the "**nard**" or sweet smelling and very expensive perfume, she is saying Solomon is precious to her. She esteems him. She goes on to say "**Behold, you are beautiful, my beloved, truly delightful**" (1:16). She goes on to describe her beloved.

Song of Solomon 1:13-14 | My beloved is to me a sachet of myrrh that lies between my breasts. [14] My beloved is to me a cluster of henna blossoms in the vineyards of Engedi.

The "**myrrh**" is an expensive spice that would have been mixed with the holy oil in the Tabernacle (Exo 30:23-33).[48] This same anointing oil was used in the Temple in first-century Jerusalem when Jesus taught there. By saying her beloved is like the holy "**myrrh**" close to her heart, she is saying her heart for holiness is knit with his heart. She reverences him.

---

[48] Carr. *The Song of Solomon,* 92.

And what about the "**henna blossoms**"? Thirty miles south of Jerusalem, Engedi was one of two freshwater springs on the western shore of the Dead Sea. Engedi's year around temperate climate and available water made it well known as an agriculture center. When the Beloved described her lover as a cluster of henna blossoms, she implied that he was beautiful and smelled good. Henna blossoms contain an essential oil used to make perfume.

Henna blossoms and myrhh aside, we are called to esteem the beauty of holiness in a potential mate. We cannot make our feelings known but must show restraint and patience. Inward holiness is infinitely more important than mere outward beauty. "Charm is deceptive, and beauty is fleeting; but a woman who fears the LORD is to be praised" (Pro 31:30, NIV). Respect, esteem, and wonder are proper for a girl of marriable age as she looks to a godly man. But this of course speaks to more than just this love story between Solomon and the poor peasant farm girl. This speaks of the beauty of holiness that Christ puts in our hearts as we come to know him. He welcomes us to him. And though we are poor and worthless and weathered by sin, our King of kings welcomes us. As he says to poor sinners like you and me, "Come to me, all who labor and are heavy laden, and I will give you rest" (Mt 11:28), we begin to see him as "beautiful" and "truly delightful." Christ is like the nard that rests upon our heart. He is at the control center of all that we do. His beauty and love are truly irresistible.

> THEODORET OF CYRUS (393-466): "'It will lodge between my breasts,' that is, in the governing part of my soul, which is located in the heart lying between the breasts. This indicates the fulfillment of the prophecy spoken by God, 'I shall dwell and walk about among them, and I shall be their God and they shall be my people, says the Lord almighty' (Eze 37:27; Rev 21:3). The bridegroom in person also makes the promise, 'We shall come, my Father and I, and shall make our abode with him' (Jn 14:23)."[49]

The Shulamite farm girl saw the king from a distance "on his couch" (1:12) in the forest; she was moved in her heart for the king. She guards her love for him "between her breasts," near her heart. Though

---

[49] Theodoret of Cyrus. *Song of Songs*. In *Early Christian Studies*, Vol 2, 51.

this girl had powerful affections for the king, she maintained a respectable emotional distance from Solomon in public.

The couch is referring to the king's dining table where he would recline for a meal. His royal tent ("the curtains of Solomon," 1:5) had likely been brought there as he travels the countryside inspecting his vineyards. We can imagine him having dinner out in the open. She is admiring him from a distance.

We have to remember that this all pictures Christ and his church. Christ does not come to soil us, but to convict us of sin, righteousness, and the judgment to come. He calls us to see the beauty of his holiness. He doesn't take his Bride to be and roll her around in the mud. He loves and respects her and protects her purity! Single men, it is your responsibility to picture this and to protect that girl's purity.

Consider this if you are single and considering marriage. You've got all these God-given feelings, but you must control them. You must be careful as the Shulamite says

> I adjure you...that you not stir up or awaken love until it pleases. — Song 2:7

I'm told that my great Uncle Jack Reed, a realtor who worked in Oregon and California was once was in partnership with a man named "Walt Disney" who wanted to build a "Disneyland" amusement park in California with help of Uncle Jack. Uncle Jack broke the partnership with Mr. Disney because he thought that the little cartoon mouse would never take off. Wow, was he wrong. Disney put out a film called *Bambi* in 1941 that in one scene had an owl explaining to everyone what it was to be in love and how powerful the emotional aspect of love is.

> Owl: "Nearly everybody gets twitterpated in the springtime. For example: You're walking along, minding your own business. You're looking neither to the left, nor to the right, when all of a sudden you run smack into a pretty face. Woo-hoo! You begin to get weak in the knees. Your head's in a whirl. And then you feel light as a feather, and before you know it, you're walking on air. And then you know what? You're knocked for a loop, and you completely lose your head!"

It's comical, but it is strikingly true. These emotions are raging and trying to get to the surface in all of us. What are we to do with them?

Remember commitment principle #3: Be patient. The joy of intimacy is the reward of commitment.

Commitment principle #4: Be thankful

It may be that as you trust in the Lord and live life according to his plan that he leads you into a committed relationship. This is a gift from the Lord, and you need to be thankful and never take it for granted. "The man who finds a wife finds a treasure, and he receives favor from the Lord" (Pro 18:22, NLT). "An excellent wife who can find? She is far more precious than jewels" (Pro 31:10). "Then the Lord God said, It is not good that the man should be alone; I will make him a helper fit for him" (Gen 2:18). Whatever your situation is in seeking a godly mate, you must trust in the Lord alone to work it out according to his will. And if he does give you the gift of a committed relationship, you ought never take his kindness for granted, but be thankful for that special someone.

We see this in Solomon's love story. There is a mutual affection that stirs between Solomon and the Shulamite. Solomon's heart is revealed to us. Again, using soliloquy (silent and unexpressed sentiments and thoughts), we find the king finds this future queen quite suitable. He exclaims (at least inwardly):

Song of Solomon 1:15 | Behold, you are beautiful, my love; behold, you are beautiful; your eyes are doves.

Solomon sees this farm girl through the eyes of grace and love. Jerusalem's king greatly esteems this woman of low estate. She is beautiful in every way to him. He even knows her eye color. He sees the innocence of the dove in countenance. He loves her. And the Shulamite girl responds (again at least inwardly) with equal joy and excitement:

Song of Solomon 1:16a | Behold, you are beautiful, my beloved, truly delightful.

What a wonderful gift it is to fall in love with a godly person. They are thankful for each other. Solomon sees beyond the lowly position of the Shulamite girl and sees a queen.

We can easily apply this to our walk with Christ. He sees us, and he says, "you have dove's eyes." This is how Christ sees you. He loves you! You are beautiful to him. You are truly delightful to him. You might think, Oh! How could he say that? He says that because he doesn't see me as I am in my flesh. He sees me as I am having been clothed in his righteousness. He has given you his beauty so he can say you are his Bride, who is the fairest among women! When you know the color of the girl's eyes you are interested in, you know you are in love. And so Christ loves us. He knows our frame. He remembers we are dust. We are accepted and welcomed by God because of Christ the Beloved One (Eph 1:7).

> JEROME (347-420), "'Ah, you are beautiful, my beloved, ah, you are beautiful: your eyes are doves!' You who are beautiful and strong, because you resemble him of whom it is sung, 'In your beauty and your splendor' (Psa 45:3), will hear from your spouse, 'Forget your people and your father's house. So shall the king desire your beauty' (Psa 45:10-11)."[50]

Christ says to you, "you have dove's eyes." He sees in you in light of his transforming grace and beauty. He's transformed us and now sees in us qualities that he finds lovely or desirable in us – the kind of spiritual beauty that is now ours in Christ.

Doves speak of meekness, of gentleness, of tenderness. The dove is mild and harmless. Perhaps he's thinking of her being chaste and faithful and humble. Those words all go along with dove's eyes. Then there's a distinctive of dove's eyes that is fascinating, and that speaks to another Christian grace, that of being single-focused. I'm told that dove's eyes focus on one thing at a time. It's not that they can't see more, but they're not easily distracted. That's why they're often referred to as "lovebirds." When they fix their attention on their mate, they're not distracted by other things going on around them. Their eyes are single focused. This bride stays focused on her beloved, and he loves that about her. You might want to pray for the Lord to give you that single devotion – "Lord, give me dove's eyes; give me undistracted devotion for only you."

PILLAR 4: DETERMINATION TO PLEASE GOD (1:16B-2:7)

The one thing you want to be careful of during courtship is that you carry through on your convictions before God. Solomon did that. He was a man of honor and purity who desired to please God in all things.

---

[50] Jerome. *Homilies on the Psalms.* In *Fathers,* Vol 57, 26.

Please God by Meeting in the Open

You must be determined in your accountability. The courtship begins! You can see that this is the first instance of the couple together in a committed way. We see this in a public meeting place, among the shade giving trees, a popular place to gather where there could be relief under the trees from the hot sun.

Song of Solomon 1:16b-17 | Our couch is green; the beams of our house are cedar; our rafters are pine.

They are together, but they are never alone. If you want to destroy your potential marriage before it starts, then have no accountability, and keep yourself in a state of temptation. If you are alone, no matter how godly you are, you will be tempted. You must be determined in your purity. The emotions are running high.

First, they are not alone, because they are meeting in the open. They are in the public gathering place in the open where the shade of trees brings shelter to the people in the public square. They are not in a private place meeting – that would have been a scandal in that day. They are meeting out in the open where all can see. But they are also not alone because the Lord is there. Ambrose speaks to the strength of the relationship whose commitment is first with Christ.

> AMBROSE (333-397), "These words point to the beautiful adornment of the beams' strong structure, which, as beams do, uphold by their excellent qualities the superstructure of the church and give charm to its façade."[51]

The church has for her structure Jesus as the chief Cornerstone and the apostles and prophets for her beams (1 Pet 2:6-7; Eph 2:20). The Word of Jesus holds up all true believers so that Christ "builds his church and the gates of hell shall not prevail against it" (Mt 16:18).

Please God by Protecting Your Purity

The courtship begins, and of course the emotions are exhilarating. Yet Solomon is meeting in the open. He is not compromising her integrity. That does not mean their emotions are not enflamed with passion. God created this wonderful journey to marriage. While God is trust-

---

[51] St. Ambrose. *Six Days of Creation.* In *Fathers,* Vol 42, 108.

worthy, the strong desires of a courting couple are not at all trustworthy. We see in Solomon's Song the explosive passions of both Solomon and his future queen, and yet there is a warning not to publicly express these sentiments or stir them up until the proper time, i.e. the wedding day.

The future queen feels treasured.

Listen to the future queen; she calls herself a rose.

Song of Solomon 2:1 | I am a rose of Sharon, a lily of the valleys.

Solomon replies...

Song of Solomon 2:2 | As a lily among brambles, so is my love among the young women.

This peasant girl refers to herself as a "rose of Sharon," which is just a common wildflower on the plain of Sharon in Judea on the Mediterranean coast. It's a fertile place, and it's famous for roses. This description is commonly ascribed to Christ. We have songs about it, poems about it, but I favor the view that it's the bride who is speaking in this verse. "I am the rose of Sharon, and the lily of the valleys."

According to this view, the rose of Sharon and the lily of the valleys are just common, ordinary wildflowers. If this is the bride speaking, she's saying in essence, "I'm just a lowly, everyday wildflower." She doesn't feel herself to be anything special. There's nothing in her that is worthy of his notice. Isn't this exactly how we feel when we come to salvation? – unworthy, undone by sin, and completely amazed to be called by Christ. Solomon's future queen has a very low view of herself.

But then Solomon responds to her, and his opinion is very high and elevated. He says, "Like a lily among brambles, so is my love among the young women." He treasures her. His estimation of her is far different than her estimation of herself. The key to a healthy self-image is coming to see ourselves as Christ sees us.

Solomon basically says to her, "You are choice to me; you are special to me. You stand out from the others. You are like a flower among the thorns." How appropriate this is. The plain of Sharon is known for its thorns, not its flowers. Yet lilies may grow there, however few they be. The lily is supposed to be pure and beautiful and simple, but lilies are found sometimes among these thorns. This is a reminder that we were once thorns, but now we are a new creation. We've been trans-formed by grace. He has made us into a work of beauty, a lily, and we are precious to him.

The future queen feels protected.

Solomon furnished his future bride with shelter and shade. She is so thankful.

Song of Solomon 2:3a | As an apple tree among the trees of the forest, so is my beloved among the young men.

He stands out like a towering apple tree in the forest, providing the protection of shade. She's able to be at home with him, to enjoy him. She's able to rest and be herself. That's what makes him stand out among the other young men. In our walk with Christ, Jesus as well stand above all others. It's not enough to just know about Christ and to talk about him. We need to experience him, to enjoy him, and to rest in his presence.

This poor farm girl finds in Solomon a resting place. She finds ac-ceptance and a place where she can feel at ease. She's able to stop the busyness and rest. How we need to slow down. As Christians, we are often "too busy" to enjoy the Lord's presence. It goes without saying that you cannot enjoy the shade unless you stop and sit down. We are so busy, but we must make time to stop and sit down in Christ's shade.

Song of Solomon 2:3b | With great delight I sat in his shadow.

Some of us have been too busy to stop and be nurtured by Jesus. There's no fellowship, there's no lingering in his presence. Stop rushing around—and sit down. Put away your iPad, put away your smart phone and your laptop. Enjoy the shade of God's presence. "In the shadow of your wings I will take refuge" (Psa 57:1).

The future queen feels provided for.

Song of Solomon 2:3c | With great delight I sat in his shadow, and his fruit was sweet to my taste.

These thoughts of the Shulamite girl reveal the security she felt with Solomon. He was king and had need of nothing. Solomon fur-nished his future bride with the best food and would have no difficulty caring for her future needs should the Lord lead them to marry. I like to say it this way: the two main requirements for a lady to enter a committed relationship with a man is that they need to love Jesus above all else, and the man must have a well providing job. Courtship should never be entered into unless there is the prospect of employment that can provide living arrangements and provision for the new husband and wife and possible future children. The suitor should not even consider the idea of marriage if he is not only gainfully employed but able to support a growing family.

In our walk with Christ, we enjoy the cooling protection of his shadow in the harsh sun of this world. Marriage reflects Christ's care for his church. We eat of his satisfying fruit. "O taste and see that the Lord is good" (Psa 34:8).

> CHARLES HADDON SPURGEON (1834-1892), "If Jesus is as an apple tree among the trees of the woods, do not keep away from him, but sit under his shadow, and taste his fruit. Jesus casts a shadow, let us sit under it: Jesus yields fruit, let us taste the sweetness of it. The spouse knew her Beloved to be like a fruit-bearing tree, and at once she sat under his shadow, and fed upon his fruit. It is a pity that we can know so much about Christ, and yet enjoy him so little. May our experience keep pace with our knowledge, and may that experience be composed of a practical using of our Lord!
>
> In the shade of Jesus we have more delight than in any fancied light of our own. The spouse had great delight. I trust that you Christian people do have great delight; and if not, you ought to ask yourselves whether you really are the people of God. But, oh, there is an intense delight in being overshadowed by Him if you know him! He is near you, and you know it. His dear presence is as certainly with you as if you could see him, for his influence surrounds you. Often have I felt as if Jesus leaned over me, as a friend might look over my shoulder. Although no cool shade comes over your brow, yet you may as much feel his shadow as if it did, for your heart grows calm."[52]

This same desire to provide for his Bride should be in the heart of every suitor as he enters into courtship. If God reveals to both parties

---

[52] Spurgeon. *Pulpit,* Vol 57, Sermon 3249, "Under the Apple Tree" (1911), 217.

that marriage is his will, the man should already be in a place to take that important step forward to engagement when the time is right. Certainly that step means a readiness and preparedness to provide that shade of security if God should lead you to marry.

The future queen feels loved.

The future peasant princess feels greatly honored, loved and celebrated as a woman.

Song of Solomon 2:4 | He brought me to the banqueting house, and his banner over me was love.

Banquets are often an expression of joy and celebration. As Solomon celebrates this poor farm girl, so Christ celebrates us.

> THOMAS WILCOX (1549-1608), "By 'banqueting house,' she means the places of rich food and feasting, but all this must be spiritually understood, that is, that our Savior brought the church to life and salvation, by the delicate food of his Word and the wine of the Spirit's power and grace. And Christ our spouse always sets up his banner of love, grace, and favor over us, however little we deserve it."[53]

> MARTIN LUTHER (1483-1546), "Soldiers in camp are assigned according to the order of their banners. So she says: I recognize my banner, which is love, under this God; I am assigned to this position." [54]

This great king honors the lowly farm girl. He has assigned his love to her. This is significant because the place of women in ancient society was very low. Solomon elevates the place of women by the way he treats his future bride. He celebrates her not only with a banquet but with a banner. A banner is a military flag. The banner over Solomon's future queen is something more precious than an ensign of cloth, but a display and commitment of self-sacrificing love. There is an almost militaristic desire to cherish and protect the future queen. He doesn't want to take

---

[53] Thomas Wilcox. *An Exposition upon the Book of Canticles* (London: Robert Waldegrave, 1585), Song 2:4.

[54] Martin Luther. *Luther's Works, Vol. 15: Ecclesiastes, Song of Solomon, and the Last Words of David* (St. Louis: Concordia Publishing House, 1971), 214.

advantage of her and defile her purity. He wants to protect her and love her and respect her.

So many misunderstand love, so be careful not to misunderstand it yourself. Most "fall in love" because they feel cared for. They love being loved. If you think about it, that is a self-centered emotion that does not measure up to biblical love. If I love someone mainly because they fit my mold and meet my expectations, then I really have something that is less like love and more like selfish desire. Some might say, "We had sex because we loved each other." That's not love but animal desire. Love respects and restrains and protects the dignity of your relationship. Real biblical love is a commitment. It goes beyond emotion to conviction and action, sacrificing self for the object of your love.

Love is not mere emotion. Love, as God defines it, is not primarily an emotion. The world says, "when the feeling stops, the love is over." Love is not a tingly sensation. Love is not sentimentalism. Love has nothing to do with how you feel. God so loved the world that he gave his only Son. He didn't look at the world and say, "I just can't resist them; I've got to get them in heaven. They're terrific." There wasn't one thing in us that was deserving. We were enemies; we hated God; we were sinful and vile, but God loved us anyway. And he loved us so much, he gave us his Son.

Solomon celebrates this lowly farm girl. She says, "his banner over me is love." Worldly men in our day and age take advantage of women. Many men speak harshly and bitterly to their wives and even abuse them and worse. The man in whom Christ dwells is gentle, loving, and kind, serving and protecting his wife in self-sacrificing love. Love is so much more than romantic infatuation. It is total self-sacrifice for the other. This self-sacrificing love points to a higher and divine love that is seen in Christ's banner which he puts over his Bride.

ARTHUR JACKSON (1593-1666), "Christ, the Captain of our salvation manifests his glorious presence amongst us and carries us with arms of love. He cheers us up with his unfurled banner of love, proclaiming his defense to us and resistance of our enemies. 'When the enemy shall come in like a flood, the Spirit of the Lord shall lift up a standard [banner] against him.' So is God's banner of love to cherish and protect us."[55]

The future queen is sick with love.

All of these strong romantic emotions tend to make a massive assault on purity. We have another soliloquy. We hear the thoughts of her heart.

Song of Solomon 2:5-6 | Sustain me with raisins; refresh me with apples, for I am sick with love. [6] His left hand is under my head, and his right hand embraces me!

Raisins and apples are ancient aphrodisiacs. As a relationship gets more serious, feelings of deep passion and romance sometimes seize our emotions. It's so strong it's painful. This love sickness and longing for the romantic love of marriage points to the "joy unspeakable" that the Christian experiences. The longing in romance points to a higher love story when our Bridegroom Jesus comes again for his precious bride.

Solomon's future queen is overcome with passion and, in effect says, "This love is too much to be contained. This is too much for me." She has a powerful sense of being loved, so much that it hurts. Have you ever been there with Christ? That's not an intensity you're going to experience in the Christian life every single day, but we can testify that there have been moments when we've experienced the power of his love – it's so divine, so great, and you think, "I can hardly stand it. It's overwhelming!"

> BASIL THE GREAT (330-379), "What reflection is sweeter than the thought of the magnificence of God? What desire of the soul is so poignant and so intolerably keen as that desire implanted by God in a soul purified from all vice and affirming with sincerity, 'I languish with love.' Totally ineffable and indescribable are the lightning flashes of divine Beauty."[56]

---

[55] Arthur Jackson. *Annotations on Job, the Psalms, Proverbs, Ecclesiastes, and Song of Solomon* (London: Roger Daniel, 1658), Song 2:4.

[56] Basil the Great. *The Long Rules*, In *Fathers of the Church: A New Translation*, Vol 9 (Washington, D.C: Catholic University of America Press, 1947-2013), 234.

AUGUSTINE (354-430), "In the Song of Songs it is said, 'wounded with love'; that is, of being in love, of being inflamed with passion, of sighing for the bridegroom, from whom she received the arrow of the Word." [57]

"The wound of love is health-giving. The bride of Christ sings in the Song of Songs, 'I am wounded with charity.' When is this wound healed? When our desire is saturated with good things. It's called a wound as long as we desire and don't yet have. Love, you see, in that case, is the same as if it were a pain. When we get there, when we have what we desire, the pain disappears, but the love doesn't cease." [58]

To be embraced by the love of Christ is better than any romantic love on earth. Romantic love is a shadow that points to our union with Christ. Christ fills and satisfies the heart beyond what any human being is capable of doing. It is for this reason we must careful not to put romantic love above where it should be. Romantic love points to divine love. It is an image of it, but a faint one. There will be no romantic love or sex in heaven because as exciting and exhilarating it is on earth, it pales in comparison to divine love. Don't mistake it for biblical love. Let's be clear – romantic love (eros) is not wrong. Within marriage, it's God's invention and his idea. It is real and certainly sanctified and wholesome and perfectly good in the bonds of marriage, but it is not to be trusted because of our weak and sometimes idolatrous hearts. Romantic love is blinding even to the most sanctified of believers. Be careful with the deep romantic feelings you have for that special someone. God created romance and sex and wants most people to enjoy intimacy when the right time comes. When the fires of romantic love are stirred up, it's hard to think of anything else. This is why physical contact should be limited in the courtship relationship. Once a kiss is given there is an unstoppable desire to consummate that kiss. A courting couple has no legitimate way to carry out those desires before God until they are actually married.

---

[57] Augustine of Hippo. *Psalms. Nicene and Post-Nicene Fathers of the Christian Church*, Vol 8, 145.

[58] Augustine of Hippo. *Sermon 298.2*. In *J. E. Rotelle, ed. Works of St. Augustine: A Translation for the Twenty-First Century*, Vol 8 (Hyde Park, N.Y.: New City Press, 1995), 225.

It is to be expected to be "sick with love" as you grow in respect and appreciation for the one you are courting. God invented romantic love. As mentioned before, the fire should remain in the fireplace, not in the middle of the living room. Take it out of the fireplace, and you might burn down the house. So it is with romantic love. Guard it and save it for your wedding night.

One day our divine Bridegroom will return for his lowly bride, and we as believers long for that day. We are "sick with love" to see him. Don't soil yourself with this world but save yourself for the world to come. "Beloved, we are God's children now, and what we will be has not yet appeared; but we know that when he appears we shall be like him, because we shall see him as he is. And everyone who thus hopes in him purifies himself as he is pure" (1 Jn 3:2-3).

The future queen does not want to stir up love too soon.

We see the strong desires of the future queen expressed in soliloquy, but when she might want to express them or give in to them, we see the right response to those desires. She exclaims to the elite women of the court.

Song of Solomon 2:7 | I adjure you, O daughters of Jerusalem, by the gazelles or the does of the field, that you not stir up or awaken love until it pleases.

The love she has for her future husband, she does not want to prostitute it and defile it by giving her sexual desires to him before they are covenanted together in holy matrimony. "Let marriage be held in honor among all, and let the marriage bed [a metaphor for sex in marriage] be undefiled, for God will judge the sexually immoral and adulterous" (Heb 13:4).

> GREGORY OF NYSSA (335-394), "She uses the oath not to assure them of the progress she herself has made but to lead the daughters of Jerusalem through their oath to a life of virtue. She adjures them to keep their love alert and watchful until his good will come to fulfillment..."[59]

---

[59] Saint Gregory of Nyssa. *Commentary on the Song of Songs.* Casimir McCambley, trans. (Brookline, Mass.: Hellenic College Press, 1987), 104-105.

The poor but dignified farm girl can't give legitimate expression to these desires and still hold on to her dignity. As these very good and godly desires flow into her heart, she is essentially saying: "Stop! Not yet. It's not the right time." Giving expression to these holy desires would have soiled them. She is saving them for her future husband.

Conclusion

I would encourage anyone beginning courtship to sign a purity covenant with their parents present, if possible. Never allow yourself to be alone. Be careful what you talk about on the phone. Let things be focused on Scripture. Memorize Scripture together. Put that passion and motivation to good use. My wife Jill and I memorized the book of James and the Sermon on the Mount together during this time. Don't let the conversations get romantic. The time will come for that. Do not awaken your love. Be very careful when you say the words "I love you." It's best to wait until you're engaged to do that. Also, I recommend short engagements. The reasons are obvious. You don't want to awaken love until the wedding night. You've got to focus your mind away from romance so you can get to know the person. You are laying a foundation for marriage. Be very careful not to have physical contact. Don't act like you're married until you are actually married. Keep your clothes on and your hands off. Be determined to please God and do nothing to compromise your convictions.

Courtship is all about building trust. If you are a car dealer, you don't let the person take the car on a trip to Florida until they have *purchased* the car. If you're in real estate, you don't let them move into the house until they've *purchased* the house. Until they are committed and have promised to care for that item, they are not allowed to act like owners.

If you are single, and one day consider beginning courtship, or your children begin courting someone, remember, you want to find out during this time if this person is trustworthy to serve God and fulfill their God-given role. This is a person you need to be able to trust. Are they a dependable, trustworthy, predictable, faithful committed Christian person? You can start by seeing if this person has the character and commitment to submit themselves to accountability, visibility, and purity. May God give us the grace to do so!

THE DATING COMMITMENT

This covenant is a good example of the many dating commitments I have been a part of as a pastor.

Purpose

To be conformed to the image of Jesus Christ and to glorify God, becoming selfless and humble, having complete dependence on the One whom they aim to glorify.

To discern, in gospel centered community, whether marriage is a viable option for <Young Lady> and <Young Man> through a season of deepened friendship.

Accountability and Encouragement

<Young Man> and <Young Lady> are to be held accountable by <Father of the Young Lady>, as he is the father and shepherd of the courtship. <Young Man> and <Young Lady> are to meet with <Father of the Young Lady> both together and individually for the purpose of accountability, to be exhorted with Scripture when appropriate. With that in mind, it will be important to note that <Young Man> is not the head or leader over <Young Lady>, that role is still designated to her father, who is <Young Lady>'s head and protector until she is given in marriage.

When <Young Man> has an opportunity to meet with <church pastor>, he should do so; this is for the purposes of accountability, but also to provide wisdom, exhortation, and healthy rebuke if necessary.

<Young Man> is highly encouraged to be held accountable by a strong Christian brother throughout the duration of the courtship, not only to provide accountability, but also to provide encouragement through the Word and support through prayer. Ideally, this brother is to hold <Young Man> accountable in matters beyond the courtship, to ensure that he is growing in holiness, grace, and knowledge. Ultimately, that <Young Man> is abiding in Christ and thus bearing fruit; loving God and loving neighbor. Moreover, it is encouraged of <Young Lady> to form as similar relationship with a strong Christian sister.

While <Young Lady> and <Young Man> are to hold each other accountable as brother and sister in Christ, they are not "accountability partners."

All involved in accountability are to ask pressing and vital questions of <Young Lady> and <Young Man>. If <Young Man> and <Young Lady> fail or violate their relationship with each other or in their relationship with God, the courtship will be suspended and ultimately concluded if they are not restored back to the Lord.

Initiatives

While <Young Lady> and <Young Man> are together, they will give testimony to how the Lord has been moving in their lives. This includes sharing Scripture they have been studying, and discussion of any Christian extrabiblical literature that is being read. Additionally, they are not to become dependent upon one another for spiritual food. They are encouraged to do ministry together, ultimately for the furthering of the gospel, of which they are only vessels through whom Christ works; <Young Man> and <Young Lady> are not needed for the advancement of the kingdom, but have the privilege to do so.

Boundaries

Verbally: <Young Man> and <Young Lady> are not to speak as though they were married. They are not to speak as though their futures' were bound; they will not verbally bind their futures. They should be careful in their expression towards one another.

Physically: <Young Man> and <Young Lady> are not to have a physical relationship. The physical relationship will be kept inside the marriage covenant. Side hugs are appropriate during courtship. It is recommended that holding hands should be reserved for engagement. The first kiss should be given at the altar when a couple enters into the marriage covenant.

Socially: <Young Man> and <Young Lady> are never to be alone. They may go out to public places in view of the people present, or with their friends. They may not drive alone in a car together but should have an approved chaperone or drive in separate vehicles. Unrelated, it is expected that <Young Man> abide with the <Young Lady>'s family to see that he is proven faithful.

<Young Lady> and <Young Man> are not allowed to court/date another while they are courting each other.

Honoring Christ

This covenant is created not because we wish to be under law, but because we wish to honor Christ with our lives, having been saved by grace, our hearts have been regenerated and our consciences have been quickened; we are new creations. Certainly, we are not under law, but grace (Rom 6:14; Gal 5:18).

In the event that this covenant becomes burdensome, the courtship will be suspended. It is recognized that this document reflects Christian principle and standard; and Christian principle and standard were never intended to be followed without faith in Christ and dependence upon His Church. Consequently, this covenant is not to be obeyed in the flesh, but the Spirit (Rom 8:4; Gal 5:25).

Signatures:

_____

Young Man

_____

Young Lady

_____

Father of Young Lady

_____

Pastor or spiritual leader

4 | SONG 2:8-3:5
PASSION, PURITY, & ENGAGEMENT

My beloved speaks and says to me: "Arise, my love, my beautiful one, and come away."
SONG 2:10

The last chapter we talked about courtship, and we'll continue a bit longer on this important subject. What's courtship all about? It's a time when you are deciding whether or not the person is someone you would consider marrying. Courtship is parental involvement, accountability, visibility, and it committed to purity. The word "courtship" comes from the Elizabethan era in which the ladies of the court were wooed and won by knights and lords of the court through a process of frequent visitation.

In courtship, there is a commitment to not go to the romantic side. It doesn't mean you don't want to! It means you have a special friendship leading to a committed relationship with lots of parental or church involvement. I was always with my wife's parents or other godly adults.

Courtship ideally leads to engagement. You've come to the place where you believe this person to be someone you can look up to spiritually. You haven't had to compromise your purity or your convictions to keep this person. Let me just say, that if you have had to compromise, put on the brakes. You don't want to hitch your wagon to a wild horse. It's not a wagon you will destroy, but your life. Make sure the person you are considering marrying is faithful, dependable, exemplary and predictable in their godliness and convictions.

Now we come to Song of Solomon 2:8-3:5, where courtship leads to marriage. She is anxious to see him! He's anxious to see her!

PREPARATION FOR MARRIAGE: COURTSHIP (2:8-13)

Courtship is a wonderful time to lay some good foundations for marriage. You say, don't you do that during the engagement? You might do some of that, but during the engagement, you are primarily planning the wedding. By the time you are engaged you should know and trust that this person is a faithful, consistent, dependable Christian person you can spend the rest of your life with.

How long should courtship go on? It should go as long as it takes to get to know what this person is really like. There are only two options in courtship—it ends in realizing that the person is not for you, or it ends in engagement. In courtship, there are several things that deepen and grow your relationship.

Anticipation

Song of Solomon 2:8 | The voice of my beloved! Behold, he comes, leaping over the mountains, bounding over the hills.

The anticipation of seeing one another is breathtaking. We see King Solomon "leaping" and "bounding" over hills and mountains.

Courtship is exhilarating. There is great anticipation for engagement and marriage. You need to be careful. There are many mountains and hills you could trip on! Courtship ought to be a time when you are focused on trying to understand the person's convictions and faithfulness. Guard your heart! Do not give your heart away! You may not get married to this person. Even the consideration that the person you are courting might be the one is intoxicating. It makes one leap and bound like a gazelle! The pursuit of a wife is a good thing!

Proverbs 18:22, "He who finds a wife finds a good thing and obtains favor from the LORD." Solomon was pursuing with great anticipation, "leaping" and "bounding" over every obstacle. So it is with Christ in his pursuit of his bride.

GREGORY THE GREAT (540-604), "The church speaks through Solomon: 'See how he comes leaping on the mountains, bounding over the hills!' ... If I can put it this way, by coming for our redemption the Lord leaped! My friends, do you want to become acquainted with these leaps of his? From heaven he came to the womb, from the womb to the manger, from the manger to the cross, from the cross to the sepulcher, and from the sepulcher he returned to heaven. You see how Truth, having made himself known in the flesh, leaped for us to make us run after him." [60]

Dedication

Dedication is good preparation for marriage. Solomon was committed. He saw something in her that helped him overcome all obstacles and persevere. Often as couples continue in courtship they must overcome obstacles quite resiliently.

Song of Solomon 2:8 | The voice of my beloved! Behold, he comes, leaping over the mountains, bounding over the hills.

Mountains and hills are probably literary images for obstacles to their love that the man overcomes. It is amazing how resilient love is. When a young couple fall in love, they always think the best and give each other the benefit of the doubt. As Proverbs 10:12 says, "love covers all offenses." When you love someone, you tend to overlook the blemishes. Truly, love is blind!

Now I'm not talking about stupidity. A godly person will want to court someone of godly character. You ought to be the type of person that no one would ever ask you to compromise your convictions. You'll be able to truly be committed and want the best for your possible mate if you know they are godly. You will easily cover their flaws. You'll "leap" and "bound" over them like a young stag or a gazelle!!

1 Corinthians 13 tells us that "love hopes all things." Love thinks the best and fills in the question marks with thinking the best of the person. Consider how Christ joyfully left heaven and "leaped" into the story of redemption to demonstrate his love for us— "In that while we were still sinners, Christ died for us" (Rom 5:8).

> JOHN WESLEY (1703-1791), "Christ's voice is the word of grace revealed outwardly in the gospel, and inwardly by the Spirit of God. He comes after us leaping. He says, leaping and skipping,

---

[60] Gregory the Great. *Forty Gospel Homilies*. In *Cistercian Studies* (Kalamazoo, MI: Cistercian Publications, 1973), 123-124.

to denote that Christ comes readily, and swiftly, with great desire and pleasure and adds, upon the mountains and hills, to signify Christ's resolution to come in spite of all difficulties." [61]

Communication

Communication is important preparation for marriage. There's a desire to spend time together. The Shulamite hears her beloved speaking. She recognizes his voice.

Song of Solomon 2:8 | The voice of my beloved!

The beloved is speaking to his bride, but in this moment, he is outside the house. She can't see him, but she recognizes his voice instantly. She knows that he is speaking to her. She knows that he's not talking to the neighbor. She knows he's talking to her. What does he say?

Song of Solomon 2:10 | Arise, my love, my beautiful one, and come away.

Solomon, asks the Shulamite, the one he loves, to "come away," to go perhaps for a walk in the countryside. It's important to enjoy time together and get to know each other. The joy of love presents a God-given escape from the cruel world. There is that time when you are able to spend frequent time together. But be careful. Don't focus on romance. There will be enough sparks flying in your heart that you need to be careful and self-controlled, or you will start a fire that you can't put out! Focus on seeing if this person is committed to the Lord. Also remember when you are together, as we already learned, there needs to be visibility, accountability, and purity.

The same is true with your relationship with Christ. He calls us to frequently "come away" with him. Is your heart often stirred by him? As often as we can, we are to come away with him and spend time with him.

> ORIGEN (185-254), "Before the bridegroom appeared before her eyes, he was recognized by the bride through his voice alone. Afterwards, however, he appeared before her eyes, leaping upon certain mountains near that place where the bride was, and skipping over the hills and mountains, not with great steps so

---

[61] John Wesley. *Explanatory Notes Upon the Old Testament* (London: William Pine, 1765), Song 2:8.

much as with great bounds, after the manner of a deer or roe, and in this manner coming with all speed to his bride. when he reached the house wherein the bride was staying, he stood a while behind the house, so that at any rate his presence might be noticed; though as yet he would not enter the house openly and for all to see but, lover-like, would first look through the windows at the bride. If, then, we too want to see the Word of God, the bridegroom of the soul, 'leaping upon the mountains and skipping over the hills,' we must first hear his voice."[62]

In courtship, you want to make sure your beloved knows Christ's voice better than anyone else's. "My sheep hear my voice, and I know them, and they follow me" (Jn 10:27). There will be a day, if God wills, when you may be married and spend days and nights together, talking into the night and waking to a "good morning" from your beloved. That day will come for we who are Christ's beloved. He is coming again soon. He says, "Come away with me!" Come away from this mess. What joy we will have when that day comes. "Behold! I tell you a mystery. We shall not all sleep, but we shall all be changed, in a moment, in the twinkling of an eye, at the last trumpet. For the trumpet will sound, and the dead will be raised imperishable, and we shall be changed. For this perishable body must put on the imperishable, and this mortal body must put on immortality" (1 Cor 15:51-53).

Affection

Affection is also good preparation for marriage. Again, I'm not speaking of the physical side of love here. I'm talking about a healthy esteem and respect for the other person. You ought to think the world of one another for the right reasons. And here we see the foundations of love and respect being established for marriage.

Song of Solomon 2:9a | My beloved is like a gazelle or a young stag.

Solomon sets the example with strength and gentleness. Are you like a strong young stag of a man that will keep his convictions? Are you gentle but firm with your special someone, so that they know you want

---

[62] Origen. *Song of Songs.* In *The Works of the Fathers in Translation*, 84.

their best? Are you graceful like a gazelle? The Shulamite trusts Solomon as a man of honor. Solomon was a man among men, but he was a true "*gentle*man." The man's affection draws him to his beloved Shulamite farm girl. His affection for her is so great, he protects her purity and her honor.

So is Christ's love and affection for his bride that he protects us as a young stag, and yet he is so gentle as to be described as a gazelle.

> AMBROSE (333-397), "Be a follower of him 'who comes leaping upon the mountains, skipping over the hills, looking through the windows,' beyond the reach of snares. The bonds of pleasure, which give delight to the eye, charm to the ear, but pollution to the mind, are evil. What temporary and worldly pleasure offers is often spurious."[63]

Truly, it is the strength of Christ's love that will keep a couple pure during their courtship. Affection for your beloved is strong, but your affection for Christ ought always be exponentially stronger.

Boldness

Listen to the poor farm girl's response to King Solomon's pursuit.

Song of Solomon 2:9b-10 | Behold, there he stands behind our wall, gazing through the windows, looking through the lattice. [10] My beloved speaks and says to me: 'Arise, my love, my beautiful one, and come away.

Solomon approached the wall around his dear beloved's home and then peered through the lattice. He was anxious to see her. But now he calls to her. His love leads him to boldness to openly declare his love for her. He wants her to get up and leave that comfortable, secure, precious place and go out with him into the mountains and hills. He scales them with ease, and he wants her to scale them with him. He's not asking her to do something scandalous with him, no. This is a beckoning for betrothal. He's hinting at what we might call engagement here. This takes courage and boldness from a young man to finally have that "state of the relationship" conversation.

Engagement is good. God calls most people to be joined in holy matrimony. "Two are better than one, because they have a good reward

---

[63] St. Ambrose. *Cain and Abel*. In *Fathers,* Vol 42, 373-374.

for their toil. For if they fall, one will lift up his fellow. But woe to him who is alone when he falls and has not another to lift him up!" (Eccl 4:9-10). Again, "The Lord God said, 'It is not good that the man should be alone; I will make him a helper fit for him...' So the Lord God caused a deep sleep to fall upon the man, and while he slept took one of his ribs and closed up its place with flesh. And the rib that the Lord God had taken from the man he made into a woman and brought her to the man" (Gen 2:18, 21-22). Adam was asleep in the will of God, and he awoke to find that special someone. So it is that Solomon awoke from his stupor of singleness to realize he ought to propose to his future bride.

Solomon calls her to "come away," to be married. The betrothal is about to begin. He's making his intentions clear: "Come away with me!" That's what we do when we get married. We leave and cleave. In order to become a bride, the girl must leave her home – leave her father and mother and the comfort of her culture and begin a new home. "Therefore a man shall leave his father and his mother and hold fast to his wife, and they shall become one flesh" (Gen 2:24).

Renewal and Hope

Whenever you see a stag bounding through forest, you know winter is past and springtime has arrived. As I write this, it is springtime. Springtime is often celebrated as a time for young people in love. This is a gift from God. Love is a lot like springtime, everything is exciting and refreshing. There is so much unbounded optimism and enthusiasm. Solomon describes the atmosphere of love:

Song of Solomon 2:11-13a | For behold, the winter is past; the rain is over and gone. [12] The flowers appear on the earth, the time of singing has come, and the voice of the turtledove is heard in our land. [13] The fig tree ripens its figs, and the vines are in blossom; they give forth fragrance...

There is great hope during a good courtship process. The winter seems to be past. You can see how you might work together. You have the same convictions. You love the Lord. You deeply feel respect and love for your special someone, and they make you feel loved and respected. All that is a good foundation for marriage. One mistake that some make is they don't know how to read the warning signs. I know of a courting couple that allowed themselves to be in tempting situations and started fooling around, so they got married. That's not good preparation for marriage.

I've heard of couples getting married because it's a quick way to get out of their parents' house. Bad idea! That's the warning sign of a tumultuous marriage. It's a tragic way to start a marriage by breaking the fifth commandment, "Honor your father and mother" (Exo 20:12).

There are those who can't get along very well as a couple. They are worn out from all their highs and lows. They think marriage will bring some stability. They conclude, "We don't seem to be doing very well in courtship. At least in marriage we'll be able to be intimate. Let's get married." That's like saying "I can't bench press 50 pounds, so I think I'll add 500 more pounds!" And you get crushed by it. I've seen marriages that start like that end in divorce.

Learn to read the warning signs, and slow down or break off the courtship altogether if you must. If you are heading in the right direction, it'll be like spring has come. Godly people are giving you the green light on the person's character. You have seen that this person walks with the Lord. You esteem them and feel so special to be loved by such a godly person. Springtime signifies something new is about to begin. Everything is sweet and blooming.

> AMBROSE (333-397), "'Arise, come, my dearest one,' that is, arise from the pleasures of the world, arise from earthly things and come to me, you who still labor and are burdened, because you are anxious about worldly things. Come over the world, come to me, because I have overcome the world. Come near, for now you are fair with the beauty of everlasting life, now you are a dove, that is, you are gentle and mild, now you are filled entirely with spiritual grace.... 'Winter is now past;' that is, pardon has come, the forgiveness of sins has arrived, temptation has ceased, the rain is gone, the storm is gone, and the affliction. Before the coming of Christ it is winter. After his coming there are flowers. On this account he says, 'The flowers appear on the earth' (2:12). Where before there were thorns, now flowers are there. 'The time of singing has come.' Where before there was

desert, the harvest is there. 'The voice of the dove is heard in our land.'"[64]

THE PROPOSAL FOR MARRIAGE (2:13B-14)

We now find a clear invitation to leave her home.

Song of Solomon 2:13b | Arise, my love, my beautiful one, and come away (*cf* 2:9-10).

This is the closest thing to a proposal we have in the Song of Solomon. Engagement is a promise to marry. Betrothal in Bible times was serious. It required a spoken and eventually written covenant that laid out the intentions for marriage. It was taken very seriously, and it was made between the two families. It was signified by giving a ring or some other token of the groom's intension to marry the bride.

There was actually a ceremony for betrothal. "The Jewish betrothal [ceremony] in Christ's time was conducted thus: The families of the bride and groom met, with some others present to serve as witnesses. The young man would give the young woman either a gold ring, or some article of value, or simply a document in which he promised to marry her. Then he would say to her: 'See by this ring [or this token] thou art set apart for me, according to the law of Moses and of Israel.'"[65]

The betrothal was "the period of engagement preceding marriage; betrothal was a binding contract established between two families and sealed by the exchange of gifts. During this period the couple did not live together; sexual relations with each other at this stage was regarded as equivalent to adultery."[66] Engagement requires the father's permission, if living and able. Both families were involved in the Jewish betrothal. It is important, if possible, that the parents be involved in the engagement. It is not mentioned here, but it must be said – in courtship and in engagement, it is the man's responsibility to seek the father's permission. "But if any man thinks he is behaving improperly toward his virgin [daughter], if she is past the flower of youth [of marriable age], and thus it must be, let him do what he wishes. He does not sin;

---

[64] St. Ambrose. *Isaac, or the Soul.* In *Fathers,* Vol 65, 29-30.

[65] James Freeman. *Manners and Customs of the Bible* (New Kensington, PA: Whitaker House, 1996), "betrothal."

[66] M. H. Manser, "Betrothal" In *Dictionary of Bible Themes: The Accessible and Comprehensive Tool for Topical Studies* (London: Martin Manser, 2009).

let them marry" (1 Cor 7:36, NKJV). We see that the father gives his daughter's hand in marriage. The father must protect his daughter and make sure she is marrying a godly man.

For modern cultures, engagement means that the woman must start thinking about leaving her parents protection and come under the protection of the groom. Solomon calls out to his betrothed.

Song of Solomon 2:14 | O my dove, in the clefts of the rock, in the crannies of the cliff, let me see your face, let me hear your voice, for your voice is sweet, and your face is lovely.

Solomon calls his beloved a dove. So it is that a young lady agreeing to engagement ought to be blameless – with an inner beauty that demonstrates her readiness for marriage.

> ARTHUR JACKSON (1593-1666), "In the spiritual sense these words, *O my dove!* are an expression of the great love that Christ bears to his Church, and the great delight that he takes in her. In many regards the Church may be compared to a dove, because the spiritual beauty of the faithful is like that of the dove; because their spiritual chastity is also like that of the dove; and because they are meek and gentle and harmless as the dove, without any gall. Also, the dove is a sociable creature, delighting to consort and dwell together; so true believers delight in the communion and assemblies of the saints."[67]

Notice Solomon calls her to come from the protection of the rocks. Doves hide in the crevasses of the rocks. This speaks to the young lady's desire for safety and the protection of her mother's home. In engagement, the couple is preparing to leave their parents and begin a new home, as Christ said (quoting Gen 2), "a man shall leave his father and mother and hold fast to his wife" (Mk 10:7). The woman has to trust that her potential suitor will protect her.

Ladies, one way you can know if this man is a man of honor and will protect you, is if he is careful to protect your purity. Is he careful to guide the conversation in a godly direction? Are his walk and talk consistent? If not, stay in the crevasses of the rocks in your parents' home! It's better that you break an engagement than you later find yourself with a broken marriage!

---

[67] Arthur Jackson. *Song of Solomon*, Song 2:14.

The betrothal is not mentioned here, but it is assumed. The courtship has been observed by godly people. The father is consulted. In this case, since the Shulamite's father does not seem to be on the scene, the mother would be consulted. Perhaps the mother would seek advice from other godly men in the family. At any rate, by this time it should be plain to godly, mature people whether or not a wedding should take place. Permission would be either granted or denied.

> NANCY DEMOSS WOLGEMUTH (1958–), "Our heavenly Bridegroom is at work doing his work in those mountains, in those hills, and he causes us to rise up and join him in working in and dealing with those circumstances and those challenges. The bride doesn't respond to the first call, so the bridegroom repeats his call. He's persistent in his appeal. I don't know about you, but I am so grateful for God's mercy and grace in pursuing me so many of those times when I was hesitant. He does not reprimand us. He sees his beloved as beautiful, chaste, meek, tender. Aren't you glad that Christ sees us positionally, as we are in him, rather than what we see ourselves to be apart from him? She is fair. She is his dove. She's in the clefts of the rock. I think how we are hidden in Christ, the Rock, who was cleft for us."[68]

THE PRESSURES OF THE ENGAGEMENT (2:15)

Engagement brings with it many pressures. It's one thing to dream about marriage. There are no imperfections in most of our dreams. But actually considering marriage is scary for most people. You really begin to see the flaws for the first time. But it's a good thing if you handle the pressures in the right way.

Solomon speaks to the keepers of the vineyards and illustrates his blossoming relationship. It's really a warning to those who are headed toward engagement.

Song of Solomon 2:15 | Catch the foxes for us, the little foxes that spoil the vineyards, for our vineyards are in blossom.

---

[68] Nancy Demoss Wolgemuth. "How to Fall and Stay in Love with Jesus," Day 9. Accessed Aug 21, 2017. https://www.reviveourhearts.com/radio/revive-our-hearts/song-solomon-day-9/

Whether he is referring to his actual vineyards is inconsequential. The vineyards here refer to his "blossoming" relationship with his beloved. Certainly in engagement, the resiliency of the relationship will be tested.

Foxes are pests that wreak havoc in vineyards (e.g., they will eat the grapes). The foxes represent some hindrances that are threatening to spoil their relationship. Many obstacles or temptations as have plagued lovers throughout the centuries. When it comes to vineyards, the big foxes aren't the problem. The big foxes attack the fruit, but the fruit can grow back. It's the little foxes that get down underneath the fruit and gnaw away at the roots, gnaw away at the vine—the heart of the relationship.

Perhaps it is the little fox of uncontrolled desire which drives a wedge of guilt between a couple. Perhaps it is that little fox of mistrust and jealousy which breaks the bond of love. Or it may be the fox of selfishness and pride which refuses to let one acknowledge his fault to another. Or it may be an unforgiving spirit which will not accept the sincere apology of the other. Those unseen little foxes of pride, discontent, complaining, murmuring, a competitive spirit, self-absorption (being consumed with myself, my needs, my desires), bitterness, unforgiveness, neglect of God's Word, neglect of prayer. These are "little foxes" that destroy your relationship with God and with others. These foxes have been ruining vineyards for years and the end of their work is not in sight. What are the little foxes in your life?

The point here is that we need to be diligent to preserve and protect the intimacy of a love-relationship—whether it's your relationship with your mate or your relationship with Christ. We need to be willing to deal with every breach in that relationship, no matter how small it may seem.

BERNARD OF CLAIRVAUX (1090-1153): "Pressing needs like little foxes steadily destroy our relationship with the Lord; anxieties, suspicions, cares, charge in from all sides. At times, I need a flood of tears to fertilize the barrenness of my soul. There are times I am unfit to take care of my own soul: here I speak of souls as vineyards. O my vineyard, what an amount of produce was robbed from me by the subtle trickery of my own deceitful heart, at the very time when I was growing more vigilant in my care of you! How many and how precious the clusters of good works either were blighted by anger, or snatched away by boasting, or defiled by vainglory! What temptations did I not endure from gluttony, from mental slothfulness, from timidity of spirit or the storm of impulsive passion! How easily the 'little foxes' can hinder and cut off the clusters of joy that proceeds from the vine, who is Christ."[69]

Engagement will bring with it little foxes that can destroy the vines of relationship. Are you able to guard your relationship from foxes? Are you able to keep your thoughts and your body under control? Even in ideal courtships and marriages most couples encounter some potentially destructive problems. Their willingness to solve them together is an evidence of their maturity. If you can't get along and solve problems with each other for a few hours a day, three or four times a week, you certainly aren't going to be able to get along with a person 7 days a week for the next 50 years!

THE PASSION OF ENGAGEMENT (2:16)

Song of Solomon 2:16 | My beloved is mine, and I am his; he grazes among the lilies.

This poor Shulamite farm girl feels the deep assurance of the king's love. It transcends the pains of this life and points (if only dimly) to a higher and divine love. Marriage at its best points to the love of Christ, from which we cannot separated.

> JAMES DURHAM (1622–1658): "'I am his, and he is mine!' The relationship that the believer has with Christ is the great ground of his happiness and deep comfort, even when we do not sense the presence of Christ with us. All believers may attain this assurance and may come to know truly that Christ is theirs. Believers should aim to be thorough in this, that their 'calling and election may be made sure' to themselves (2 Pet 1:10). Believers when they have attained clearness in their assurance, should acknowledge it and comfort themselves in it, and not raise new disputes about it. This clearness may continue even with the absence and lack of Christ's manifest presence for a time. Indeed,

---

[69] Bernard of Clairvaux. *Commentary on the Song of Solomon*, "Sermon 30: Mystical Vineyards and the Prudence of the Flesh."

there is no case wherein a believer should hold tighter to his confidence than in such a situation, when under the feeling of desertion and absence, as the spouse does here, for our assurance is based on faith through the Word, not on feeling through the flesh. If Christ be yours, where is he? 'Among the lilies.' Here all believers are so called, as partaking of that same beauty, and because they are planted in the same true garden. Christ was called a lily, for he became like one of us. We must never forget that here all believers are called lilies, showing that all believers have a conformity to Christ, and partake of the divine nature and Spirit that is in him."[70]

THE PATIENCE OF ENGAGEMENT (2:17)

Song of Solomon 2:17 | Until the day breathes and the shadows flee, turn, my beloved, be like a gazelle or a young stag on cleft mountains.

She strongly desires marriage, and yet she hesitates. Her passions are strong. Yet she may not be ready to leave with him just yet. She wants him to come to her, but she's not prepared to go with him. Wait **"until the day breathes and the shadows flee away."** Wait until these life circumstances clear out, wait until things aren't so difficult. Wait just a little longer, but please, wait for me. I may not be ready now, but I want no one else."

Even in the most promising of relationships, our hearts can be unsure. Everything lines up, the engagement is moving along fine, and all the sudden, it's shaky. I've seen that especially with the Christian ladies. They want to be married to that godly man, but they need just a little more time. The man must be patient yet persistent, gentle as a **"gazelle"** and as persistent and strong as a **"young stag."** Brother in Christ, you must demonstrate patience and persistence in your engagement. Her heart may at times be unsure. We don't encourage exceedingly long engagements, but we also don't want to rush it. Trust the Lord to lead you in his perfect timing.

So it is with Christ. We often feel shaky in our walk with him. Does Christ really love me? Has he truly called me? Am I really his? He is so

---

[70] James Durham. *Clavis Cantici*, 147-148.

patient with us. He holds us fast to himself. He "will never leave us nor forsake us" (Heb 13:5).

Just as a godly couple may be shaky at times as to the timing, so they may also want to speed things up! Sometimes the engagement seems far too long. Here (in 2:17) it may also be that the future bride is waiting for the night shadows to hasten and "**flee**." She wants the morning dawn of her new married life to hurry up and arrive.

Isn't that also how our walk with Christ is? We long for his coming, when he makes all things new and wipes all our tears away. We desire him to make our night into day.

> JAMES DURHAM (1622–1658): "Though there be shadows (she says) and vails between him and me, in this night of uncertainty; yet there is a day coming when these, by the Bridegroom's presence, shall be made to flee away, and I shall see him as he is. So it is with Christ. There is a twofold day spoken of in Scripture. First, a day of Christ's presence here upon earth, in his incarnation – his first coming when 'the day-spring from on high has visited us" (Lu 1:78). Second, the day of his glorious appearing, when he comes a second time – commonly called the great day, because it has no night of interruption. It goes so far beyond what believers possess now, as day exceeds the night; therefore, it's called the morning."[71]

THE PURITY OF ENGAGEMENT (3:1-3)

Strong, soul-clenching desires often grip the hearts, emotions and bodies of engaged couples. In Song of Solomon 3, the woman dreams of her future husband.

Song of Solomon 3:1-3 | On my bed by night[72] I sought him whom my soul loves; I sought him, but found him not. I will rise now and go about the city, in the streets and in the squares; I will seek him whom my soul loves. I sought him, but found him not. The watchmen found me as they went about in the city. 'Have you seen him whom my soul loves?'

---

[71] James Durham. *Clavis Cantici*, 151.
[72] very strong in the Heb. lit. 'night after night'

The wedding is approaching. Night after night she thinks about marriage to her king. It has now become crystal clear that she truly cannot live without him. She dreams of losing him and cannot bear it. The wedding can't get here soon enough, so that she can hold him and bring him into her "**mother's house**" (3:4). It is clear that this girl is still an unmarried virgin. She's still at her mother's house, but she is gripped by the mysteries of her fast approaching wedding night. She's dreaming about pursuing him. She can't live without him. So tender and special are her thoughts to her future husband.

The soon-to-be bride is not content to be without he beloved. She's not content to stay separated from him. Listen, an evidence that we belong to Christ is that when you lose the sense of his presence, you go seek him. You go looking to have that relationship restored.

> NANCY DEMOSS WOLGEMUTH (1958–), "How badly do you desire fellowship with Jesus? Do you have a seeking heart? Or are you content with where you are, what you have, and what you know of Jesus? How badly do you want his fellowship? Are you desperate to find him? Are you willing to leave your bed and go about the city? Are you willing to go to greater lengths to find him? Are you willing to make sacrifices, to extend yourself, to be inconvenienced?"[73]

Are you willing to deny yourself in order to have a more intimate relationship with Christ? Food? Sleep? Pleasure? Friends at times? Is anything too great a price to pay in order to find the supreme treasure—Christ? The passions of the bride-to-be are powerful, yet not enslaving. She is a godly woman. These are pure and holy passions, but she knows they must be reserved and guarded for the soon coming marriage, and so she says again, "I adjure you, O daughters of Jerusalem, by the gazelles or the does of the field, that you not stir up or awaken love until it pleases" (3:5). She dreams of married life, but she is careful with her desires. She guards her passions. A fire in the hearth is beautiful because it is controlled and in the right place. It gives warmth and light. But if you take the logs and burn them in the middle of the living room, you'll lose everything. So it is with passion. You must guard it!

---

[73] Nancy Demoss Wolgemuth. "How to Fall and Stay in Love with Jesus," Day 10. Accessed Aug 21, 2017. https://www.reviveourhearts.com/radio/revive-our-hearts/song-solomon-day-10/

THE PRECIOUSNESS OF ENGAGEMENT (3:4)

Song of Solomon 3:4 | Scarcely had I passed them when I found him whom my soul loves. I held him, and would not let him go until I had brought him into my mother's house, and into the chamber of her who conceived me.

You may be saying right now about a special relationship God has given you, "I found him whom my soul loves" or if you are a man, "I have found *her* whom my soul loves" (3:4). How precious it is to find the one your soul loves! You want to hold them and never let them go. But can you say that about Christ? "I found him whom my soul loves." Can you say, "I love Christ, and whether I ever find a spouse on earth, my soul is content in Jesus"? Whether a believer ever gets married or finds love on this earth, he or she can say, "I have found Christ, because he first found me. My soul loves Jesus. No one else on earth could be as sweet as my walk with him."

> CHARLES HADDON SPURGEON (1834-1892), "Ardent lovers of Jesus must diligently seek him. The chapter before us says that the spouse sought him, sought him on her bed, sought him in the streets, sought him in the broadways, sought him at last at the lips of the watchmen, sought him everywhere where he was likely to be found. We *must* enjoy the perpetual fellowship of Jesus. We who love him in our souls cannot rest until we know that he is with us. I fear that with some of us our sins have grieved him. It may be our lax living, our neglect of prayer, or some other fault, has taken from us the light of his countenance. Let us resolve at this moment that there shall be no rest unto our souls until once again he has returned unto us in the fullness of his manifested love, to abide in our hearts. Seek him, brother, seek him, sister. He is not far from any of you, but do seek him with an intense longing for him. Labor to bring Jesus into the chambers of the church, but first be sure that have known him yourself, or your zeal will be hypocrisy."[74]

---

[74] Spurgeon. *Pulpit,* Vol 18, Sermon 1035, "The Real Presence of Christ" (1872), 85.

ROBERT MURRAY M'CHEYNE (1813-1843) "Have you found
him whom your soul loves? Have you this day seen his beauty,
heard his voice, believed the record concerning him, sat under
his shadow, found fellowship with him? Then hold him, and do
not let him go. Why seek after Christ and find him whom your
soul loves?

Motives. 1. Because peace is to be found in him. Justified by
faith, we have peace with God – not peace with ourselves, not
peace with the world, with sin, with Satan, but peace with God.
True divine peace is to be found only in believing, only in keeping fast hold of Christ. If you let him go, you let go your righteousness; for this is his name. You are then without righteousness, without a covering from the wrath of God, without a way
to the Father. The law will again condemn you; God's frown will
again overshadow you; you will again have terrors of conscience. Hold him then, and do not let him go. Whatever you let
go, let not Christ go; for he is our peace, not in knowledge, not
in feeling, but trust in him alone. 2. Holiness flows from him. No
true holiness in this world, but it springs from him. A living
Christ is the spring of holiness to all his members. As long as we
hold him, and do not let him go, our holiness is secure. He is
engaged to keep us from falling. He loves us too well to let us fall
under the reigning power of sin. His word is engaged: "I will put
my Spirit within you" (Eze 36:27). His honor would be tarnished
if any that cleave to him were suffered to live in sin. If you let
him go, you will fall into sin. You have no strength, no store of
grace, no power to resist a thousand enemies, no promises. If
Christ be for you, who can be against you? But if you let go His
arms, where are you? 3. Hope of glory is in him. We rejoice in
hope of the glory of God. If you have found Jesus this day, you
have found a way into glory. A few steps more, you can say, and
I shall be forever with the Lord. I shall be free from pain and
sorrow, free from sin and weakness, free from enemies. As long
as you hold Christ, you can see your way to the judgment seat.
"Thou wilt guide me with thy counsel, and receive me to thy
glory" (Psa 73:24). This gives you such joy, such transporting
desires after the heavenly world! But let Christ go, and this will

be gone. Let Christ go, and how can you die? The grave is covered with clouds of threatening. Let him go, and how can you go
to the judgment – where can you appear?

Means. Christ promises to keep you holding him. If you are
really holding Christ this day, you are in a most blessed condition, for Christ engages to keep you cleaving to him. "My soul
followeth hard after thee, and thy right hand upholdeth me"
(Psa 63:8). He that is the Creator of the world is the upholder of
it, so he that new creates the soul keeps it in being. This is never
to be forgotten. Not only does the Church lean on her beloved,
but he puts his left hand under her head, and his right-hand
cloth embrace her (Song 2:6). "I taught Ephraim, how to go, taking them by their arms" (Hos 11:3). It is good for a child to hold
fast by its mother's neck; but ah! that would be a feeble support,
if the maternal arm did not enfold the child, and clasp it to her
bosom. Faith is good; but ah! it is nothing without the grace that
gave it. "I will put my fear in your heart" (Jer 32:40). 2. Faith in
Christ. The only way to hold fast is to believe more and more.
Get a larger acquaintance with Christ, with his person, work,
and character. Every page of the gospel unfolds a new feature in
his character, every line of the epistles discloses new depths of
his work. Get more faith, and you will get a firmer hold. A plant
that has a single root may be easily torn up by the hand, or
crushed by the foot of the wild beast, or blown down by the
wind; but a plant that has a thousand roots struck down into the
ground can stand. Faith is like the root. Many believe a little concerning Christ, one fact. Every new truth concerning Jesus is a
new root struck downward. Believe more intensely. A root may
be in a right direction, but, not striking deep, it is easily torn up.
Pray for deep-rooted faith. Pray to be established, strengthened,
settled. Take a long intense look at Jesus – often. If you wanted
to know a man again, and he was going away, you would take
an intense look at his face. Look then at Jesus, deeply, intensely,
till every feature is graven on your heart. 3. Prayer. – Jacob at
Bethel (Gen 28). "Take hold of my strength" (Isa 27:5). You must
begin and pray after another fashion than you have done. Let it
be real intercourse with God, like Hezekiah, Jacob and Moses. 4.
By not offending him. First, by sloth. When the soul turns sleepy

or careless, Christ goes away. Nothing is more offensive to Christ than sloth. Love is an ever-active thing, and when it is in the heart it will keep us waking. Many a night his love to us kept him waking. Now, can you not watch with him one hour? Second, By idols. You cannot hold two objects. If you are holding Christ today, and lay hold of another object to tomorrow, he cannot stay. He is a jealous God. You cannot keep worldly companions and Christ too. "A companion of fools shall be destroyed" (Pro 13:20). When the ark came into the house of Dagon, it made the idol fall flat. Third, by being unwilling to be sanctified. When Christ chooses us and draws us to himself, it is that he may sanctify us. Christ is often grieved by our desiring to reserve one sin. Fourth, By an unholy house. "I brought him into my mother's house" (Song 3:4). Remember to take Christ home with you, and let him rule in your house. If you walk with Christ abroad, but never take him home, you will soon part company forever."[75]

The day before Puritan theologian John Owen departed to be with Christ (23 August, 1683), he dictated his last letter to a friend: "I am going to him whom my soul has loved, or rather who has loved me with an everlasting love, – which is the whole ground of my consolation."[76]

This is the preciousness of human love, to remember you are reflecting the highest divine love. This begins to bud in engagement.

Conclusion

Engagement is a sacred time, so be very wise in how you proceed. Let us consider a few encouragements and warnings.

First, don't jump into an engagement too quickly. If you are not very, very sure that this person truly is what they say they are, wait. Don't jump in too quickly. Listen to godly people around you. Make sure you are desire marriage for the right reasons. Physical attraction is not strong foundation. There must be consistency, godliness, and biblical conviction. Is the man able to provide for his potential bride

---

[75] Robert Murray M'Cheyne. "Holding Christ Fast" In *Memoir and Remains of the Rev. Robert Murray M'Cheyne* (Edinburgh and London: Oliphant, Anderson & Ferrier, 1892) 454.

[76] John Owen. Christologia, or, *A Declaration of the Glorious Mystery of the Person of Christ* (Glasgow: M Grey Booksellers, 1790), xi.

and possible future children? Does the person you are interested in speak and live openly about their walk with Christ? If it is not the center of their life now, you cannot expect anything to get better when you are married. You can certainly expect things to likely get worse.

Look for the warning signs. Can your relationship survive misunderstandings, arguments, and the pressures of life? If not, you may need to put the engagement on hold. This goes back to your walk with the Lord. Are you mature? If not, your marriage will be a clear barometer of where you are with the Lord.

Plans should move quickly if you are engaged. The time to discover if this is the person to marry is during courtship. I believe in a long courtship but a brief engagement. If you are engaged, try to make it a short engagement, if possible, with lots of accountability. Once the decision is made to marry, it is very difficult to restrain passion. Do *not* be alone together. The passions are too high. More than a year of engagement is not wise unless there is great distance between you. I was engaged to Jill for a year and two months, but she was 1000 miles away in college. We were both very busy during our engagement. A short engagement is advisable. Keep busy planning the wedding and get on with the marriage!

Here's a word of advice to you men. Get to know the girls' parents well during the courtship time and especially the engagement time. Schedule some time with her parents while she is away. You are not only marrying her, but you are marrying her family.

The Bible tells us that we are betrothed to Christ, and we need to be a "chaste bride." This is true in engagement, but it is also true in our Christian life. We are not yet in heaven. We have not yet partaken in the marriage supper of the Lamb. Keep yourself unspotted from this world. Let your heart be set on the Beloved One Jesus Christ! Walk closely with him, because he is coming very soon to bring his Bride to the wedding feast. "Then I saw a new heaven and a new earth, for the first heaven and the first earth had passed away, and the sea was no more. And I saw the holy city, new Jerusalem, coming down out of heaven from God, prepared as a bride adorned for her husband. And I heard a loud voice from the throne saying, 'Behold, the dwelling place of God is with man. He will dwell with them, and they will be his people, and God himself will be with them as their God. He will wipe away every tear from their eyes, and death shall be no more, neither shall there be mourning, nor crying, nor pain anymore, for the former things have passed away'" (Rev 21:1-4).

5 | SONG 3:5-11

A WEDDING DESIGNED BY GOD

Go out, O daughters of Zion, and look upon King Solomon,
with the crown with which his mother crowned him on the
day of his wedding, on the day of the gladness of his heart.
SONG 3:11

The wedding ceremony is symbolic of the marriage of Christ and his church. A Christian wedding is the earthly anticipation of the heavenly wedding that is to come between Christ and his Bride when we will fully be united eternally with Christ. What a day that will be! In every way, the wedding day should display the Church's relationship with Christ. It is the day when two people become one in every way: spiritually, emotionally, physically, and socially. The wedding ceremony is so important because it lays the secure foundation for your family, and for many generations to come. I often remember my wedding vows.

> "I Matthew take you Jill to be my lawfully wedded wife, to have and to hold from this day forward, for better or for worse, for richer or for poorer, in sickness and in health, to love, honor, protect, and cherish, abandoning all others and dedicating myself wholly to you 'till death do us part."

Jesus will never leave or forsake his Bride. We men must never leave or forsake the bride God gave us. The wedding ceremony is special because it is a vow before God and witnesses. It symbolizes the union between Christ and his Church. That vow is a vow of fidelity, devotion to God, protection and provision for the wife, and the permission and blessing of the parents.

A VOW OF FIDELITY TO ONE ANOTHER (3:5)

The wedding ceremony symbolizes the couple's fidelity to each other. The Shulamite farm girl has more anticipation of love than most young marriable women. She is a poor peasant girl about to be a queen. And yet, she demonstrates self-control. Some people say, "I just can't help myself." That is not true! You can and you must. Listen to this young lady's words.

Abandoning All Others

The bride encourages patience to express romance and passion for a second time.

Song of Solomon 3:5 | I adjure you, O daughters of Jerusalem, by the gazelles or the does of the field, that you not stir up or awaken love until it pleases (*cf* 2:7, 8:4).

She is calling out to the ladies of the royal court to follow her example – don't awaken the strong emotions of love until the right time. In my wedding vows, Jill was mine "to have and behold from this day forward." In my vows I said, "abandoning all others and dedicating myself wholly to you 'till death do us part." That's why this young lady was controlling herself. She was reserving what was most precious for her king and soon-to-be husband. Once I was married, I abandoned any friendships of the opposite gender I might have had. That is an obligation for all married people. At that time, my wife was all mine, and we could awaken love fully and completely. Until that day, purity had to be carefully guarded. Love is not to be awakened until after the marriage vows. It is for this day the couple has preserved themselves. God said in Genesis 2:24, "Therefore a man shall leave his father and his mother and hold fast to his wife, and they shall become one flesh." It is not until you leave and cleave through a marriage covenant before God and witnesses that you may become one flesh. The marriage day marks a transformation of pathways. No longer will they be two, but one flesh. Two souls will now be mingled together.

Staying pure in engagement is hard work, but it is worth it a thousand times over. The wedding is the day that you have reserved yourself for each other. You have kept yourself from the world's lusts. You have remembered Hebrews 13:4, "Let marriage be held in honor among all, and let the marriage bed be undefiled, for God will judge the sexually immoral and adulterous." You have remembered Proverbs 5:15, "Drink water from your own cistern, flowing water from your own well." And now, this is the day that God has given you your own cistern that will fulfill you and by his grace bring you many generations of godly children.

A VOW OF DEVOTION TO GOD (3:6)

Listen to the description of someone coming up from the wilderness.

Song of Solomon 3:6 | What is that coming up from the wilderness like columns of smoke, perfumed with myrrh and frankincense, with all the fragrant powders of a merchant?

Since the description is neutral ("what is that?") it could refer to the bride or so Solomon himself. If it is Solomon, then he is being described as one who is devoted to God and led by him into this marriage.

Devoted First to God, Then to Each Other

It is clear from this description (if it is speaking of Solomon) that he was led to this marriage by God. In great contrast to Solomon's hundreds of political marriages later in life, this woman is the wife of his youth. He was directed to this marriage by God. We see this by the description, as he comes with God's presence—signified by the "**columns of smoke**." In the Old Testament, the Lord led his people with his glory cloud in the wilderness. It is vital for anyone to consider that marriage is God's idea, and just as he led his people of old, he will lead you. It matters that you first follow him and be guided by his presence.

Many times we think of marriage in the wrong way. When we are young, we are prone to think of marriage as a fantastical story of romance. For many, marriage is thought about in terms of one's own happiness. Yet so many enter marriage and the hang ups, the quirks, the insults, and the misunderstandings all take us by surprise. We often do not think of those things before marriage. St. Paul tells us that marriage will most certainly complicate life and bring "worldly troubles" (1 Cor 7:28). Those who get married will have trouble. The Greek word for trouble, means pressed together, squashed or squeezed. What Paul is teaching here is simple. Anytime you press two sinners together in a marriage relationship, there's trouble! This is not rocket science. There's a greater potential for misery in marriage. It's true. If you are single, the only person that can make you miserable is you. In marriage, that potential is doubled! "Marriage presses two sinners together in the closest possible ways. The two become one, but they are still two personalities, two distinct people with their own likes and dislikes, their own characteristics, emotions, temperaments, and wills. We bring our sinfulness into the marriage and it sometimes creates war. That is true even of the best marriages. When one partner is immature, self–centered, temperamental, or domineering, every conflict is magnified." [77]

Marriage works best between two Holy Spirit-filled believers. We all need to be like Solomon, moving forward with God's presence in us, like two columns of smoke, filled with that Old Testament glory cloud. Marriage is ordained of God, good, holy, and fulfilling; but it does not solve all problems. It actually brings more. Marriage never should be used as a way of escape, even from loneliness. Many people carry their loneliness right into marriage and end up making another person lonely.

Marriage is about more than happiness. It is about holiness. God uses marriage to humble us and see our infinite need for him. My vows were: "for better or for worse." If I am married, I do not have the authority to split in two what God has put together. Every lawful marriage is put together by God. "What God has joined together, let not man separate" (Mk 10:9). When two believers commit to marriage, they are committing to God first and then to each other.

Devoted to Spiritual Nourishment

Solomon is the shepherd-king, but more importantly, he is identified as someone filled with the presence of God. **"What is that coming up from the wilderness...?"** (3:6). Here the wilderness is not a

---

[77] John MacArthur, Jr, *1 Corinthians. MacArthur New Testament Commentary* (Chicago: Moody Press, 1984), 181.

desert but the green pastures around Jerusalem. The image of the green wilderness pastures where the shepherds would feed their sheep is given. They would literally "come up" to Jerusalem, which was truly the beautiful royal city set on a hill. Like a sheep, Solomon could say with his father David, "The Lord is my Shepherd" (Psa 23:1). The point is this was a man entering into marriage that was already being fed by the Good Shepherd. He was "coming up from the wilderness" – the green pastures and the still waters.

Devoted to Authentic Worship

God is the true shepherd king. Solomon and his bride-to-be are described as "columns of smoke" coming up from the wilderness. **"What is that coming up from the wilderness like columns of smoke?"** (3:6). This is a striking reference to the leading of the Spirit of God who manifested himself through a pillar of smoke by day and a pillar of fire by night in the wilderness – his *shekinah* glory – his manifest presence! Those who worship together have a joy that is not bound to all the quirks, weaknesses and even failures that marriages are prone to.

The wilderness the Jews would have understood reading this passage may not just refer to the green pastures around Jerusalem, but perhaps refer to a region south of Palestine toward Egypt. And in the Scripture, Egypt is usually a picture of the world. We see a picture here of God leading his people out of the wilderness of Egypt (where there was false worship). God manifests himself as a pillar – a fiery glory cloud. The presence of God, manifested by the glorious columns of smoke led them safely to the promised land where they would learn true worship (Exo 40:34-38).

> JAMES DURHAM (1622–1658): "These words (smoke coming out of the wilderness) contain an encouragement to the Church. The commendation has two parts. First, Christ ascends from the wilderness; Before this manifestation of Christ, the Church was dry and withered-like, in a wilderness condition, without any beauty or luster; but now that condition is changed. When Christ appears, he ascends out of the wilderness to wed his Bride. And this wilderness (considering his ascent from it) signifies the world, wherein he rescues his Bride. It is in this wilderness be-

lievers sojourn on their way to Heaven (as Israel did in the wilderness to Canaan). In the wilderness, there is no true contentment for Christ's Church, nor satisfying rest sought by them, nor to be found by any. Therefore, their back is toward the world, though before they knew Christ they seemed to be settled in it with the rest of mankind. Thus, the heavenly mindedness of believers in their lives and thinking is set out. Second, she joins Solomon, as he arrives like pillars of smoke. This is not ordinary smoke, but the smoke of the incense of temple worship, where the glory cloud rests in the Tabernacle. This heavenward smoke of incense is commanded in God's worship, and is acceptable to him. The Church, warmed by God's fiery presence and freshly inflamed and made alive with Christ's fellowship, cannot but send out a sweet aroma, which ascends upward from the world (which is but a wilderness) as smoke ascends from the earth."[78]

As the Tabernacle imagery in the Song of Solomon demonstrates, marriage is not just between you and your spouse. It is between you, your spouse and God. You are his holy temple. Marriage then is a holy, unbreakable vow before the divine Author of marriage. If you enter into marriage, do so only by following the Lord's leading.

Devoted to Living Separate from the World

Solomon comes out of **"the wilderness"** to bring his bride into the palace. Christ too came for his bride, leaving his royal throne to enter the wilderness of humanity (Phil 2) and brings his bride out of that wilderness of sin to a new creation where righteousness dwells. We are not at home in this world of sin, but we are at home in Christ.

> J. HUDSON TAYLOR (1832-1905): "May we all, while living down here, in this wilderness world, but not of it, find our home in the heavenly places to which we are seated together with Christ. Sent into the world to witness for our Master, may we ever be strangers there, ready to confess him, the true object of our soul's devotion. There is no room for love of the world here, for union with Christ has filled the heart; there is nothing for the gratification of the world, for all has been sealed and is kept for the Master's use.

---

[78] James Durham. *Clavis Cantici*, 172.

> *Jesus, my life is Thine!*
> *And evermore shall be hidden in Thee.*
> *For nothing can untwine Thy life from mine."*[79]

Today, Christ is bringing his Bride, the Church, out of the world—out of that which she was born into—out of her natural state in Adam—out of the wilderness of idolatry of materialism, substance abuse, co-dependent relationships, and even addictions of various sorts. He's taking his Bride safely to a place of true worship, a place of abundance and fruitfulness in Christ. The secret to a long and loving marriage is not mainly compatibility, communication or agreeing on proper roles in marriage. Those things are important, but they are the fruit, not the root. The root of a godly, loving and lasting marriage is worship. Both husband and wife will rebel against all the above ideas if they are not mutually submitted to Christ in worship.

The statistics support the idea that those submitted to Christ's Word will have a strong foundation for a lasting marriage. "A recent survey concluded that 80 percent of relationships in which couples were living together without marriage vows end in separation. Sixty (60) percent of those who are married by a justice of the peace are divorced later. Forty percent of those who are married in churches eventually divorce. But those who regularly read their Bibles together divorce only at the rate of 1 out of 1,050."[80] It is so important that a marriage be founded upon devotion to God. Think of the joy when the Church's wedding day comes, and we see the King of kings and Lord of lords coming for his Bride (Rev 21:1-4).

A VOW OF PREFERENCE (3:6A)

Let's return back to our question.

Song of Solomon 3:6 | What is that coming up from the wilderness like columns of smoke, perfumed with myrrh and frankincense, with all the fragrant powders of a merchant?

---

[79] J. Hudson Taylor. *Union and Communion: Thoughts on the Song of Solomon* (Edinburgh: R & R Clark, 1893), 36.
[80] Nelson. *The Book of Romance*, 71.

The ESV uses a neutral pronoun but may likely refer not just to Solomon but to the bride as well. "Who of all people is that coming up from the wilderness with King Solomon."

> NANCY DEMOSS WOLGEMUTH (1958–), "In the eastern culture, the bride and the groom would travel together to the wedding—a journey as we've said might take some period of time. So we have in verse 6 some observers, some of those bystanders who say, 'Who is this coming out of the wilderness like pillars of smoke, perfumed with myrrh and frankincense with all the merchant's fragrant powders?' Now, as we get into this passage we know that these bystanders are aware that the bride is in this processional. Because when they say, 'Who is this?' in the original language, that's a feminine singular word. They are thinking of the bride. 'Who is this bride coming out of the wilderness like pillars of smoke perfumed with myrrh and frankincense with all the merchant's fragrant powders?' Observers see the wedding train in the distance. And of course, as you might imagine, they are eager to get a closer look, eager to identify who's coming. As the processional approaches, they see these pillars—these columns of smoke which may be incense being burned from the front of that processional. And as the processional gets closer, they could smell the fragrance—the myrrh, the frankincense. Now they say that she is the one who's perfumed. But remember all through this book that whenever she is fragrant or she is beautiful she gets all that from him. He's the one who is fragrant."[81]

All that Solomon is and all that he has he gives to his bride. He prefers her above all others, so much that people are quite surprised. "Who is this poor farm girl with the king?" So it is with all who are in Christ. We can rejoice when all else fails and crumbles that all that we could ever want is in Christ. In his sovereign election, he has chosen us. We are completely unworthy, yet all that Christ is and has, he has given to us. He has looked upon our poverty and in spite of having nothing, he loves us and prefers us. Our Lord has sought a bride – he became

---

[81] Nancy Demoss Wolgemuth. "How to Fall and Stay in Love with Jesus," Day 11. Accessed Aug 21, 2017. https://www.reviveourhearts.com/radio/revive-our-hearts/song-solomon-day-11/

lowly to demonstrate his preference for her. Miracle of miracles, he loves his precious bride and prefers her above all others.

A VOW OF PERMANENCE (3:6B)

The wedding ceremony symbolizes the sacredness of marriage. The bride is described as "...**perfumed with myrrh and frankincense, with all the fragrant powders of a merchant**" (3:6b). This marriage was extravagant. This extravagance points to the permanence of marriage. You don't spend all this money and have this kind of lavish display for some overnight fling. This marriage is "'till death do us part." The costly fragrances point to the sacredness and significance of the marriage. The Scriptures teach that marriage is permanent.

> CYRIL OF ALEXANDRIA (375-444): "The myrrh mixed with frankincense was used for burying our Lord. Frankincense is mentioned because whoever is risen with Christ in the new birth is a partaker in the divine nature (2 Pet 1:4). The soul of Christ's church is imbued not only with these divine fragrances but also with everlasting principles of wisdom and insight by the Spirit (Eph 1:8). The one who does not live according to the flesh but according to the Spirit, whose heart has not been hardened, generates and preserves various sweet smells of Christ, rendering a good aroma from all the sweet herbs which are now called perfumes. Likewise, the soul of Christ's church, a daughter formerly destitute of God, ascends from the wilderness of the Gentiles, that is, from the desert of those who were formerly remiss in sound doctrine, words and deeds, having in times past abandoned God, but now rise as sweet-smelling fragrances to God."[82]

> JAMES DURHAM (1622–1658): "Solomon is perfumed with myrrh and frankincense, and all the fragrant powders of the merchant. As precious powders are used to make one smell savory, so the believer is replenished with the graces of Christ's spirit. These graces of the new birth are made alive by his presence, and they cast a delightful aroma to everyone with whom

---

[82] Cyril of Alexandria. *Fragments of the Commentary on the Song of Solomon*, In J.P. Migne, ed. *Patrologiae cursus completus. Series Graeca.* 166 vols., Vol 69 (Paris: Migne, 1857 – 1886), 1286-1287.

believers converse. Those who belong to Christ have such a powerful influence, as to be a sweet savor in every place (2 Cor 2:14-
15). They leave the Spirit's fragrant conviction upon people's
consciences. What can so perfume a person or place, as the
aroma of the Gospel?"[83]

The merchants here refer to the traders that would have brought
the very best of the perfumes from across the world. Solomon spares
no expense to make this wedding one never to be forgotten for his
bride. The marriage is special and sacred. It is to be celebrated. It is
extravagant. "The Scriptures teach that marriage is one of the most important events in a person's life. Therefore, it is fitting that the union of
a couple be commemorated in a special way."[84]

Consider the extravagance of Christ's love to us! "He who did not
spare his own Son but gave him up for us all, how will he not also with
him graciously give us all things?" (Rom 8:32).

A VOW OF PROTECTION (3:7-8)

Song of Solomon 3:7-8 | Behold, it is the litter[85] of Solomon!
Around it are sixty mighty men, some of the mighty men of
Israel, all of them wearing swords and expert in war, each with
his sword at his thigh, against terror by night.

Solomon arrives on his chariot-chair with sixty groomsmen beside.
The king's royal litter is the couch upon which he was carried by his
servants. This is a royal, full-dress military wedding. These are the navy
seals or green berets of Solomon's army.

> BEDE THE VENERABLE (672-735): "Solomon arriving at his
> wedding carried upon his royal chair is symbolic of Jesus, our
> King of peace, whose presence and protection brings rest to his
> saints. The rest is only partially enjoyed while the King's beloved,
> that is, the church, strains daily through the desert of this world
> awaiting the final marriage when her Bridegroom comes again.
> Though the day has not yet come, believers already partly enjoy
> this rest, insofar as he gives his faithful a foretaste of their future

---

[83] James Durham. *Clavis Cantici*, 173.
[84] Walvoord, *The Bible Knowledge Commentary*, Vol 1, 1017.
[85] the couch on which servants carry the king

reward. But they will receive it fully only when, at the end of the age, the founder and King of the heavenly city gathers the elect from the four winds, and as was said elsewhere, 'girds himself and makes them recline at table and serves them' (Lk 12:37)."[86]

"The king was taking no chances with the safety of his bride. If bandits would appear at night and terrorize the bride, the soldiers were ready for them. The lesson is valid today for a would-be husband. He should give proper thought and planning to protect his bride. One form this takes is providing economic security for her."[87]

Husbands, love your wives, as Christ loved the church and gave himself up for her, that he might sanctify her, having cleansed her by the washing of water with the word, so that he might present the church to himself in splendor, without spot or wrinkle or any such thing, that she might be holy and without blemish. In the same way husbands should love their wives as their own bodies. He who loves his wife loves himself. For no one ever hated his own flesh, but nourishes and cherishes it, just as Christ does the church. — Ephesians 5:25-29

The word cherish means "to warm with body heat." It has the idea of not leaving the body vulnerable. A man is to protect his wife. What does Paul mean about nourishing and cherishing his own body? Well, when your body is vulnerable you cherish it. When you hit your thumb with the hammer you carefully protect it and shelter it. You make sure no one and nothing can do it any more injury.

Solomon brought his bride great protection – sixty of the finest soldiers of Israel! So Christ protects his Bride as well.

CHARLES HADDON SPURGEON (1834-1892), "*Sixty valiant men are about Solomon's royal chair* – There are always enough men chosen of God to guard the Church. Let the Lord say unto thee as he did unto Elijah—'Yet have I left me seven-thousand in Israel, all the knees which have not bowed unto Baal' (1 Kings 19:18). There shall be just as many warriors as the crisis shall require. We do not know where the men are to come from, but the Lord will provide. There may be sitting in the Sunday school

[86] Bede the Venerable. *Commentary on the Song of Songs*, In *Corpus Christianorum. Series Latina*, Vol 119B (Turnhout, Belgium: Brepols, 1953), 237-238.
[87] Walvoord, ibid.

today a child who shall one day shake this nation from one end to the other; there may be even here, unknown, obscure, and unobserved, the man whom God will make strong to rebuke the infamous infidelity of our age. We know not where the anointing rests. We, in our folly, would anoint Eliab or Abinadab, but God has chosen David (1 Sam 16:1-13), the shepherd's boy, and he will bring him forth and teach him how to hurl the stone at Goliath's brow. Tremble not, neither be afraid; God who makes man and makes man's mouth, will find the sixty men when the sixty shall be needed. 'The Lord gave the word, great was the company of them that published it' (Psa 68:11). 'The glory of the Lord shall be revealed, and all flesh shall see it together, for the mouth of the Lord hath spoken it' (Isa 40:5)."[88]

Christ has an infinite love for his Bride. Of course, all Christians will suffer and go through various trials (Jas 1:1-3). Some will die of sickness or even die as martyrs, but we can say in the end "no weapon formed against you shall prosper" (Isa 54:17). We may lose our health or even our physical life, but when Jesus comes, both body and soul of the believer will be preserved eternally. He died to secure his Bride. He protects us at all costs. He is our shelter and our refuge and our high tower (Psa 61:3). Christ cherishes and protects his Church. Do you realize what Christ has done for us? He satisfied the wrath of God for our sins (1 Thess 1:10). He took the shame of our sin upon himself (2 Cor 5:21). He intercedes for us (Heb 7:25). He guides us and sanctifies us by his truth (Jn 17:17). He says, "I will never leave you or forsake you" (Heb 13:5). We abide under the shadow of the Almighty (Psa 91:1). We can say **"I am his and he is mine"** (2:16).

When a man vows to cherish his wife, it is a vow of protection. He is mirroring the love of Christ by guarding his wife from harm. He is to treat her gently and lovingly and preserve his dear wife from harm.

A VOW OF PROVISION (3:9-10)

Song of Solomon 3:9-10 | King Solomon made himself a carriage from the wood of Lebanon. He made its posts of silver, its

---

[88] Spurgeon. *Pulpit,* Vol 8, Sermon 482, "The Royal Pair in Their Glorious Chariot" (1862), 661.

back of gold, its seat of purple; its interior was inlaid with love by the daughters of Jerusalem.

The Song of Solomon here describes the royal carriage which is adorned with the finest quality materials for this occasion, so extravagant that it is said to be "inlaid with love." Purple cloth for the seat was made using a pigment from the murex shellfish which is said to be even rarer than silver and gold at that time. The women of the court have lovingly contributed to this day. Everyone shared the joy of King Solomon's wedding with his poor, but now rich Shulamite bride.

We travel with Christ our Bridegroom and enjoy all the provisions in his chariot. The seat of purple. Purple represents royalty, kingly authority. This is a carriage fit for a king and a reminder that because we are married to the King of kings, we travel with him and receive all his riches and benefits.

> J. HUDSON TAYLOR (1832-1905): "In these verses the bride is not mentioned; she is eclipsed in the grandeur and the state of her royal Bridegroom; nevertheless, she is both enjoying and sharing it. The very air is perfumed by the smoke of the incense that ascends pillar-like to the clouds; and all that safeguards the position of the Bridegroom himself, and shows forth his dignity, safeguards also the accompanying bride, the sharer of his glory. The car of state in which they sit is built of fragrant cedar from Lebanon, and the finest of the gold and silver have been lavished in its construction. The fragrant wood typifies the beauty of sanctified humanity, while the gold reminds us of the divine glory of our Lord, and the silver of the purity and preciousness of his redeemed and peerless Church. The imperial purple with which it is lined tells us of the Gentiles—the daughter of Tyre has been there with her gift; while the love-gifts of the daughters of Jerusalem accord with the prophecy, 'Even the rich among the people shall entreat thy favor' (Psa 42:5)."[89]

All that we are and all that we have is a result of our union with Christ. We have all things in Christ, being "heirs of God and co-heirs with Christ" (Rom 8:17-18). St. Paul probably has the most expansive recounting of all we have in Christ.

---

[89] Taylor. *Union*, 38.

Blessed be the God and Father of our Lord Jesus Christ, who has blessed us in Christ with every spiritual blessing in the heavenly places, even as he chose us in him before the foundation of the world, that we should be holy and blameless before him. In love he predestined us for adoption to himself as sons through Jesus Christ, according to the purpose of his will, to the praise of his glorious grace, with which he has blessed us in the Beloved. In him we have redemption through his blood, the forgiveness of our trespasses, according to the riches of his grace, which he lavished upon us, in all wisdom and insight making known to us the mystery of his will, according to his purpose, which he set forth in Christ as a plan for the fullness of time, to unite all things in him, things in heaven and things on earth. —Ephesians 1:3-10

Solomon shows us that a man must be ready and willing to provide for his wife. It is his responsibility, not hers. Lack of money is one of the greatest causes of tension in life, and it certainly is true in marriage.

If anyone does not provide for his relatives, and especially for members of his household, he has denied the faith and is worse than an unbeliever. — 1 Timothy 5:8

In the New Testament, husbands are called to lay down their life for their bride and to nourish, or provide for them (Eph 5:29). David said, "The LORD is my shepherd; I shall not want" (Psa 23:1). Christ, our good Shepherd is the believer's provider. Indeed, "no good thing does he withhold from those who walk uprightly" (Psa 84:11). Christ will nourish and care for his Bride, laying his life down for her. He provides for her in every way.

A VOW WITH PROPER APPROVAL (3:11A)

The wedding ceremony symbolizes the permission and blessing of the parents.

Song of Solomon 3:11 | Go out, O daughters of Zion, and look upon King Solomon, with the crown with which his mother crowned him on the day of his wedding, on the day of the gladness of his heart.

Solomon's mother Bathsheba crowned him with the wedding crown that a groom wore in those days, usually a laurel crown of leaves.

It was a sign of her approval that he was marrying a woman she valued and would love as a daughter. It is also a sign to the general public that he would be leaving his parents' home and making a home of his own.

For centuries upon centuries, crowning was a part of marriage ceremonies. Today, the bride is crowned with her veil. The bride even in ancient times would be crowned with a garland of flowers by her father.

All of this symbolizes the parent's permission and blessing. Today, usually the wedding ceremony begins with the minister asking, "Who gives this woman to be married to this man?" The father normally gives permission by saying, "Her mother and I do." 1 Corinthians 7 demonstrates the importance of the father's permission. It's clear in the NKJV. A bride must have her father's permission.

> But if any man thinks he is behaving improperly toward his virgin, if she is past the flower of youth, and thus it must be, let him do what he wishes. He does not sin; let them marry. —1 Corinthians 7:36, NKJV

If a young lady has come to physical maturity and has the desire to marry, the father should take serious consideration of her desire and, if the man is a proper godly suitor who can provide for his daughter, he should permit them to marry.

> Nevertheless he who stands steadfast in his heart, having no necessity, but has power over his own will, and has so determined in his heart that he will keep his virgin, does well. So then he who gives her in marriage does well, but he who does not give her in marriage does better. —1 Corinthians 7:37-38, NKJV

Why was this such a big deal? Why would Paul have to remind the fathers that they were not "sinning" when giving their daughter in marriage? The context is that some father's in this church had dedicated their daughters to the Lord's service as single people. At the time, some of the girls came to physical maturity and wanted to be married. Paul said, you are not sinning if you dedicated your daughters, and later on, they want marriage. Let them marry. The father should consider the daughter's desire for marriage, and if the young man is godly, the father should consider the daughter's desires.

The giving of the bride is the father's prerogative. "He who gives her in marriage does well, but he who does not give her in marriage does better" (vs. 38). If the daughter has no necessity of getting married, the father still has the prerogative to encourage her in marriage or to encourage her to remain single. It's fine if the father encourages his daughter or son in marriage, but it is even better if parents encourage singleness if they can bare it. Matthew 19:12, "...there are eunuchs who have made themselves eunuchs for the sake of the kingdom of heaven. Let the one who is able to receive this receive it." A wedding that is approved by the parents is one that God blesses!

What if the parents are not alive (such as for Solomon's bride)? Then we look for approval from the Lord's congregation. This should be sought regardless, for in Christ we have many fathers and mothers. When a wedding has been designed by God it will always have the approval of God's people.

A VOW OF PREPARATION (3:11B)

Finally, the wedding ceremony symbolizes the great joy that God gives a couple who have diligently prepared to enter into marriage the right way. The wedding guests observe the tremendous happiness of King Solomon: "...**on the day of his wedding, on the day of the gladness of his heart**" (3:11b). You will not regret all the sacrifices and care you took during your courtship and engagement. Do it right and you will have gladness of heart. Do it wrong and you will have questions and even confusion and serious consequences. Those who diligently seek the Lord in their lives and especially in marriage, will not be disappointed. Long term happiness and stability does not come by finding "Mr. Right" or "Miss Perfect." Happiness and stability come from obedience to God and commitment to him. Let his rule and reign extend to your courtship, engagement, and your marriage.

Are you planning a wedding? Put God first. If God's not in this, call off the wedding. You must live by the "God First" Principle. We see it throughout the Word of God. "Delight yourself in the LORD, and he will give you the desires of your heart" (Psa 37:4). If you are seeking the Lord and delighting in him, then you are going to be longing for his will. Seek the Lord's kingdom and righteousness, and everything else will be added to you (cf. Mt 6:33), and that includes the right kind of marriage.

The NIV says that it's "**the day that his heart rejoiced**" (3:11). More important than the details of your wedding, the colors you choose, the people who celebrate it with you is the God who gives the gift of marriage. On that day we want to say, "it's the day" God's heart rejoiced! We want to please him and not ourselves.

Of course, the most important wedding – the most beautiful love story – is not the one you are planning with your future spouse here on earth, but the wedding that's coming when Jesus comes a second time.

> NANCY DEMOSS WOLGEMUTH (1958–), "This king is utterly awestruck with the sight of his bride. He's awestruck at the thought that he gets to be married to her. He finds great joy and great delight in her. And keep in mind that through this book, the king, Solomon, the groom is a picture of our heavenly Bridegroom, of Christ on whose head are many crowns. Praise him! Praise Him! Crown him with many crowns. And we're seeing here the picture of his marriage to the Bride that he has chosen for himself which is a cause for great joy. Revelation 19 tells us about that wedding. It says, "Let us be glad and rejoice and give him glory for the marriage of the Lamb has come and his wife has made herself ready." I want to remind us of the day the Lord Jesus took you to be his bride, His heart rejoiced. Can you imagine that we give him joy?"[90]

Conclusion

If you have any question about entering into marriage, wait! Don't go forward until you have all the green lights. Make engagement a time of further preparation. A wedding designed by God is one truly to rejoice in.

The most important wedding you should be planning for is meeting the true Bridegroom Jesus Christ. Revelation 19 tells us about that wedding. It says, "Let us be glad and rejoice and give him glory for the marriage of the Lamb has come and his wife has made herself ready." The day the Lord Jesus took you to be his bride, his heart rejoiced. Can you imagine that we give him joy? Let us rejoice that if we know him, the day of death or the day he comes again will be a day of rejoicing and not of wrath. Christ has made all the preparations, and he vows that

---

[90] Nancy Demoss Wolgemuth. "How to Fall and Stay in Love with Jesus," Day 11. Accessed Aug 21, 2017. https://www.reviveourhearts.com/radio/revive-our-hearts/song-solomon-day-11/

because of his sacrifice we are welcomed and accepted and even celebrated in his presence. What a wedding that will be when we see our eternal Bridegroom face to face.

6 | SONG 4:1-5:1

THE BEAUTIFUL BRIDE'S HONEYMOON

Behold, you are beautiful, my love, behold, you are beautiful! Your eyes are doves behind your veil.
SONG 4:1

How does God see you? It is here in Song of Solomon 4 we realize how God views us. You may say, he sees everything, right? He sees all my failures. He sees the remaining sin and deceit and defilement of my heart. Oh no, dear child of God, you are in Christ. God has a vision of you that is so much greater than yours. God is infinite, outside of time. He sees you as you will be in his presence in eternity, perfected and complete in Christ. You are complete right now in Christ. He's applying his chisel in a thousand ways in your life – through trials and pain and difficulties – in weakness, in difficult relationships, in difficult circumstances. He's working the perfect image of Christ upon your soul. He sees you as the Bride of Christ, without spot or wrinkle. If we are going to become radically transformed, we need to focus our eyes on Christ.

I learned this principle of focus when I was a student at Ponchatoula High School in Louisiana. One of my most transformative and life shaping-classes was Art class with Mrs. Kim Zabbia. One of the lessons she taught me that if I wanted to replicate an object, I had to be totally committed to it. I had to get my eyes and my mind off myself and with my pencil, replicate each part of the object with its minute details. I had to be committed to every detail, every turn and shape of that object. I had to get my eyes and my mind off myself and on to that object, taking in every detail into my mind, and drawing it with my hand.

This is the secret to marriage – not only on the wedding night, but during the entirety of your marriage, till death parts you. Get your eyes off yourself and onto Christ.

Marital Intimacy is a Picture

Chapter four of the Song of Solomon is breath taking. It describes the wedding night of Solomon and his bride. Lovers look forward to their wedding night for the unexplored mystery of romance and intimacy. God said that in marriage, the man and his wife are "naked and unashamed" (Gen 2:25).

Only in marriage, a man is encouraged by God to look upon the unclothed beauty of his bride. Although there may be many beautiful women in the world; in marriage, the husband has vowed to take an interest in her womanly beauty in particular. It is important that the husband regularly praises his wife's beauty. We see this here at the honeymoon for Solomon and his new bride. Though every wife has her imperfections, Solomon does not see those of his lover. In a profound way, Solomon is acting out God's love story. Through Solomon, we see how God sees Christ's Bride, the Church. This beautiful and sacred vulnerability in marriage, as powerful and electrifying as it is, is but a faint picture of the reality of the wedding night for Christ's Bride. When we see Jesus, the love and joy and exhilaration will be even greater than what we find in Solomon's Song.

As we look at this chapter, we want to be careful to keep the sacredness of marital romance mysterious as the Holy Spirit has written through Solomon. We don't want to "unclothe" this love story and make it less than exalted. Many have ruthlessly raped the romance in Song of Solomon by the way they have presented the delicateness of the marriage bed.

Let me reiterate that God has a plan for intimacy. It is very simply this: sexual expression is beautiful only in marriage. All sexual intimacy outside of marriage is sin. A couple who has waited for marriage to give themselves to each other will be on solid ground emotionally, socially, and sexually. Great sorrow is avoided for those who have made the decision to wait.

Intimacy outside of marriage is ugly and cheap. Within marriage it is the most exalted form of human love. Outside of marriage it is taking something beautiful and dragging it through the mud. It is taking a beautiful face and scarring it up! It is taking the sacred and spitting on it. Marital intimacy is beautiful in God's sight.

God designed intimacy to be between one man and one woman in a monogamous relationship for the entirety of life. God made marital intimacy to be pure and undefiled and holy. It is designed by God. Hebrews 13:4 summarizes the message in Song of Solomon 4 when the writer says this: "Let marriage be held in honor among all, and let the marriage bed be [kept] undefiled, for God will judge the sexually immoral and adulterous."

So many do not have a clue how sacred marital love is, and they have become sexually immoral. Our society is saturated with sexual immorality. Intimacy is reserved for marriage alone. Let me try to explain how powerful physical love is and how it should be carefully guarded and protected. I want to do this by sharing a little parable I once heard by a pastor by the name of Tom Nelson.

The Parable of the Crocodile

Once upon a time there was a man that went to live among the people a great River. And he sat by to eat with these people. Then he noticed out of the corner of his eye was a 1700-pound crocodile. As the crocodile approached the table, the man yelled out: "There's a crocodile coming at us!" As he did that a woman shushed him and said, "We don't talk about crocodiles—it's impolite."

If you walked around town, you could see many people who were torn up by these crocodiles. Some wounds were fresh. Others were scarred over and over again. But there were no signs to warn the people of crocodiles. And no one wanted to talk about it. It was something they all just lived with.

That's how many churches deal with intimacy. Most young people learn about God's gift of marital intimacy on the playground and on the streets. Young people see it in magazines and hear about it through standup comedy.

Many young people never really understand that God's gift of intimacy is only beautiful in marriage. They don't hear that if it is hatched before marriage, it is overwhelming and destructive. They never hear God's perspective on it. Then when a young person is about 14 or 15 a crocodile comes out of the river and puts a permanent scar on them. They have the most powerful overcoming urge that comes upon them, and it is something that can cause untold pain and heartache and tears with long lasting wounds and unhealed marks. And the young person gets married, but they've never talked about it. They've learned to sweep it under the rug in the home and in the church. They're not to talk about it.

But all of the sudden he gets married and the problem is glaring in neon lights every day. And if this is not talked about, you can have singles and married people who go through years of silent pain and anxiety and maybe even anger and bitterness and frustration. It can become the bar of leverage that separates and sears couples or makes a single person who's messed up think they could never enter into marriage.

We are talking about God's plan for intimacy in this chapter. It is reserved for marriage. But some of you—single and married people need to know that God can cleanse every wound of sin. He can purify all of us today. We need to come to the healing fountain of Jesus' blood. No matter what has happened to you in your life, understand, where sin abounds and heart ache and pain because of sin abounds, grace much more abounds (Rom 5:20).

God gives us an entire chapter of his word to tell us how beautiful marital love is, and why marital intimacy is reserved for marriage. God's gift of intimacy can be a great blessing to married people, but he will judge and is judging people every day for defiling it. Internet pornography and the steamy lust of many television commercials is destroying marriages and keeping people from eternal life. Marital intimacy is not something to play with. It is something to guard and reserve for the right time. It is designed by God, and it is special.

Yet as beautiful as sexual intimacy is, it pales in comparison to the love that we have in Christ. The love of Christ is exalted far above all human love. Marital love and intimacy is a faint picture of the powerful love that we have in and through Jesus Christ. If you are married, you need to keep the marriage bed pure and undefiled. That's done through listening to each other, forgiving each other, and keeping a very close relationship with one another. If you are unmarried, to keep the marriage bed undefiled means you have a vow of chastity until you say "I do" at the wedding altar. That's on the human level.

This chapter is not simply about marital love. Oh that you would experience the exalted love that God has for you if you are in Christ. God has used marital love to be a beautiful picture of his love for the church. He has made the marriage bed pure, undefiled, and holy. This chapter does describe the wedding night of the royal couple, but it does so in a very dignified way, not so that it can be a manual for relations in marriage, but so that it can point to a far more exalted reality – the reality of our marriage to Christ. Marriage then is a picture of something much greater. The joy and love and intimacy of marriage points to how Christ sees his bride whom he has redeemed. "Christ loved the church and gave himself up for her, that he might sanctify her, having cleansed her by the washing of water with the word, so that he might present the church to himself in splendor, without spot or wrinkle or any such thing, that she might be holy and without blemish. In the same way husbands should love their wives as their own bodies" (Eph 5:25-28).

What is happening in this passage? The king comes to his wedding in glory in 3:6-11, and upon his arrival he sings a song of praise to his beloved (4:1-5), followed by a declaration of both her beauty and his desire (4:6-16). O how he loves his new bride. Some have said, "Love is blind." Solomon sees this ordinary peasant girl through eyes of love that covers any blemishes. There is great comfort that the Greater Solomon (Jesus) sees us with eyes that, because of his work on the cross, covers our sins and fallenness. Because of the tender mercies that flow from the cross, God sees us as flawless.

THE BRIDE'S BEAUTY (4:1-7)

The real question of this passage then is not "how does Solomon see his bride," but "how does God see you?" Marriage gives us a faint look at how God takes pleasure in you. You may be married and can relate with the heightened love language that this couple enjoys. All of the words of this chapter except for the last verse is by Solomon. This is a picture of God's love for us. God sees you as beautiful. The day the

Lord Jesus took you to be his Bride, his heart rejoiced. Can you imagine that we give him joy?

You may not feel beautiful. You feel so unworthy. You feel at times dirtied and soiled and trampled by the world. In Song of Solomon chapter 4, Christ now sees his Bride as eternally beautiful. You are loved by God right now. If you are in Christ, you are eternally beautiful to him from beginning to end. Solomon looks upon his bride behind her veil (4:1) and expresses his love to her.

Song of Solomon 4:1 | Behold, you are beautiful, my love, behold, you are beautiful! Your eyes are doves behind your veil. Your hair is like a flock of goats leaping down the slopes of Gilead.

The honeymoon begins! They have just been married, and Solomon is delighted with his new bride. He tells her of her beauty! As you read this passage, you are going to find how strange Solomon's comparisons are for his bride. The imagery which Solomon uses in praising his Shulamite bride are drawn from a setting she would have been familiar with: the green pastures that his shepherdess bride was familiar with. Though Solomon is a king, and he knows of gold and silver and palaces, he does not use that language. He uses her language—that of doves, goats, sheep, pomegranates, fawns, gazelles, mountains, hills. Solomon's bride was raised in the country, and she would have so appreciated these images.

If you are a married man, you need to speak in words your wife will appreciate. You need to work on your communication with her. She needs to know she is loved, first by God and then by you. Are you one who complains about your spouse? Do you look at the negative and hold the person you married to impossible expectations? How can you know? Simple: if you have high, unmet expectations of your spouse, you will likely have many toxic and negative emotions like self-pity, anger, sharp criticism of your spouse and complaining. Often married couples instead of accepting one another in a spirit of contentment and gratitude, they lash out at each other in a spirit of envy (wishing they had married someone else) or a spirit of self-righteousness (believing they are right, and their spouse is the real problem).

A believing spouse sees their mate how Christ sees them (if they are born-again). If your spouse doesn't know Christ, then you have the privilege of living a faithful example to them by loving them in spite of their brokenness. Married couples are called to see each other through God's eyes of love. This praise and admiration of Solomon's new bride would bring a sense of peace and security to her heart. Married men, is your wife secure in your marriage? Do you speak to her with words of gentleness and love? More importantly, we need to hear Christ's words to us as his bride. When Christ sees you as his Bride, he rejoices over you

God Sees You as Beautiful

With Solomon's first view of his bride, he was overwhelmed by her beauty. Have you ever grasped the fact that you, as Christ's bride, are precious to him, and that he takes great delight in you? Listen to the words of Solomon to his new bride on their wedding night.

Song of Solomon 4:1a | Behold, you are beautiful, my love, behold, you are beautiful!

He's going to repeat this thought two more times in this chapter. In verse 7, he says, "**You are altogether beautiful, my love; there is no flaw in you.**" He says it again in verse 10.

God loves you. He rejoices over you. Even though you run and hide at times, he is a relentless Redeemer. He's got you. You cannot outrun or overcome his love for you. You love him because he first loved you (1 Jn 4:19). There's no other reason. He drew you with his love. He called you to himself. There are so many verses in the Bible that paint for us a great salvation that is by God grace and pleasure and love.

John says of you: "I saw the holy city, new Jerusalem, coming down out of heaven from God, prepared as a bride adorned for her husband" (Rev 21:2). You are adorned by Christ, beloved saint of God! He's lavished his grace on you (Eph 1:7-8). He's rich in mercy because of the great and infinite love he has for you (Eph 2:4-5). He takes delight in you with gladness. With his love, he will calm all of your fears. He will rejoice over you with joyful singing (Zeph 3:17). "Nothing in all creation, is able to separate us from the love of God in Christ Jesus our Lord" (Rom 8:39). He did this not because you are so worthy. You and I are totally depraved and blind and wretched apart from his redeeming love. But once he glances upon us, he makes us new. We are his new creation (2 Cor 5:17).

All throughout the New Testament, we are told that we are no longer depraved sinners but saints. Yes, we have a struggle with our old flesh, but that is no longer our identity. We have a new identity! Just look at the first chapter of Ephesians, and we see the same glimpse that God has for his Bride. You are the Bride, and you are beautiful in his sight! You can say...

Because of Christ living in me...

- I am faithful (Eph 1:1)
- I am blessed in the heavenly realms with every spiritual blessing (Eph 1:3)
- I am chosen before the creation of the world (Eph 1:4)
- I am holy and blameless (Eph 1:4)
- I am adopted as his child (Eph 1:5)
- I am given God's glorious grace lavishly and without restriction (Eph 1:5, 8)
- I am in him (Eph 1:7; 1 Cor 1:30)
- I have redemption (Eph 1:8)
- I am forgiven (Eph 1:8; Col 1:14)
- I am included (Eph 1:13)
- I am sealed with the promised Holy Spirit (Eph 1:13)
- I have been brought near to God through Christ's blood (Eph 2:13)
- I have access to the Father (Eph 2:18)

In this chapter, the groom goes to great lengths to express the deep love he has for his bride, and how beautiful she is to him, and how much he delights in her. It's heavy language. We saw in chapter 1 that this bride does not see herself as beautiful or lovable or worthy of his love. Remember, she was just a plain, ordinary country girl whose skin had been scorched and toughened by doing menial labor on her family farm out in the hot sun. That's how she saw herself, and that's how she was (1:6, "They made me keeper of the vineyards, but my own vineyard I have not kept). But her bridegroom sees her through eyes of love—his love.

God Has Clothed You with Beauty

In the betrothal time, Solomon promised to get his bride ready for the wedding. He promised to bejewel her (1:10-11). I'm certain he got her ready with skin treatments, rings of precious jewels, strings of pearls, a head-dress with "**ornaments of gold, studded with silver.**" And so it is that right now you may not feel beautiful as God's child, but God is in the process of conforming us to Christ's glory and beauty. Don't despair saint of God, you are beautiful in God's sight!

God's love is so strong – so intense! There is so much more to God's love that is not yet revealed to you and me. "But, as it is written, 'What no eye has seen, nor ear heard, nor the heart of man imagined, what God has prepared for those who love him'" (1 Cor. 2:9). Of course, God has revealed some of these things to us by his Spirit. But we "see in a mirror dimly, but then, face to face" (1 Cor. 13:12).

God Loves Your Doves' Eyes

Solomon admires his new bride's eyes.

Song of Solomon 4:1b | Your eyes are doves behind your veil.

The dove represents a bird that usually likes to hide away in rocky places where it remains safe. In a beautiful picture here, the young bride is peeking out from behind the veil and her flowing hair, which covers some of her face. Solomon can see her eyes of innocence and sincerity. She has doves' eyes. There is an innocence to doves. Doves portray meekness, gentleness, and tenderness. The dove is mild and harmless. Perhaps Solomon is thinking of her being chaste and faithful or humble.

The bride feels free and peaceful in the presence of Solomon, her husband and king. And so it is with the church. We know that there is freedom and safety in Christ! No matter what our past, we are made innocent and harmless in him. He has transformed our evil eyes into doves' eyes. There is no condemnation for those who are in Christ (Rom 8:1), but only welcome and access to the grace that transforms us. "For through him we both have access in one Spirit to the Father" (Eph 2:18).

> MATTHEW HENRY (1662-1714): "The doves' eyes are somewhat covered by the locks of the Bride's hair, so that, she cannot fully see everything in front of her. As long as we as Christians are here in this world, we know but in part, for a hair hangs in our eyes; and we cannot order our speech by reason of darkness. But be encouraged, because death will shortly cut those locks, and then we shall see all things clearly. The future things God has for us cannot be fully seen at this moment. They are like the

stars that shine through the thin clouds. The doves' eyes may intimate the bashfulness of the church's looks; she does not allow her eyes to wander after this world, but limits her vision within her locks."[91]

God Loves Your Covering

Solomon admires his new bride's hair.

Song of Solomon 4:1c | Your hair is like a flock of goats leaping down the slopes of Gilead.

This hardly sounds like a complement! Seen from a distance the dark hair of Palestinian goats was beautiful in the sunset as a flock was descending from the mountains. Probably she had dark, flowing hair and it made him think of Mt. Gilead. It's a plateau area that has very high cliffs coming off of it. Solomon is overcome by her hair, her covering! Long hair for a woman is a very outward display of devotion and submission to God. It was clear that she honored her God.

Do you realize you are covered by Christ's righteousness? When we finally see God, and he says, "Well done, good and faithful servant (Mt 25:23), I can imagine hearing those words and looking around saying, "Me, Lord? Are you sure? I don't feel so faithful." But it's true, and just behind us will be Jesus smiling, saying – "I did it all for you. I lived for you. I died for you. Your life wasn't perfect, but I was at the center of it. Enter into your rest my dear child." From beginning to end, Christ is our righteousness. We are made the "righteousness of God in him" (2 Cor 5:21).

> ARTHUR JACKSON (1593-1666), "The hair points to spirituality that flows from the Church's faith and trust in Christ, which is indeed a great ornament to her. She is righteous inwardly because of Christ, and out of this fountain proceed good works, and more particularly, the pure and holy thoughts and meditations in the minds and heads of the faithful, still ascending heavenward, which though they be innumerably many, yet by the watchfulness of the saints, are kept in good order, as a flock of goats by the shepherd. Still further, in the hair, we see the multitude of true believers, numberless as the hairs upon a man's

---

[91] Matthew Henry. *Commentary*, 1064.

head are, who when they meet together in full assemblies to wait upon God in his ordinances, and are as goodly a sight as a flock of goats upon mount Gilead."[92]

God Loves Your Teeth (Spiritual Appetite)
Solomon admires his new bride's teeth.

Song of Solomon 4:2 | Your teeth are like a flock of shorn ewes that have come up from the washing, all of which bear twins, and not one among them has lost its young.

This would have been particularly amazing in that culture where they didn't have all the dentists and the dental care. People's teeth would be falling out and yellowed with age. It was rare to have all your teeth in the ancient world! And not only did this girl have all her teeth, they were very well aligned, like "twins." It seems that this bride had a sweet smile on her face. She felt happy being married to the king! O the joy that the church has in Christ.

Solomon says, "There's a purity in my bride's teeth. There's whiteness, cleanness. Her teeth are symmetrical; no teeth are missing. She's lovely; she's beautiful." What do you do with teeth? Well, among other things, they're used for taking hold of and chewing food. Maybe this speaks of our ability to take in spiritual food. To chew it, to digest it, to take the Word and appropriate it into our lives and get it into our system through meditation and prayer.

It seems that this bride had a sweet smile on her face and she felt happy being married to the king! O the joy that the church has in Christ.

> JAMES DURHAM (1622–1658): "The teeth properly understood, are useful for furthering the nourishment of the body. They are the instruments that prepare food for digestion. What beauty is in them is not immediately obvious. A person's teeth are not always seen or discerned in their size or shape. Unless the lips are moving the teeth are hidden. In Scripture, the teeth are used to evidence and signify these various things. What comes out of the mouth reveals the nature and disposition of a person's heart, as good or evil. For example, evil men are said to have lions' teeth, and their teeth are as spears (Psa 57:4). The

---

[92] Arthur Jackson. *Song of Solomon*, Song 4:1.

beast in the book of Daniel (Dan 7:5, 7) is said to have three ribs in his teeth, manifesting its cruel disposition. The teeth have the evidence of healthy or unhealthy food that the person feeds on. The teeth of Judah are said to be "white with milk" demonstrating a healthy diet and appetite (Gen 49:12). When a person comes to Christ, their new nature is often compared to eating, because it furthers the soul's nourishment, and is the means by which the soul lives on its spiritual food. For example, Jesus is said to be the "bread of life" (Jn 6:35) and the "water" whereby one will never thirst again (Jn 4:14). A true and living faith brings with it an appetite for heavenly things. Just as we feed our physical body, so the inner man must also have food for sustenance and health. Not only this, but the believer actually eats, and makes use of the spiritual food in the Bible. The new birth has furnished him with teeth for that end, that he should not only look on Christ, but feed on him. The bride's teeth may also refer to meditation on God's Word, serving much to the feeding and filling of the soul. "My soul shall be filled as with marrow and fatness," how? "while I meditate on thee on my bed, and think of thee in the night watches" (Psa 63:6-7). Meditation is the soul's ruminating and chewing its cud, feeding upon, and digesting what is understood and eaten, as the clean beasts did. This may be one reason why her teeth are compared to a flock of sheep, which were among the number of clean animals in the Old Testament. Meditation is exceptionally useful for a believer's life, and they who are strangers to it, are not like Christ's sheep."[93]

Pray to the Lord, "My relentless Redeemer, thank you for a new appetite and sharp shining spiritual teeth to chew on and savor your Word and your presence." Cry out: "Oh, taste and see that the Lord is good. Blessed is the man who takes refuge in him" (Psa 34:8). We are "like newborn babies, long for the pure milk of the word, so that by it you may grow thereby" in our salvation and walk with God (1 Pet 2:2). Pray to the Lord: "O precious Jesus, give me a hunger and a thirst for righteousness, that I may be filled. Grant me a spiritual appetite for you and your Kingdom."

---

[93] James Durham. *Clavis Cantici*, 204-205.

God Loves Your Lips (Communication)
Solomon admires his new bride's lips.

Song of Solomon 4:3a | Your lips are like a scarlet thread, and your mouth is lovely.

The lips are a vehicle of expression. Your mouth is a means of communication. Solomon says, "Your mouth is lovely." That's in contrast to so much of the speech you hear among people today, even Christian people. Marriages today are plagued with mouths that destroy the soul of their spouse. "Let no corrupting talk come out of your mouths, but only such as is good for building up, as fits the occasion, that it may give grace to those who hear" (Eph 4:29). The true believer is one that has a mouth that reveals a transformed heart. A lost person cannot produce consistent godly communication. "How can you speak good things, when you are evil? For out of the abundance of the heart the mouth speaks" (Mt 12:34). "The mouth of the righteous is a fountain of life, but the mouth of the wicked conceals violence" (Pro 10:11). The mouth of the believer is lovely. It reveals a transformed heart. "The good person out of the good treasure of the heart produces good, and the evil person out of evil treasure produces evil; for it is out of the abundance of the heart that the mouth speaks" (Lk 6:45)

Pray to the Lord. Ask the Lord to guard your mouth. Ask him to fill your mind and heart with him so your words will be pure. Pray to the Lord – praise him for giving you a new heart with new words. Your mouth is lovely in Christ, because your heart is renewed. Ask him to give you lovely speech for him. We need to pray for edifying speech, joyful speech. We need to praise and thank the Lord at all times. His praise should continually be in our mouths (Psa 34:1).

God Loves Your Innocent Countenance
Solomon admires his new bride's cheeks.

Song of Solomon 4:3b | Your cheeks are like halves of a pomegranate behind your veil.

All of this is while she is still behind her veil. Perhaps the vows have been made, but the honeymoon has hardly begun. Yet he is admiring her as if for the first time. Her face beams with purity, integrity and sincerity.

Let me say a word about purity and how preserving yourself is worth the wait. Solomon, it seems, has a clear conscience. He has preserved himself for marriage, and now that he has vowed his love to this girl he is free to look upon her and admire her. This is not a cheap glance of lust, but a deep gaze of love. Solomon is not in this for some quick thrill, but he has now pledged his life to this girl. Now he admires her behind her veil. Husband and wife are now "naked and unashamed" (Gen 2:25). Solomon says in essence to his tender bride, "Your face shines with the holiness of God; your countenance reveals that you walk with God; your cheeks are flush with the reflection of the Holy One." We might say that Solomon recognized that his bride "had been with Jesus" (Acts 4:13).

The child of God stands before God with sincere pomegranate cheeks. All your heart and life are naked before him, and in Christ we are pure and unashamed. No matter what regrets and dirtiness we experienced before Christ, we are now cleansed and justified and glorified in Jesus (Rom 8:29-30). Your countenance is now pure in Christ. We who once were shameful harlots are now a covered bride for Christ. Child of God, I don't know what sins you committed before you knew Christ, but they are gone. Even the sins you struggle against day by day, God promises to progressively deliver and sanctify you (Heb 12:1-2, Phil 1:6). "Now may the God of peace himself sanctify you completely and may your whole spirit and soul and body be kept blameless at the coming of our Lord Jesus Christ. He who calls you is faithful; he will surely do it" (1 Thess 5:23-24). You heart is changed. Your face is beaming with the love of Christ. Your smile speaks of a joy that is not from this world, "unspeakable and full of glory" (1 Pet 1:8). Thank the Lord that he has lightened upon your countenance, with cheeks that tell that your life is hidden in Christ.

> BERNARD OF CLAIRVAUX (1090-1153): "The bride's modesty is a delicate thing. At the Bridegroom's glance, a warm flush covered his bride's face, so heightening her beauty that she was immediately greeted with: 'Your cheeks are like halves of a pomegranate behind your veil.' We ought not give a merely earthbound meaning to her face. Her flush cheeks reveal her pure soul. The substance of the soul is, of course, incorporeal and invisible, possessing neither bodily limbs nor any visible coloring. Try then to grasp the nature of this spiritual entity by means of

this spiritual insight. The heart's purity is at times manifested through the face. So then, we may see in this flush on the cheek an unassuming disposition where the virtue and beauty of God thrive, and grace increases."[94]

God Loves Your Fortified Neck

Solomon admires his new bride's neck.

Song of Solomon 4:4 | Your neck is like the tower of David, built in rows of stone; on it hang a thousand shields, all of them shields of warriors.

This doesn't sound like a complement, but it surely is. Upon David's tower in Jerusalem would have hung thousands of shields of those warriors who had fought for him. They were a sign of allegiance and love. What good is a beautiful face if it is not connected to the body. The bride is intact. The life is a person is demonstrated by the neck, which connects the head to the rest of the body.

The king had seen many fortified places, but upon seeing the jewelry on his bride's neck, he expresses his undying loyalty to her with this military metaphor. The purity of her mind and body had been protected like the towers of Israel constructed by Israel's warrior king. She had guarded her mind and body for her husband. "In this picture of her neck like a warrior's tower, Solomon sees his bride as unassailable. No man could 'conquer' her, and her suitor is awed by the dignity she carries. Her love is a gift; it could never become plunder."[95] The bride then freely gives her love to Solomon.

Why is this description of the bride's neck so important? Because this woman had guarded herself with military-like fortification so that she might freely give herself to her husband. Her body and brains belong only to her husband. As guarded as she has been she freely invites her king alone to traverse the "rows of stones" on her neck. Though her neck was decorated with what are portrayed as thousands of warriors' shields, that well-guarded neck now belongs to the king.

The Christian has a well-guarded neck that we freely give to Christ because it belongs to him and no one else. The neck vitally connects the

---

[94] Bernard of Clairvaux. *Commentary on the Song of Solomon*, "Sermon 40: The Face of the Bride."

[95] Garrett. *Song of Songs*, 405-406.

head to the rest of the body. For all believers, we have a fortified neck that is protected and shielded through our union with Christ. Nothing can sever or injure our union with Christ. St. Paul exclaims, "I am sure that neither death nor life, nor angels nor rulers, nor things present nor things to come, nor powers, nor height nor depth, nor anything else in all creation, will be able to separate us from the love of God in Christ Jesus our Lord" (Rom 8:38-39). Your neck – your connection with Christ – will never be severed.

Christ is so dedicated to you, he laid down his life so that you would be forever protected by his love. He has brought you into union with himself and has made sure you are vitally connected to him. The Scripture tells us that all blessings flow from our union with Christ. John Calvin said, "For this is the design of the gospel, that Christ may become ours, and that we may be ingrafted into his body, participants not only in all his benefits but also in himself."[96]

You as a believer are gloriously connected to Christ – you have an illustriously fortified neck connecting you to Christ your head, and that connection can never be severed. Indeed, the Father "has blessed us in Christ with every spiritual blessing in the heavenly places" (Eph 1:3). When we are born again, we are baptized into Christ by the Spirit of God (Rom 6:3). We find literally hundreds of places where the Bible speaks of the believer's union with Christ. Here are a few more – believers are created in Christ (Eph 2:10), crucified with him (Gal 2:20), buried with him (Col 2:12), baptized into Christ and his death (Rom 6:3), united with him in his resurrection (Rom 6:5), and seated with him in the heavenly places (Eph 2:6). Christ is formed in believers (Gal 4:19) and dwells in our hearts by faith (Eph 3:17). The church is the body of Christ (1 Cor 6:15; 12:27). Christ is in us (2 Cor 13:5), and we are in him (1 Cor 1:30). The church is one flesh with Christ (Eph 5:31–32). Believers gain Christ and are found in him (Phil 3:8–9).

So often we allow the assaults of the world to cut off our windpipe. We can't breathe because of fear, despair, lust, or anger. We have forgotten our union with Christ. Pray to the Lord to have a neck that is protected from the world. Ask Him that you might breathe the breath

---

[96] John Calvin. *Institutes of the Christian Religion, The Library of Christian Classics* (Louisville: Westminster John Knox Press, 1960), Kindle Locations 14581-14582.

of the Spirit. Receive refreshing and invigorating wind of life from the Spirit.

God Loves Your Fruitful Form

Solomon admires his new bride's form.

Song of Solomon 4:5 | Your two breasts are like two fawns, twins of a gazelle, that graze among the lilies.

This is shockingly intimate to us, but the point Scripture is making is not merely erotic but practical: marriage is a place of comfort and procreation. A woman's bodily form is precious and should be revealed to her husband alone. When she is revealed to her groom, what she has carefully guarded (her body, her form) is now freely utilized as a refuge and a comfort for her husband.

Then, in most marriages, her body also becomes an incubator for life and nourishment. Her breasts are like "**twin gazelles that graze among the lilies.**" There is something happening here. Gazelles and lilies are characterized by life. The wife's breasts, while comforting to the husband and life giving to the new infant child.

God sees his people as those who edify and encourage with supernatural comfort. One of the most profound fruit of our union with Christ is the spiritual fruit of evangelism, whereby we bring comfort to the repentant sinner with the merits of Jesus Christ. The believer's only lasting and meaningful comfort is Christ in our heart, in our very bosom, as the one we love above all others. This love is so attractive that it's aroma can convert and transform the heart of a person. "we are the aroma of Christ to God among those who are being saved and among those who are perishing, to one a fragrance from death to death, to the other a fragrance from life to life" (2 Cor 2:15-16). People want to know how to obtain the contentment of a heart filled and satisfied with Christ. William Perkins, the systematic theology professor who taught many Puritans said that he taught "the science of living blessedly forever." That's the nourishment and comfort that all Christians offer. The offspring of that love brings forth spiritual children when others see our love and come to Christ through the new birth.

> JAMES DURHAM (1622–1658): "A believer is, as it were, a nurse with breasts, fitted to edify others. Believers are to be use-

ful to all the saints for their edification. This is a particular evidence that they are truly converted. Believers as well give off the warmth and kindness of Christ. When Christ is brought into our bosom and received into our hearts by faith the believer experiences his warm affections."[97]

Married People – a Living Picture

The admiration of the married man for his wife is a picture of Christ's love and admiration for his bride. The love between a married couple is the highest human love there is. But Christ's love for his church is infinitely more exalted than the greatest human love. We read in Song of Solomon 8:6, "...love is strong as death, jealousy is fierce as the grave. Its flashes are flashes of fire, the very flame of the LORD." This love is so strong, it is described as the very flame and essence of God's person and essence. God is love. This is who he is.

Marriage then has one purpose: to promote, reveal and introduce people to the person of God by being a picture of Christ's love for his church. We are to be a living proclamation of God's redemptive and unrelenting love for unworthy people. How is it that God can love a rebellious people to the point where they are transformed by a supernatural love that far surpasses human love?

You are Flawless in God's Eyes

The Christian is so profoundly transformed that he becomes spotless and lovely in the eyes of Christ. Christ tells us the flawless beauty he sees in his bride.

Song of Solomon 4:7 | You are altogether beautiful, my love; there is no flaw in you.

The One who has saved you has made you this way. He has declared you to be like this. He shed his blood for you. Perhaps you are a believer, and you are struggling against sin. Your heart's desire is to please Jesus Christ, but you look in the mirror and you see all the ways you come short. Perhaps you are depressed because you see all your failings and all your blemishes. You need to know this: "where sin abounds grace much more abounds" (Rom 5:20).

---

[97] James Durham. *Clavis Cantici*, 209.

When Christ looks at you he sees no blemish because he himself has put away your blemishes with his own scars—his own wounds, with the wrath of God that he took on that cross in your place. You are all together lovely in his sight. You are "justified by faith apart from works of the law" (Rom 3:28). You are "cleansed with the washing of water by the word" (Eph 5:26). You are "accepted in the Beloved One" (Eph 1:6).

God treasures you in Christ. He has reserved a universe that he has not yet even created. He wants to freely and "graciously give us all things" (Rom 8:32). We are called "the apple of his eye" (Psa 17:8). If you are in Christ, if you have been united to him by faith, then you are loved with an infinite eternal love. "I have loved you with an everlasting love; therefore I have continued my faithfulness to you" (Jer 31:3). God is faithful to us because of his unrelenting love for us, not because of our feeble love for him.

Yet we often struggle with the idea that God loves us. We feel that we haven't done as much as others, so God must love us less. God must love Tyndale and the martyrs and the missionaries and Paul more than me. Listen, the love of God is not a ladder to climb. There is not a love scale that God measures us by. That's all our American mentality. God's love for us is not dependent upon us. His love for you is based on his work for you, not your work for him.

You are precious to him because of Christ's work. You cannot do anything to make him love you less. You cannot do anything to make him love you more. You didn't perform the righteousness that makes you lovely. Jesus paid it all. Your sin is gone, and Jesus' lovely righteousness make you lovely.

God loves you because you are in Christ. You don't deserve this love. If you plant 1000 churches you still will not deserve this love. You are loved because you are God's child. He's made you into his own likeness in Christ. He loves you because you are now his child.

There is no flaw in you. You are sinless and perfect before his almighty holy throne in Christ. Rejoice in his love for you. You are altogether lovely in his sight. But you say, "I don't feel holy." In Christ, we are positionally righteous. "There is no condemnation" (Rom 8:1).

AMBROSE (333-397), "God the Word says to the church, 'You are all fair, my love, and there is no blemish in you,' for guilt has been washed away. 'Come here from Lebanon, my spouse, come here from Lebanon, from the beginning of faith you will pass through and pass on,' because, renouncing the world, she passed through things temporal and passed on to Christ."[98]

Yet if we say we have no sin, "we deceive ourselves, and the truth is not in us" (1 Jn 1:8). God says, "I see no flaw in you," yet we see so many flaws in ourselves. How do we reconcile this? For one thing, we need to understand that when God says, "there is no condemnation" or "I see no flaw in you," he is not saying – you have reached sinless perfection. He is not saying you no longer struggle with sin. He's speaking of the finished work of Christ on your behalf. In other words, there is a difference between positional sanctification and progressive sanctification. We might say it this way – there is a difference between your covenant with God and your relationship with him. When I get married, I have a covenant with my wife. If I hurt her feelings, the covenant is fine, but the relationship is injured. So it is with our relationship with God. As Christians, we sometimes sin. It is of course not our way of life. We have been forever changed and cannot continue in sin. Yet we do sin. And when we do, our relationship with God is disturbed, yet our covenant in Christ can never be affected. Indeed, a mystery exists. We are sinners, saints, and sufferers. We have been forever changed, but we still struggle against sin. We are transformed, but not completely sinless until Jesus comes. There is still an element of sin that is disturbing to us. Some of God's people become so scrupulous over their sin that they lack assurance of their own salvation. Paul wrote to the Roman church for us, "where sin abounds, grace much more abounds" (Rom 5:21). So there is a struggle and a fight to "walk in the Spirit," and because of our new nature we will be preserved by God in holiness and a holy lifestyle. But what we must never lose our grasp on is that we are completely righteous in Christ.

Positionally, we are blameless in the eyes of God. You, child of God, are flawless through Jesus Christ. Your sin – all of it – is imputed to Christ, and all his righteousness has been imputed to you. What love is this? There is an awesome, glorious day coming in which the Son of Man will command his angels to cut down all those who dwell on the earth with a sickle (Rev 14:18). You may be afraid that you will be cut down. Let not your heart be troubled. Those who have come in humble, hopeful faith in Christ will not only be spared, but will be protected as

[98] Ambrose of Milan. *On the Mysteries.* In *Select Works,* Vol. 10, 322.

God's treasured possession. Yet God insists we are his treasured possession, and we belong to him.

> They shall be mine, says the Lord of hosts, in the day when I make up my treasured possession, and I will spare them as a man spares his son who serves him. —Malachi 3:17

Can it be that we are spotless in God's sight? Positionally, we are perfected in Christ through his righteousness which he obtained through his righteous life and atoning death on the cross. Any sin in our lives does not affect our position, but our relationship with God. This is why a true Christian can never live comfortably in sin. But never forget that we he glances at us, he sees His spotless Bride.

> THOMAS WILCOX (1549-1608), "No spot! Here is an astounding commendation of the church, containing also in it a promise, specially of sanctification and holiness to be bestowed each believer in this life. When God says, 'there is no spot in thee,' he promises us eternal blessedness. This applies specifically to all in Christ's church who are true believers who are now righteous in Christ through his merits, and who shall remain holy in the life to come. They have no spot who are true Christians, whose sins are forgiven, and Christ's righteousness is imputed, who has washed us in his own blood from all sin (1 Jn 1:7; cf. Eph 5:26-27)."[99]

> NANCY DEMOSS WOLGEMUTH (1958–), "'You are all fair, my love, and there is no spot in you.' That is the power of redeeming love—that our Solomon, our King Jesus, our Bridegroom could say to us, 'You are all fair my love, and there is no spot in you.' You know, there was a time when it could have been said of us what we read recorded in Isaiah 1:6, 'From the sole of the foot, even to the head, there is no soundness in it, but bruises and sores and raw wounds. They are not pressed out or bound up or softened with oil.' That describes our condition before Christ, but because of his amazing love and his grace and his mercy and his forgiveness, he can now look at us and say, 'You are all fair, my love, there is no spot in you.' God is rich in mercy. He has

---

[99] Thomas Wilcox. *Canticles*, Song 2:7.

cleansed us, forgiven us, restored us. He says there is no spot in
us. Have you ever really grasped the fact that you are precious
to Christ, that he takes great delight in you, that you are beautiful
to him? Now, we all know that it's not that we have any natural
beauty to offer him. Anything of value that he or others see in us
is all the result of his mercy and his grace. But once you realize
how much he loves you, your life will never be the same. You'll
be set free from fear, from comparison, from striving to perform
and measure up to others. You'll be able to enjoy Christ, to be
secure in his love, and to truly love him and others."[100]

THE BRIDE'S BED (4:6-11)

Lovers look forward to their honeymoon. It is so blissful that they
never want it to end. Newly married lovers want to spend every hour
together, day and night. Listen to Solomon's invitation to his new bride.

Song of Solomon 4:6-8a | Until the day breathes and the shadows
flee, I will go away to the mountain of myrrh and the hill of
frankincense. You are altogether beautiful, my love; there is
no flaw in you. Come with me from Lebanon, my bride; come
with me from Lebanon.

He's saying, let's reside together. He is gazing upon the bed he's
going to share with is bride. He's going to be sleeping in it with her for
the first time.

The heightened language of union is profound. Solomon speaks of
retreating to the bliss of a mountain and a hill. Marriage can be that
paradise, if only dimly. As we will see, marriage is only a faded reflection of a greater reality. The sweet communion, the physical pleasure,
and the escape that romance provides is not the ultimate answer to
man's loneliness and fears. People have tried to turn spouses into sav-
iors. It never works. And yet, marriage has a beautiful part to play in
pointing to the true Savior.

---

[100] Nancy Demoss Wolgemuth. "How to Fall and Stay in Love with Jesus," Day
12. Accessed Aug 21, 2017. https://www.reviveourhearts.com/radio/revive-our-
hearts/song-solomon-day-12/

J. HUDSON TAYLOR (1832-1905): "Separation never comes because the Lord has departed. Christ is always ready for communion with his heart prepared. In this happy communion the bride
becomes ever fairer, and more like to her Lord. She is being progressively changed into his image, from one degree of glory to
another, through the wondrous working of the Holy Spirit."[101]

The marriage of two lovers lasts until death. Sometimes the romance of man and wife can be dimmed by tragedy or health or age. Not
so with Christ. Nothing separates us from his love. In human intimacy
there are delights, dangers, desires and devotion that reflect our eternal
intimacy in Christ.

The Delights of Intimacy

Song of Solomon 4:6 | Until the day breathes and the shadows
flee, I will go away to the mountain of myrrh and the hill of
frankincense.

The honeymoon begins. Solomon desires to consummate the marriage. The king wants to sleep all night with his new bride, "until the
day breathes and the shadows flee." He wants to view the sunrise for
the first time with his first love.

The king wants to go to the "**mountain of myrrh**." What is that?
Myrrh was used in burials because it could overcome the smell of death,
so powerful was its aroma. Myrrh is said to be a fragrance of intimacy
and romance (Prov 7:17). It was brought to Jesus as an infant to symbolize his humanity. So then, what is this "mountain of myrrh" on the
honeymoon? It points to the couple's shared humanity as two become
one flesh. There is a sweetness, a heavenly fragrance to this depth of
sexual intimacy in marriage. Myrrh points us to the fact that once a
person is married, they are pressed together and are no longer two, but
one flesh. This mountain of myrrh points to the ultimate mystery of
marriage – that of Christ's union with his church. Christ shared our
humanity to the point of death. He was not only born as a man, he died
as a man – living and dying in our place.

Solomon then declares, "**I will go... to the hill of frankincense.**" Frankincense was a costly, beautiful-smelling incense that

---

[101] Taylor. *Union and Communion*, 41.

was used only for the most special of occasions. It was used in the grain offerings at the Tabernacle and Temple (Lev 2:2, 15-16), and in Solomon's royal processions (3:6-7). Origen, the great church father, suggested that frankincense was the incense of deity. In the Old Testament, it was stored in a special chamber in front of the Temple and was sprinkled on certain offerings as a symbol of the people's desire to please the Lord.[102] Frankincense was brought to Jesus as an infant to symbolize his deity. What does it mean then for Solomon go to the "hill of frankincense" but that God himself is present and pleased with this union. Man and wife can be "naked and unashamed" (Gen 2:25). It is God's will for man and wife to consummate their marriage with a physical union. "Let marriage be held in honor among all, and let the marriage bed be undefiled, for God will judge the sexually immoral and adulterous" (Heb 13:4). God invented the sexual union, but notice how mysterious and delicately it is spoken of here in Song 4:6. Marital intimacy is to be treated with all holiness and dignity. It is not to be prostituted, but rather protected and preserved, shared by husband and wife alone.

As delightful as the myrrh and frankincense of sexual union in marriage can be, it cannot hold a candle to the intimacy we have in God. What makes the marriage bed delightful is not merely the biological pleasure it provides, but rather the vulnerability of sharing one's whole life and body and soul with one another and in response to be welcomed and celebrated, needed and adored.

This marriage bed is but a faint reflection of the eternal joy we have in Christ, not just till the sun rises in the morning for one night or even one lifetime. We have a Savior that we can bring our prayers to and lift our praise to that with an intimacy that literally lasts forever. We have a Savior that will bring full contentment and satisfaction to us for all time and for all eternity.

> HENRY LAW (1797-1894): "The mountain and the hill are pre-
> eminent as a place delightful fragrance. Here myrrh and frank-
> incense flourish and abound. Here is luxuriant growth of all that
> cheers and charms the senses. The sweetest aromas float around
> them. This view leads to the truth, that Christ finds delightful

---

[102] John MacArthur, Jr. *Matthew*. MacArthur New Testament Commentary (Chicago: Moody Press, 1985), 35.

solace in his people. In this fragrance, we are led to see that prayer and praise are as sweet beds of spices. It is joy and gladness to the Lord, when believers thus pour forth the incense of their hearts. He delights to listen to their supplicating voice, and to bow attentive ears when they open out their need, and in sweet communion, beseech the Lord to render help. Their praises, also, are as fragrant as the myrrh, and as satisfying as the scent of frankincense. It is indeed a mighty mystery, but faith clings to the truth, that in prayer and praise we glorify and gratify our Lord. Shall we ever, then, be silent? Let it be our constant effort, and our ceaseless wish to besiege the mercy-seat with prayer, and to encircle the throne with praise. May we thus stand prominently out as mountains of myrrh, and hills of frankincense!"[103]

Marriage was never meant to bring true happiness. That comes through Jesus. In fact, when Jesus comes, marriage will be no more. There will be no more sexual activity – neither "marriage or giving in marriage" (Mt 22:30). Why? As beautiful as marriage and intimacy is, something greater will satisfy us. "In your presence is fullness of joy, and at your right hand there are pleasures forevermore" (Psa 16:11).

Marriage is not primarily based on sexual union. It cannot be. In our vows, we promise to love each other "for better or for worse, for richer or poorer, in sickness and in health, till death parts us." Sickness often takes away the ability for intimacy. There are ebbs and flows to our health, especially as babies come and the years pass by. Sexual union should be enjoyed as each spouse desires, but in reality, it is not always possible. Sex can be a joyful escape from this painful world, but sex, even in marriage, is not a savior. It is meant to point to the Savior. Sexual union gives us the perception that all is well, that each is committed, loyal and unrelenting in their love and devotion to the other. Yet human love cannot sustain this devotion forever. We all eventually die. Our bodies are fading like a leaf. Marriage was never meant to give people perfect happiness. It points to something much grander that can truly satisfy the soul. Marriage points to the one who will "never leave you nor forsake you" (Heb 13:5).

---

[103] Henry Law. *Song of Solomon: for Sunday Reading* (London: Hamilton, Adams & Co., 1879), 99.

Our true mountain of refuge is the holy hill of the Lord. This is where we find true intimacy. "He who takes refuge in me shall possess the land and shall inherit my holy mountain" (Isa 57:13). "As for me, I have set my King on Zion, my holy hill" (Psa 2:6). "I will bring to my holy mountain, and make them joyful in my house of prayer; their burnt offerings and their sacrifices will be accepted on my altar; for my house shall be called a house of prayer for all peoples" (Isa 56:7). "I cried aloud to the Lord, and he answered me from his holy hill" (Psa 3:4). "Great is the Lord and greatly to be praised in the city of our God! His holy mountain" (Psa 48:1). "Exalt the Lord our God, and worship at his holy mountain; for the Lord our God is holy" (Psa 99:9).

There is no place like the feet of Jesus where you can find peace, satisfaction, and deep contentment. "And we all, with unveiled face, beholding the glory of the Lord, are being transformed into the same image from one degree of glory to another" (2 Cor 3:18). It is not the joy of work or home or even merely being around other Christians that gives us strength, but the joy of the Lord in all our activities that gives us strength.

The Dangers of Intimacy

In marriage, we come down from dangerous places to the place of God's protection. Strong desires outside of marriage easily turn into lust, and lust will kill your spiritual life! We hear the groom, King Solomon calling to his Jewish bride.

Song of Solomon 4:8 | Come with me from Lebanon, my bride; come with me from Lebanon. Depart from the peak of Amana, from the peak of Senir and Hermon, from the dens of lions, from the mountains of leopards.

The way Solomon addresses his new bride is stunning. He paints her as dwelling in the most dangerous mountain ranges with goddess like qualities, having power over these mountain ranges and beasts, portrayed in the pagan myth of Venus, the goddess of love who ruled from the high mountains over the **"lions"** and **"leopards."**[104] What

---

[104] Marvin H. Pope. *Song of Songs* (The Anchor Yale Bible Commentaries) New Haven, CT: Yale University Press, 1995) 475–77.

meekness the king embodies as he, the sovereign of the land could command any woman he wanted. Yet, he has such an exalted view of his bride.

Lebanon is an interesting place in the northern most part of ancient Israel. There is astounding beauty in there, but also wild animals. The Lebanon mountains are a very high and dangerous mountain range which includes the peaks of the Amana, Senir and Hermon mountains. These mountains are in northern Israel, and they are more than 9,000 feet high. Within those mountains there are many dangers such as lions and leopards that will tear you apart. There are hideouts where the wild animals live. Solomon asks his exalted bride to come away from these mountains that she rules and join him. He is pursuing her as if he is helpless and unable to have her unless she herself departs from Lebanon and joins him. How beautiful this gentle pursuit. Solomon is a king and could have any woman he wanted. Yet he does not command his bride. Instead he comes humbly, meekly, and helpless to her, humbly asking her permission, that she might join him in the marriage bed. We see the great power the wife has over this area of married life. She has the power to grant or deny permission and through this can spare the marriage great danger if she will head the calls of her husband. If she denies him, she leaves him in a place of great danger.

Indeed, a good marriage will keep you from the misery of a life ravaged by this world. Proverbs 5:15 tells us, "Drink water from your own cistern, flowing water from your own well." Fill your cup at home. Don't fill it through lustful thoughts. Don't fill it through other friendships. Don't fill it by working longer hours and ignoring problems. Come down from the dangerous mountains and fill your cup at home!

This is not the voice of a drill sergeant or a task master. This is the voice of one who deeply loves you saying, "Stay away from those mountains. Come to the place of safety." It is a father calling a child away from the edge of a cliff. It is a lover calling his love away from lust that can destroy and pillage and do harm that cannot be undone.

God has designed marriage to be a place of refuge. As husbands, it is our responsibility to make our home a place of love and security and safety for our wife. She is vulnerable, and the husband ought to make the home a place of sweet refuge, a retreat from the world for him and his bride. Make your bedroom a refuge. "Let marriage be held in honor among all, and let the marriage bed be undefiled, for God will judge the sexually immoral and adulterous" (Heb 13:4). Marriage protects us from the defilement of lust and fornication. God has given all of us a legitimate way to allow our passions to burn. You may ask, what if my wife is sick or not interested in sex? Sickness will most certainly rob your marriage of romance at times. Yet you must fill your cup at home and not be looking at or thinking about someone outside your marriage covenant. Pornographic activity of any sort is forbidden and should not be once named among the saints (Eph 5:4). It is the wife's responsibility to help her husband and the husband's responsibility to help his wife achieve sexual fulfillment. While the physical act of coitus is not always possible because of sickness, other suitable sexual activity may regularly take place, but strictly within the marriage covenant. No third party, whether in the imagination, through a provocative image, or through actual physical adultery ought ever violate the marriage covenant. Christ was clear that even looking upon another person to lust after them is adultery in the heart (Mt 5:27-30).

What if my spouse is not interested in sex? Sadly, this is more common than most would like to admit. The answer is to humbly and lovingly talk about it with your spouse. If you are both committed to the Lord, it is highly advisable to consult with your church pastor or biblical marriage counselor. Even if it costs you money, it will be well worth it. If your spouse is unwilling to talk about it, the root may be a lack of commitment to the Lord. Jesus is Lord and Master of every area of the Christian's life, even over the sexual relationship. Remember God invented sex, and one of his first commands to us was to "be fruitful and multiply and replenish the earth" (Gen 1:28). Submitting to Christ's lordship includes serving him by serving my spouse in normal, loving sexual relations. To avoid danger, the husband and wife should be looking out for each other's purity. Paul gives very helpful instructions to the married couple. "Do not deprive one another, except perhaps by agreement for a limited time, that you may devote yourselves to prayer; but then come together again, so that Satan may not tempt you because of your lack of self-control" (1 Cor 7:5).

How often should couples be together? The Bible does not give specific but only general parameters. According to Paul's instructions in 1 Corinthians 7, couples should be together enough so that they may not be tempted by Satan because of a "lack of self-control." They should only be apart from the sexual bond during times of prayer and fasting.

A time of prayer and fasting will not often last more than three to seven days. We might deduce that most couples should be together sexually at least once a week. Some spouses desire it more often. Let me give a warning. While sexual relations should be regular, sex is not a savior. It should never be demanded by a spouse. Relations should always be careful, gentle, and loving. If there are health issues or pain in intercourse, sex should be postponed. One should not use the Scripture to mandate your conjugal rights, even though you have them. The marriage bed should be entered into freely and willingly. Demanding sex borders on abuse. Ultimately if a spouse is unwilling to fulfill your sexual needs, it may be a reflection on their lack of submission to the lordship of Jesus. If after biblical marriage counseling your spouse is still unwilling to care for you sexually, you must rest in the Lord to do the work in your spouse's heart.

Let me go further and say, all sex outside of the marriage covenant is not only sinful, but abusive. Pornography is a serious abuse and offense against the person in the image and against your spouse. By viewing a dirty image, the offender is adding to the "supply and demand" of smut. If people would refuse to look at these images, the industry would die. The Bible commands us to abstain from sexual immorality (*pornea*, unlawful sexual activity): "This is the will of God, your sanctification: that you abstain from sexual immorality; that each one of you know how to control his own body in holiness and honor, not in the passion of lust like the Gentiles who do not know God; that no one transgress and wrong his brother [or sister] in this matter, because the Lord is an avenger in all these things, as we told you beforehand and solemnly warned you. For God has not called us for impurity, but in holiness. Therefore whoever disregards this, disregards not man but God, who gives his Holy Spirit to you" (1 Thess 4:1-6).

Christ says, "**Depart from the peak of Amana**" (4:8). Have you viewed pornography recently? If so, you need to "depart" from it. You need to "pluck out your eye," "cut off your hand," and "lop off your foot" in order to enter the kingdom of heaven (Mt 5:27-30). You need to get rid of your smart phone with internet access. At the very least, all godly men and women should have a monitored internet connection (i.e. Covenant Eyes, etc.). But if you are involved in looking at pornography, you need to be willing to undergo radical amputation. It may mean cutting your internet and your cable. If you have a job in IT, you may need to get a new career. If you are looking at porn, it's killing your spiritual life.

If you are regenerate, you know you cannot mock the Holy Spirit. He's convicting you, telling you what to do, and you need to do it. If you have no conviction, but only excuses, you need to "examine yourself to see whether you be in the faith" (2 Cor 13:5). If you are constantly turning to porn as your savior and escape, then you ought to seriously consider you cannot serve two masters and Christ may be a mere ceremony or curiosity to you. He may be a tag on to your life. Christ was not meant to be a tag on, but the blazing center of who you are. If so, you cannot serve both Christ and pornography. Yet be encouraged. Even if Christ is only a tag on in your life, you may renounce all other masters for Christ at this moment. Be willing to exalt him as Lord through radical amputation. Let the engrafted Word be implanted in you. Trust Christ as your deliverer. You cannot make this transformation yourself. You are powerless to help yourself. You must rest on the power of Christ to save you and sanctify you.

Christ himself is faithful to do this work in each of his elect people. Paul says, "the God of peace himself sanctify you completely, and may your whole spirit and soul and body be kept blameless at the coming of our Lord Jesus Christ. He who calls you is faithful; he will surely do it" (1 Thess 5:23-24). We are "called, and chosen, and faithful" (Rev 17:14). God chooses and calls sinners to be saints, and he will empower and preserve his people so they might be faithful until the end.

What shall we say to all of this? Simply this: sex is not the savior. Your spouse is not the savior. Being rejected sexually in marriage is painful. Don't do that to your spouse. But if you are the one offended, take courage. You don't need sex to be a to be happy. God is using anything you are deprived of to help you destroy the idols in your life. Even sex in marriage can be idolatrous. Married people should serve each other in the sexual union, but we must never make it a substitute for Christ. We ought instead to find our primary refuge in Christ.

Christ says to his church—come away from all your busyness and your crowded life and your overburdened thoughts and come away with me. Depart from the dangerous mountain ranges of sexual idolatry and find rest in me.

J. HUDSON TAYLOR (1832-1905): "'Come with me.' It is always so. If our Savior says, 'Go ye therefore and disciple all nations,' he precedes it by, 'All power is given unto me,' and follows it by, 'Lo, I am with you always.' Or if, as here, he calls his bride to come, it is still 'with me,' and it is in connection with this loving invitation that for the first time he changes the word 'my love,' for the still more endearing one, 'my bride.' 'Come with me… from the lions' dens.' What are lions' dens when the Lion of the tribe of Judah is with us; or mountains of leopards, when He is at our side! 'I will fear no evil, for thou art with me.' On the other hand, it is while thus facing dangers, and toiling with him in service, that he says—'thou hast ravished my heart, my sister, my bride.' Is it not wonderful how the heart of our Beloved can be thus ravished with the love of one who is prepared to accept his invitation, and go forth with him seeking to rescue the perishing?"[105]

The Desire for Intimacy

Marriage can be a place of satisfying joy in a dangerous and difficult world. As the couple leads up to marriage, there is an intense desire for intimacy. As the two lovers enter marriage, there is a sort of waltz to romance that is helpful to understand. The man takes the lead. God made men to be initiators. Women are responders. This expression of love begins as a self-sacrificing effort on the part of the man (Eph 5:25; 1 Cor 13:1-8; 1 Pet 3:7). It is the man in Scripture who leads the way, even and especially in romance. It is only appropriate then that we see King Solomon initiating the romance on his wedding night with sincere words from the depths of his heart.

Song of Solomon 4:9 | You have captivated my heart, my sister, my bride; you have captivated my heart with one glance of your eyes, with one jewel of your necklace.

How joyful it is for young newlyweds to be captivated with each other. The word "captivate" here could be literally translated, "to make the heart beat faster" (as in the NASB). Just one glance from my wife, and my heart beats faster.

> JAMES DURHAM (1622–1658): "She captivates Solomon not with both her eyes, but he says with 'one of thy eyes,' that is with

---

[105] Taylor. *Union*, 42.

a squint-look. He caught barely a glance of the bride that was so overpowering, it prevailed thus with him. One eye (a mere glance) is here mentioned, to shew what excellent beauty is in her, and much more what infinite love is in him, that he could not (because he would not) resist a look of one of her eyes cast toward him."[106]

God's Heart Beats Faster for Your Fellowship

Of course, this is a picture of our communion with God. Just as my heart is captivated by Jill's glance, so God's heart "beats faster" with one glance to him through earnest prayer. Consider the motivation for communing with God. With just a glance to heaven, and we make God's heart beat faster. God is pleased when you pray—when you commune with him. He tells us in Jeremiah 33:3, "Call to me and I will answer you, and will tell you great and hidden things that you have not known."

What else is Solomon captivated by? **"You have captivated my heart... with one jewel of your necklace"** (4:9). Where did the bride get a necklace? She gets it from her husband. It is just like when Rebekah met Isaac. She was not embarrassed. Isaac had already given her something to wear. He had given her "jewelry of silver and of gold, and [costly] garments" (Gen 24:53). Now look at Solomon's joy in communing with his wife:

Song of Solomon 4:10 | How beautiful is your love, my sister, my bride! How much better is your love than wine, and the fragrance of your oils than any spice.

Solomon delights in his bride. Her beauty overwhelms him. Her love is intoxicating. Her fragrance is more valuable to him than the most expensive spices. This woman is supremely valued.

MATTHEW HENRY (1662-1714): "Christ esteems the love of his children as better than wine. No expressions of love can be more passionate than this here, in which Christ manifests his affection to his church; and yet that great proof of his love, his dying for it, that he might present it to himself a glorious church, goes far beyond them all. A spouse so dearly bought and paid for could not but be dearly loved. Such a price being given for her, a high

---

[106] James Durham. *Clavis Cantici*, 223.

value must needs be put upon her accordingly; and both together may well set us a wondering at the height and depth, and length and breadth, of the love of Christ, which surpasses knowledge, that love in which he gave himself for us and gives himself to us."[107]

Precious saint, God is overcome with the intoxication of joy at how beautiful you are to him. "The LORD your God is in your midst, a mighty one who will save; he will rejoice over you with gladness; he will quiet you by his love; he will exult over you with loud singing" (Zeph 3:17). This is not a man-centered statement, because it is the work of his beloved Son that makes God rejoice over you. God has great joy in communing with you and delights in your love to him. It is better than wine or perfume. This is not just "nice." This is exalted!

> ARTHUR JACKSON (1593-1666), "The Bridegroom here gives the reason why he had so earnestly pursued his spouse in the mountain ranges Lebanon, namely, because he was so exceedingly transported with love towards her. Never was love like the love of Christ to his Church; He speaks here as a man overcome with love, *Thou hast ravished my heart*, implying, that her beauty had made such a strong impression upon his heart, that he was no longer himself. Having seen her, he now had no command of his own heart, it was so wholly gone out after her; as indeed the love of Christ for his Church made him no longer regard himself but give himself completely to his bride to the point of death for her."[108]

God Does Not Merely Tolerate You, He Loves You

However exalted Solomon's love for his bride was, God's is higher, greater and deeper. God does not just tolerate you. He welcomes you. He loves you. He longs to lavish his mercy and grace and kindness on you. When I see my children, especially when they are so little and vulnerable my heart just leaps for joy. I walk into the door of my home, and my kids run to me and shout Daddy! They know I delight in them. I deeply delight and rejoice in them. In that way, God rejoices in you. His banner over you is love (2:4). You are more precious to him than

---

[107] Matthew Henry. *Commentary*, 1065.
[108] Arthur Jackson. *Song of Solomon*, Song 4:8-9.

all the gold or silver. You are the apple of his eye (Zech 2:8). You are precious. He says, "I have engraved you on the palms of my hands" (Isa 49:16).

The Devotion of Intimacy

Marriage is a place where words are said that can be said to no one else. Words are communicated that refresh the soul, like an oasis. Intimacy is not just sharing the bed but sharing the inmost desires of one another. For the Christian couple, the highest and most exalted desire they have is not for each other (as beautiful as that is) but for Christ.

Lips Dripping with Words of Life

Song of Solomon 4:11a | Your lips drip nectar, my bride.

You don't just say these words to anyone. You don't kiss just anyone. At least I hope you don't. There are certain words we don't say to anyone of the opposite gender until we marry them. Solomon describes this woman's lips and voice like honey and milk. There is a fullness and a happiness and a joy in the sweet words of lovers. Isn't it amazing how young lovers, if they are away from each other can spend hours and hours on the phone with one another! Christ loves the lips and words of his blood-bought people. They drip with prayer and his presence. They cannot hide that the Spirit dwells in them. Love's preciousness is too powerful to hold in.

> CHARLES HADDON SPURGEON (1834-1892), "Christ's people are not a dumb people, they were once but they *talk* now. I do not believe a Christian can keep the secret that God gives him if he were to try; it would burst his lips open to get out. When God puts grace into your heart you may try to hide it, but hide it you cannot. It will be like fire in the bones, and will be sure to find its way out. Now the church is a talking church, a preaching church, and a praising church; she has got lips, and every believer will find he must use his lips in the service of Christ. Now it is but poor, poor matter that any of us can speak. When we are most eloquent in our Master's praise, how far our praises fall beneath his worth! When we are most earnest in prayer, how powerless is our wrestling compared with the great blessing that we seek to obtain! When our song is loudest, and it begins to be

something akin to the chorus of the angels, even then how marred it is with the discord of our unbelief and of our worldliness! But Jesus Christ does not find any fault in what the Church speaks. He says, 'No, Thy lips, O my spouse, drop us the honeycomb.' You know the honey that drops out of the honeycomb is the best—it is called the life-honey. So the words that drop from the Christian's lips are the very words of his life, his life-honey, and they ought to be sweet to everyone. They are as sweet to the taste of the Lord Jesus as the drops of the honeycomb."[109]

Our communion with Christ overflows to our lips from our heart. When you pray, do your lips drip nectar, or are your prayers as dry and dead as ever? The secret to nectar lips is a heart filled with the love of God and the joy of the Spirit. How much effort have you made to spent time with God? Do you hear his voice? Does he hear your voice? Have you gotten down on your knees and asked God to speak to you? Are you willing to bombard the gates of heaven until he that sweetness returns to your heart and you have returned to your first love?

A Tongue Flowing with Scripture

Solomon continues:

Song of Solomon 4:11b | ...honey and milk are under your tongue.

How sweet and fulfilling for the couple to enjoy intense affection. It is from God. It is holy. Perhaps in Solomon's mind is the landscape of Canaan of old, flowing as well with honey and milk (Exo 33:3). It is interesting because at this point, Solomon is merely inviting his new wife to come to bed, but he has not yet touched her. All of this is in his imagination. He longs with deep desire to kiss his bride and to taste her lips. Perhaps there was a brief kiss at the altar, but he has not tasted that prolonged and intimate kiss. He can only imagine it. He is waiting on his bride to respond.

This speaks of many things. First, that a husband ought to romantically pursue his wife with gentleness and never with pressure. Also, when applied to our redemption, the Christian has not yet tasted the joys of heaven in their fullness but ought always to imagine it. Indeed,

---

[109] Spurgeon. *Pulpit,* Vol 5, Sermon 2469, "Christ's Estimate of His People" (1859), 457.

the heart of God's child flows with milk and honey of the Scriptures, like the land which God gave to his ancient people. The Scriptures may not always be pronounced, but they are like milk and honey under the tongue. We meditate and enjoy the savor of the Word of God.

The Scriptures have the power to produce life and healing, so they ought always to be under the tongue of the believer, flowing like milk and honey.

> ARTHUR JACKSON (1593-1666), "The people of God have speech that is wholesome and nourishing, such as may minister grace unto the hearers (Eph 4.29), like wholesome food for the nourishing both of Christ's little ones, and those also that are of riper years. God's Word on the believer's tongue is effective for the curing of the spiritual distempers of the souls of men."[110]

> CHARLES HADDON SPURGEON (1834-1892), "The things that are under the tongue of the believer are sometimes thoughts that have never yet been expressed; they do not get to the top of the tongue, but lie there half formed and are ready to come out; but either because they cannot come out, or we have not time to let them out, there they remain, and never come into actual words. Now Jesus Christ thinks very much even of the Christian's thoughts; he says, 'Honey and milk are under thy tongue;' and Christian meditation and Christian contemplation are to Christ like honey for sweetness and like milk for nourishment."[111]

Clothes Fragrant with Christ

The king goes on to celebrate the fragrance of his bride.

Song of Solomon 4:11c | The fragrance of your garments is like the fragrance of Lebanon.

The cedar trees of Lebanon had an attractive aroma. Solomon loves the scent of his bride's garments, because they told the story of where she'd been. She'd been in Lebanon. Similarly, Christ's bride has an aroma that speaks of where we have been. "For we are the aroma of Christ to God among those who are being saved and among those who

---

[110] Arthur Jackson. *Song of Solomon*, Song 4:11.
[111] Spurgeon. *Pulpit*, Vol 5, Sermon 2469, "Christ's Estimate of His People" (1859), 457.

are perishing, to one a fragrance from death to death, to the other a fragrance from life to life" (2 Cor 2:15-16). We are, as it were, wrapped in the scent of Christ.

> THEODORET OF CYRUS (393-466): "The fragrance of your garments is like the fragrance of Lebanon.' The bridegroom himself became her garment, and blessed Paul confirms it in the words, 'All of you who were baptized into Christ put on Christ' (Gal 3:27). Now, the bridegroom is both God eternal and was born a man from the holy virgin in the last days. While remaining what he was, he took as well what is ours, and clothed the bride who was formerly left naked—hence his saying to her, 'the fragrance of your garments like the fragrance of Lebanon.' She is clothed with Christ, who is both God and man. Now, 'the fragrance of Lebanon' is a symbol of the true doctrine of God, since under the norms of the Old Testament law, the incense taken from the cedars of Lebanon was offered up to God (Lev 2:1-2, 15-16)."[112]

THE BRIDE'S BOUNTY (4:12-16)

Solomon is very aware that his bride has kept herself pure for her wedding night. Anticipation is heightened. He may not proceed without permission.

Song of Solomon 4:12-15 | A garden locked is my sister, my bride, a spring locked, a fountain sealed. Your shoots are an orchard of pomegranates with all choicest fruits, henna with nard, nard and saffron, calamus and cinnamon, with all trees of frankincense, myrrh and aloes, with all chief spices— a garden fountain, a well of living water, and flowing streams from Lebanon.

See what deep respect King Solomon has for his new bride. He is in awe of her purity. He is so humbled that she has kept herself for him. Keep in mind, he could have had any woman he wanted. What a picture of Christ and his bride. When she was single, she said, "my own vineyard I have not kept" (1:6), but with the king she has the riches to be all a woman can be. It is in Christ that God has "has blessed us in the heavenly realms with every spiritual blessing in Christ" (Eph 1:3).

---

[112] Theodoret of Cyrus. *Song of Songs*. In *Early Christian Studies*, Vol 2, 83-84.

The shepherdess queen compares sharing her life with her king to a magnificent garden. Marital love truly is a delightful garden. Before supermarkets, people could only dream of these kinds of gardens that seemed to have every kind of delightful food and spice imaginable. The picture is one of incredible joy and fullness. She speaks in a very dignified and mysterious way of that which is sacred and reserved by the woman to be given to her husband on her wedding night. She speaks of that which is fruitful (perhaps a more bountiful friendship in marriage as well as the possibility of children). The bride describes her life and love as a garden that is private, protected, and productive.

A Private Garden

Song of Solomon 4:12 | A garden locked is my sister, my bride, a spring locked, a fountain sealed.

Here Solomon speaks of a beautiful garden, but it is locked. He observes a flowing, living fountain (4:15), but it is sealed. The spring is inaccessible. This garden is a private garden. It's not a public garden for everyone to come into, take a look at, and pick fruit from the trees. This is a garden that exists only for the pleasure of one person – her bridegroom. The fountain of her life is rich and flowing, but she is reserved for Solomon alone, her husband and king.

> AMBROSE (333-397), "'A garden enclosed' pictures the bride shut in on all sides by the walls of chastity. 'A fountain sealed up' is virginity, for it is the fount and wellspring of modesty that keeps the seal of purity unbroken, in whose source there may shine the image of God, since the pureness of simplicity coincides with the chastity of the body."[113]

Our lives are a garden that exists for the pleasure of our heavenly Bridegroom. "You are worthy, O Lord, to receive glory and honor and power: for you have created all things, and for your pleasure they are and were created" (Rev 4:11, NKJV). We are to love the Lord our God exclusively and completely, with all our heart, soul, mind, body, and strength. And even this is a response to his love to us. "We love him, because he first loved us" (1 Jn 4:19, KJV).

---

[113] St. Ambrose. *Letter 59, To Priests*. In *Fathers*, Vol 26, 334.

A Protected Garden

Song of Solomon 4:12 | A garden locked is my sister, my bride, a spring locked, a fountain sealed.

This garden is not only private, it's protected – "**a spring locked.**" It has boundaries. It's a garden enclosed. Some beautiful gardens have high privacy hedges around them or walls around them. Walls enclose. They define the boundaries. They protect that garden from people or things that might threaten the garden.

The new queen has reserved herself for her husband. One of the most profound aspects of this wedding night is that the king continues to wait on her to give herself freely to her king. She is locked and sealed. He pursues her, and he is waiting for her response. Solomon is so meek and mild, a genuine gentleman and gentle lover. She has reserved herself and kept her purity for him alone.

> CHARLES HADDON SPURGEON (1834-1892), "The king's bride is a spring shut up, a fountain sealed, like some choice cool spring in Solomon's private garden around the house of the forest of Lebanon — a fountain which he reserved for his own drinking, by placing the royal seal upon it, and locking it up by secret means, known only to himself. The legend has it that there were fountains which no one knew about except Solomon, and he had so shut them up that, with his ring he touched a secret spring, a door opened, and living waters leaped out to fill his jeweled cup. No one knew but Solomon the secret charm by which he set flowing the pent-up stream, of which no lip drank but his own. Now, God's people are as much shut up, and preserved, and kept from danger by the care of Christ, as the springs in Solomon's garden were reserved expressly for himself. Beloved, this is a cheering thought for all believers, that the Lord has set apart him who is godly for himself. He has taken measures to preserve all his chosen from all those who would defile and destroy them. He walled them all around with his divine decree of old, saying, "I have chosen this people for myself." He then issued his command that no one should injure them, saying, "Do not touch my anointed, and do my prophets no harm." He sets a hedge around them in providence, so that nothing shall by any means harm them. He has shut them up from

the enemy and sealed them up for perpetual preservation. The wandering Bedouins in the East plunder the open fields; but a king's garden, enclosed and protected, is safe from their ravages. So are the saints enclosed from all invading powers. The Lord has especially walled them around with grace."[114]

We find in Job that God put "a hedge around Job, his family, and everything he owns" (Job 1:10). God protects his people. He surrounds us with his blessing and his covering and his hand so that nothing can come into this garden that he is cultivating, apart from his permission.

We are the garden of the Lord and he is our hedge, he himself is our protection. "As the mountains surround Jerusalem, so the Lord surrounds his people" (Psa 125:2).

A Productive Garden

Song of Solomon 4:13-15 | Your shoots are an orchard of pomegranates with all choicest fruits, henna with nard, nard and saffron, calamus and cinnamon, with all trees of frankincense, myrrh and aloes, with all chief spices — a garden fountain, a well of living water, and flowing streams from Lebanon.

This peasant girl turned queen kept herself for the Lord, and secondly for her husband. Her garden has not been trampled on or robbed of its fruit. She has kept her garden private and protected so that it could be blessed and overflowing with fruit and spices. Outward purity always speaks of inward obedience. She has an obedient heart for the Lord, and it has paid off. Blessing follows obedience. It was certainly true for God's ancient people. "If you faithfully obey the voice of the Lord your God, being careful to do all his commandments that I command you today, the Lord your God will set you high above all the nations of the earth. And all these blessings shall come upon you and overtake you, if you obey the voice of the Lord your God. Blessed shall you be in the city, and blessed shall you be in the field. Blessed shall be the fruit of your womb and the fruit of your ground and the fruit of your cattle, the increase of your herds and the young of your flock. Blessed

---

[114] Spurgeon. *Pulpit*, Vol 33, Sermon 1957, "The Lord's Own View of His Church and People" (1887), 205.

shall be your basket and your kneading bowl. Blessed shall you be when you come in, and blessed shall you be when you go out" (Deut 28:1-6).

If you follow God's design for purity and marriage, your life will be blessed and fruitful. You will be blessed by God. With disobedience comes regret and scars. This girl has been careful and comes to her wedding night not only without regret, but as a woman bursting with joy and all the benefits of obedience.

The fruit of the Spirit is a natural outflow of your new nature in Christ. You may not receive material blessing, but "if anyone is in Christ, he is a new creation. The old has passed away; behold, the new has come" (2 Cor 5:17). The new is produced supernaturally because I am a new creation in Christ. Ironically, in times of greatest fruitfulness, I have often exerted less – much less – effort. Paul testified, "I will boast all the more gladly of my weaknesses, so that the power of Christ may rest upon me" (2 Cor 12:9). In my union with Christ, fruit just comes naturally. You don't see apple trees out there doing calisthenics. All blessing flows from our union with Christ. As Jesus himself said, "Abide in me, and I in you. As the branch cannot bear fruit by itself, unless it abides in the vine, neither can you, unless you abide in me. I am the vine; you are the branches. Whoever abides in me and I in him, he it is that bears much fruit, for apart from me you can do nothing" (Jn 15:4-5).

Solomon describes his queen as a living cornucopia of fruits and spices. "The catalog of exotic spices in this 'garden' serves to suggest that the pleasures of the woman's love are abundant and especially that they are varied; he could never grow bored in such a garden."[115] Let us be careful – this is not a catalog of the woman's body – Solomon has already admired his wife's form (4:1-7). He is equating his wife's love with a profusion of garden delights, well-cared for. This well of living water is found in the Proverbs, presumably written by Solomon. "Drink water from your own cistern, flowing water from your own well. Should your springs be scattered abroad, streams of water in the streets? Let them be for yourself alone, and not for strangers with you. Let your fountain be blessed, and rejoice in the wife of your youth, a lovely deer, a graceful doe. Let her breasts fill you at all times with delight; be intoxicated always in her love" (Prov 5:15-19).

---

[115] Garrett, *Song of Songs*, 407.

Let me say this. Guard your heart and guard your body for marriage. Flee youthful lusts. Be a fountain sealed. Let the time that you awaken your sexual passions be your wedding night.

> NANCY DEMOSS WOLGEMUTH (1958–), "'You shall be like a watered garden, like a spring of water, whose waters do not fail' (Isa 58:11). As this bride's garden is watered, it not only produces beautiful fruit for him, but ultimately it's going to overflow and bring blessing to others, and it will draw others to him. This provides for us, I think, a picture of the fullness of the Holy Spirit here: a fountain of gardens, a well of living water and streams from Lebanon—not just the garden enclosed, but now overflowing, bringing blessing to others. The New Testament equivalent to this passage, I think, must be in John 7, where Jesus Himself said, 'If anyone thirsts let him come to me and drink. Whoever believes in me, as the Scripture has said, 'Out of his heart will flow rivers of living water.' This he said about the Spirit, whom those who believed in him were to receive' (Jn 7:37-39). The picture there is not of just a trickle, but of rivers of living water—huge, immense, unbelievable great blessing that flows out of our lives to others when we are filled with the Spirit of Jesus. We're not supposed to containers of blessing, we're supposed to be channels of blessing. God wants to flow His blessing through us to others. Everything He has done for us, He wants it to flow out in refreshing, life-giving streams of grace to those around us."[116]

THE BRIDE'S BLESSING (4:16-5:1)

Finally, the chapter ends with the bride giving herself to her husband. These are the first words uttered by the new queen in the chapter.

The Blessing of Permission

For the first time in this honeymoon scene, the bride responds, and it is with great boldness she grants permission to her husband.

---

[116] Nancy Demoss Wolgemuth. "How to Fall and Stay in Love with Jesus," Day 14. Accessed Aug 21, 2017. https://www.reviveourhearts.com/radio/revive-our-hearts/song-solomon-day-14/

Song of Solomon 4:16 | Awake, O north wind, and come, O south wind! Blow upon my garden, let its spices flow. Let my beloved come to his garden, and eat its choicest fruits.

Both the cool north winds and the balmy south winds are needed for a plentiful harvest. The bride gives the invitation for her beloved to share in her garden, "and eat its choicest fruits." She chooses him above all others to share her life with. She's saying, "My garden is his garden." She's saying, "I want you to come into my life. I want you to be at home. I want you to belong here. I want you to eat freely. I want you to be pleased and satisfied with the fruit you find in my life."

That's a reminder that our lives are not ours; we belong to the Lord. My life is his garden. We desire him to find the godly fruit of holiness in our garden. Whatever is there, we want it to be pleasing to Christ, produced by the Spirit. Of course, that fruit of Christlikeness is cultivated by the warm south winds of God's kindness and blessing. But we also need the north winds of God's pruning and discipline. In order for that to take place, we need to yield ourselves to God. "Present yourselves to God as those who have been brought from death to life, and your members to God as instruments for righteousness" (Rom 6:13). "Present your bodies as a living sacrifice, holy and acceptable to God, which is your spiritual worship" (Rom 12:1).

Often, the Spirit of God is pictured as wind. Ezekiel preaches to the wind, and the Wind (Spirit) of God makes dry bones live (Eze 37:9-14). At Pentecost, the Spirit came as a "mighty, rushing wind" (Acts 2:2). In the new birth, the Spirit is pictured as the Wind of God (Jn 3:8). The effects of the wind are constantly moving us one direction or another. Sometimes the Spirit brings an encouraging wind from the south – a wind of comfort and joy. Other times he brings a north wind of chastisement and conviction. The winds of our lives come from God. "A man's steps are from the Lord; how then can man understand his way?" (Prov 20:24). We don't understand the suffering and difficulties in our lives. How can we? But we do know that man's steps are from the Lord. The Lord is the Master Gardener and all that he does in his "garden" will make us more fruitful and fragrant.

JONATHAN EDWARDS (1703-1758): "Let nothing that is said against high transports discourage the highest degree of a spiritual sense. Be filled as full as you will. Let the effect on your bodies be what they will."[117]

The Blessing of Preference

Now here is something very important. She has made a garden for a king. And this isn't just any king. This king has thousands of people making gardens for him. He has employed thousands upon thousands of people to prepare the gardens in his palace. What on earth does he need with a little puny garden from a young woman? Do you think King Solomon cares about this garden she's made for him? Yes! He prefers it above all others. Solomon makes a joyous exclamation.

Song of Solomon 5:1 | I came to my garden, my sister, my bride, I gathered my myrrh with my spice, I ate my honeycomb with my honey, I drank my wine with my milk.

He may have 30,000 gardeners working on a garden. He's the king. But the one that he loves the most is the garden that his wife has cultivated. There was some myrrh and spice that she had planted. There was honey and grapes and wine. Even milk was available. Perhaps a personal garden wasn't impressive, but because of love, and because he knew it was her best and it was done out of pure love, this would have been the greatest gift he could have received from his new bride! King Solomon is not just putting up with this garden. He is relishing it. Why? Because it came from the one he loves.

Think about the stick man your child drew for you. I have this picture of my daughter Katie and I and it hangs in my office. She drew it when she was six or seven. It's not the Mona Lisa, but it is more precious to me than any of the great masters' paintings. Why? Because my daughter drew a picture of her and her dad together. There's a smile on both our faces.

God delights to hear your voice in prayer. Your prayers may seem pitiful to you, but know that he loves your prayers. He loves your effort.

---

[117] Harry S. Stout, Nathan O. Hatch and Kyle P. Farley, eds., *Jonathan Edwards: Sermons and Discourses, 1739-1742*, Vol 22 of *The Works of Jonathan Edwards*, ed. John E. Smith (New Haven and London: Yale University Press, 2003), 534 (From Edwards' sermon on 2 Corinthians 15:1-2, April 1742).

Because he loves you. You may feel unlovable, but God prefers you. Why? Because he delights in loving the unlovely. He delights in transforming selfish sinners into saints. Why did God prefer Israel? "The Lord your God has chosen you to be a people for his treasured possession, out of all the peoples who are on the face of the earth. It was not because you were more in number than any other people that the Lord set his love on you and chose you, for you were the fewest of all peoples, but it is because the Lord loves you..." (Deut 7:6-8).

The Blessing of Praise
The guests of the wedding shout with joy.

Song of Solomon 5:1b | Eat, friends, drink, and be drunk with love!

What celebration of the couple's love! The most important guest to this wedding is the Lord God Almighty. Perhaps this is his divine commendation. God has brought this couple together. He stamps his, "Well done" upon the royal pair (Mt 25:21). His approval is what all Christians seek after. In everything, we want to "do all to the glory of God" (1 Cor 10:31). To bring glory (*doxa*) to God literally means to *give the right opinion* of God. [118]

A godly wedding is to be celebrated. The honeymoon should be a time of great joy, not of regret. There is a place where there is total freedom in marital love. It is the marriage bed. Keep it undefiled and you will be blessed. Enjoy it, it's a gift from God. Defile it, and God will remove his blessing. You'll experience the misery and tyranny of the flesh if you give into it. But if you guard it, you will experience the "Well done" of God. This commendation to eat and drink sends our minds to the marriage supper of the Lamb.

> JONATHAN EDWARDS (1703-1758): "If we choose Christ for our friend and portion, we shall hereafter be so received to him, that there shall be nothing to hinder the fullest enjoyment of him, to the satisfying the utmost cravings of our souls. We may take our full swing at gratifying our spiritual appetite after these holy pleasures. Christ will then say, as in Song 5:1, 'Eat, O friends. Drink. Ye drink abundantly, O beloved.' And this shall be our entertainment to all eternity! There shall never be any end

---

[118] C. Spicq, & J. D. Ernest. *Theological Lexicon of the New Testament*, Vol 1, (Peabody, MA: Hendrickson Publishers, 1991), 362.

of this happiness, or anything to interrupt our enjoyment of it, or in the least to molest us in it! Christ eats of the same feast with believers, and he eats with them. They sit with the king at his table (Song 1:12). Christ tells us that if we will open the door, he will come in and sup with us, and we with him (Rev 3:20). Christ sat with his disciples at his first sacrament, which signifies that he always has communion with them in the same spiritual blessings. In Song 5:1 we read first of Christ's eating and then commanding his friends to eat ... And believers are also partakers of the same glory with Jesus Christ, they shall sit with him in his throne."[119]

So this meal points to a greater and more lasting reality. There is an extravagant meal the Lord has prepared for all who trust in Jesus: the marriage supper of the Lamb. "Then I heard what seemed to be the voice of a great multitude, like the roar of many waters and like the sound of mighty peals of thunder, crying out, 'Hallelujah! For the Lord our God the Almighty reigns. and give him the glory, for the marriage of the Lamb has come, and his Bride has made herself ready; it was granted her to clothe herself with fine linen, bright and pure'— for the fine linen is the righteous deeds of the saints. And the angel said to me, 'Write this: Blessed are those who are invited to the marriage supper of the Lamb.' And he said to me, 'These are the true words of God'" (Rev 19:6-9).

What should I do if I have messed up?

God didn't come to the earth to save the righteous. There's no one who hasn't messed up in one way or another. There is victory. You can have victory if you've chosen a practice of uncleanness instead of purity. I'll give you the secret. It is through prayer. It is through radical amputation. It is through careful accountability and transparency. If you don't want to give up all for Christ and experience victory then don't complain about your misery. There is victory in Jesus.

---

[119] Minkema, ed., Jonathan Edwards: *Sermons and Discourses, 1723-1729*, Vol 14 of *The Works of Jonathan Edwards*, ed. John E. Smith (New Haven and London: Yale University Press, 1997), 287. (From Edwards' sermon, "The Spiritual Blessings of the Gospel Represented by a Feast")

Conclusion

If you are single reserve those passions for marriage. If you are married, delight in your spouse. Whether you are single or married, re-joice in your walk with Christ. If you are married, remember your mar-riage is a picture of Christ and the church. Marriage is not about hap-piness, but holiness. Husbands, display Christ's love for the church. Wives, submit to your husbands. May God guard us, both married and single people, to follow his perfect design for passion and intimacy. It was designed by God to be reserved for marriage alone.

Remember the joy of marriage is but a faint picture of the joy of heaven in our relationship with Christ. Be content in Christ, whatever state you are in. Marriage will not make you happier, but more miser-able, if you are not first content and infinitely joyful in Christ.

7 | SONG 5:2-8

CONFLICT IN MARRIAGE

I opened to my beloved, but my beloved had turned and gone. My soul failed me when he spoke. I sought him, but found him not.
SONG 5:6

The union of two sinners in marriage can be a revealing experience. Often a godly young man and woman both think they are progressing spiritually and growing in Christ. He's found his Proverbs 31 woman. She's found her pious prince charming. They both think so highly of each other. On the honeymoon while the couple is experiencing the novelty of marriage, things are going well. Then the two sinners begin life together with all the pressures and hurts and even cruelties that life brings.

Reality sets in. Insecurities and selfishness begin to rise to the surface here and there. The sparkle begins to fade. The shine and superficial varnish and newness of immature love wear away, and conflict begins. The ugly reality that you are married to a selfish sinner hits you. The person you married is far from perfect. And because you love that person and marriage requires you to be vulnerable to that person, you find that the joy your spouse can give as well as the pain they can cause you is more any other relationship in your life.

The greatest breaches in a relationship can come on the heels of the greatest seasons of intimacy. You may have experienced that in your marriage. Whether you're married or not, you have probably experienced it in your relationship with the Lord. I can go from the mountaintops down to the depths of the sea, in five minutes some-times, it seems. You have these great encounters with the Lord, these great mountaintop moments, and then come these challenges and our flesh takes over, or we give in to the enemy or to the world, and we find that the relationship has really suffered a great blow. It's alarming to discover how quickly fervor can give way to coolness.

Is there a purpose for marital conflict? Marriage is one of God's tools for making us like Jesus. Husbands are told in Ephesians 5:25-26: "Love your wives, as Christ loved the church and gave himself up for her, that he might sanctify her, having cleansed her by the washing of water with the word..." He finishes in verse 28 by saying, "In the same way husbands should love their wives..."

Marital conflict is a way that God shows us we are not as far along in our sanctification as we thought we were. Marriage is made to sanctify you. What do you do when you are hurt? How do you react when you feel cut by the one you love? Are you really Christlike? What should I do when I have a serious disagreement with my spouse?

Let us consider some timeless truth that I hope will help you make the most of your marriage when you feel hurt. I want to show you how not to waste marital conflict. Now this is also for single people too, because you too will be hurt in life. This is a study in how you can respond to conflict instead of being controlled by negative emotions. First, we need to understand the root and cause of conflict by sinners.

THE CAUSES OF CONFLICT (5:2-5)

"What causes quarrels and what causes fights among you? Is it not this, that your passions are at war within you?" (Jas 4:1). We are all by nature selfish. Our entire society is geared toward selfishness. Have it your way. Comfort is the goal. You and I as human beings are fundamentally selfish. The only question is to what degree. Only through the power of Christ in us can we lay down our lives and be selfless and serve as He served. Through the grace of Christ, we can move from selfishness to servanthood.

We are selfish sinners by nature and by choice. Our entire society encourages selfishness. We've all graduated from "Me" University with a master's degree in selfishness. The highest goal that our culture promotes is to make enough money so that everybody else serves you. The utopia and aim of living is to make it to paradise, which would be a place where the world revolves around me and my comfort. Selfish people are terrible friends, terrible spouses, inconsistent Christians, terrible parents, and they leave a terrible legacy.

This leads us to the Song of Solomon 5. The honeymoon is over. Reality is setting in. Pressures weigh upon the marriage. You know what's happening. The fantasy world of that we created in our mind about ourselves and our spouse now has some serious cracks in it. We have high expectations for our spouse to serve us, to love us, to make us happy. They fail. They might even sin against you. Mostly there are a lot of misunderstandings. What do you do?

Let's check out what Solomon does. Solomon arrives home. He does not have a nine to five job. He has a lifestyle job. He's king. In this time-period, it was common for husbands and wives to have separate bedrooms. Solomon gets home to his palace, and he wants to spend time with his wife. It's late at night. Her door is locked. She is half asleep, tired, and in the twilight of her mind, she can kind of hear her beloved husband knocking. She's not in a terrible tiff with her husband; she is just sleepy. Sometimes that happens in our walk with God. There many things that cause our love for Christ to falter. Spiritual sleepiness is a big one.

Spiritual Sleepiness

Song of Solomon 5:2 | I slept, but my heart was awake. A sound!
My beloved is knocking.

She had given up on Solomon coming home at a reasonable hour, and so she was sacked out and sleeping! Of course, being a loving husband, he would want his new bride to get plenty of beauty sleep. It would be inconsiderate to bother her at this hour of the night.

How does she become indifferent and unresponsive to her beloved? The peasant princess says, "I slept, but my heart was awake" (5:2a). This scene takes place at nighttime. The bride is at home in bed. She's just falling off to sleep, and notice she's not out running around with other men. She's not doing anything flagrantly immoral or sinful that causes this breech in the relationship. She's just half asleep. She has become indifferent and unresponsive to the advances of her beloved one.

We soon forget of the preciousness of Christ, don't we? We often go to great mountaintops and then so quickly descend to the ash heaps of spiritual defeat. What a picture we have here of how spiritual sluggishness and decline takes place in the Bride of Christ, in the Church, in us as believers. So often we find ourselves half asleep, not out there doing something flagrantly wicked, but just complacent, indifferent to our Beloved's voice.

A couple of years ago I had a corneal transplant. I had a disease called Keratoconus that deteriorated the cornea in my left eye. In order to replace it, they had to remove the defective cornea with a laser, and surgically affix the donor's cornea. I was awake, but my eye was asleep. I was conscious for the whole thing. I remember every part. But my eye was numb. That's ok when you have a medical professional to numb the affected area. But it is not ok to be spiritually numb!

Have you grown spiritually sleepy or complacent? If so, what kinds of things have "lulled you to sleep" and dulled your responsiveness to Jesus? What are some ways we become spiritually complacent?

Absence of Christian fellowship. "If we walk [together] in the light, as he is in the light, we have fellowship with one another, and the blood of Jesus his Son cleanses us from all sin" (1 Jn 1:7)

Love for this world. Demas forsook Paul being "in love with this present world" (2 Tim 4:10).

Wrong associations/friendships. Example: Solomon loved many women who drew his heart away from God. "When Solomon was old his wives turned away his heart after other gods, and his heart was not wholly true to the Lord his God, as was the heart of David his father" (I Kings 11:4).

Worldly success can cause you to forget God if you love it. The love of money which often comes by worldly success is the root of all evil. "For the love of money is a root of all kinds of evils. It is through this craving that some have wandered away from the faith and pierced themselves with many pangs" (1 Tim 6:10).

Shallowness. You start to make excuses which dull you to the Holy Spirit's conviction, and like stony ground hearer, you receive the Word with joy and then never change (Lk 8:13). "If anyone is a hearer of the word and not a doer, he is like a man who looks intently at his natural face in a mirror. For he looks at himself and goes away and at once forgets what he was like" (Jas 1:23-24).

Idleness and a lack of service for Christ. If you are not accountable to serve Christ in the local body of believers, you will become complacent and wander into the world. "And let us consider how to stir up one another to love and good works, not neglecting to meet together, as is the habit of some, but encouraging one another, and all the more as you see the Day drawing near" (Heb 10:24-25).

It's so easy to become spiritually sluggish. We get lulled to sleep with all kinds of distractions. We become more enthralled with God's extravagant gifts than with our amazing God. We become satisfied with our excesses here in comfortable America. We become filled with rich food, with million-dollar entertainment, with professional sports. We replace our fellowship with God with so much meaningless conversation, meaningless plots of television and movies. We even fill our heads with rich theology and our hearts with shallow prayers to placate our consciences.

But where is Christ in our thoughts? He is sometimes absent. Where is our ravishing love for Christ? What happened to it? We have rich theology, but where is our precious Christ? He is with us, but we've lost the conscious realization of his presence. All of that can fill us up so that we become satiated with cotton candy instead of real food that nourishes our souls. We're just stuffed so full we cannot move. We are filled with spiritual cement. We don't have room for Christ and don't really have a desire for him. We've become complacent.

This brings to my mind the picture of Jesus in Gethsemane who sweat as it were great drops of blood, and the disciples – what are they doing? They are sleeping and sluggish in the hour of their greatest trial. Remember Jesus warned the disciples to watch and pray. "Watch and pray that you may not enter into temptation. The spirit indeed is willing, but the flesh is weak" (Mt 26:41). We read about his travail and the anguish of soul as he was about to fulfill his Father's will and the plan of redemption.

Sometimes we are like those sleeping disciples who take their Master for granted. We are like the Ephesian church. St. John received a message from our Lord Jesus on the Isle of Patmos. The Lord said that the Ephesian believers had lost their first love. "I have this against you, that you have abandoned the love you had at first. Remember therefore from where you have fallen; repent, and do the works you did at first. If not, I will come to you and remove your lampstand from its place, unless you repent" (Rev 2:4-5). If God wrote you a letter today, what might he say to you?

How easy it is to become sleepy in our marriage and in our spiritual walk. We must always be awake and walking carefully. "Awake, O sleeper, and arise from the dead, and Christ will shine on you. Look carefully then how you walk, not as unwise but as wise" (Eph 5:14-15). We can easily become distracted. Spiritual sleepiness is a serious cause of conflict in marriage. It also hinders our love for Christ.

Forgetfulness

Apparently, Solomon missed his wife and needed to be near her. It's very late at night, when there is dew on the ground—certainly after midnight. He's worked long hours ruling the kingdom. He wants to enjoy the company of his wife. She is his sanctuary. He speaks to her with great tenderness and affection. She means the world to him.

Song of Solomon 5:2b | Open to me, my sister, my love, my dove, my perfect one, for my head is wet with dew, my locks with the drops of the night.

> MATTHEW HENRY (1662-1714): "Solomon not only gives her no hard names, nor upbraids her with unkindness in not sitting up for him, but, on the contrary, studies how to express his tender affection to her still. Those that by faith are espoused to Christ he looks upon as his sisters, his loves, his doves, and all that is dear; and, being clothed with his righteousness, they are undefiled. This thought should induce this peasant princess to open to him. And Christ's love to us should engage ours to Him, even in the most self-denying instances. *Open to me.* Can we deny entrance to such a friend, to such a guest? Shall we not converse more with one that is infinitely worthy of our friendship, and so affectionately desirous of it?"[120]

---

[120] Matthew Henry. *Commentary*, 1067.

Solomon's love is strong and intense. But the bride is forgetful of his love. She is ready for bed and does not want to be inconvenienced by his love. How quickly she has forgotten of their love story.

Selfishness

Like most men, Solomon was working in the hard, cruel, and cold world, and he wanted to come home to some tenderness and appreciation at the end of his difficult day. And he asks her to let him in. He's been outside toiling, and as we mentioned, his head and his hair are drenched with the heavy dew of the night. He wants to commune with her. But the peasant princess starts making excuses:

Song of Solomon 5:3 | I had put off my garment; how could I put it on? I had bathed my feet; how could I soil them?

What a bunch of sorry excuses. She's not descent. She doesn't want to dirty her feet. What is going on here? She's making excuses. "It's not convenient." Now, her response to his call is so different than the responsive, love-struck bride that we've seen earlier, where she says, "Let my beloved come into his garden and eat its pleasant fruits" (4:16). Now all she can think of is *I, me, and my*. She's left her first love. She's in a palace, not in a dirt floored shack. She wants him to know she is in control. She's not going to give way to his every whim. After all she's now a princess. She may feel a bit wronged and neglected since Solomon did not come home at a descent hour. These feelings are all very common in marriage. He powerful love is faltering because of her own selfishness. Solomon wanted to express his love, and all he got were excuses. "I'm already in bed! I'm sleeping. I don't want to get my feet dirty." The bride was thinking of herself more highly than she ought to. She was taking the love of her king for granted.

Our walk with Christ is susceptible to selfishness as well. There are times in our walk with the Lord when we think, I'll never not love the Lord. My love will always be fervent. That's what Peter said. Right? "I'll follow you even though everybody else forsakes you." Peter said emphatically, "If I must die with you, I will not deny you" (Mk 14:31). Sometimes we can allow that sweet righteousness of Christ to turn into a self-serving self-righteousness. Who gave you your righteousness? We take Christ's love for granted and become proud and cold and self-righteous. We begin to make excuses: "I don't want to serve Christ in the world. I just want to stay in my comfortable Christian bubble." How about you? Are you in the Christian bubble of ease and comfort? Have you drifted into self-righteousness and pride and complacency?

We see the root of conflict is selfishness. I want my way. We look at marriage asking what we can get out of it. How can I change my spouse to my likings? That attitude will always bring with it contention and conflict. Pride and selfishness bring great pain in marriage.

Delayed Responsiveness

Song of Solomon 5:4-6a | My beloved put his hand to the latch, and my heart was thrilled within me. I arose to open to my beloved, and my hands dripped with myrrh, my fingers with liquid myrrh, on the handles of the bolt. I opened to my beloved, but my beloved had turned and gone.

When he could not prevail with her by persuasion he put in his hand to the latch of the door, to unbolt it, as someone who was weary of waiting (5:4). But in the end, though he wants to commune with her, he leaves – apparently to go to another part of the palace. We find out later that perhaps after some rest, he goes to their secret place – to a garden that is reserved only for them.

It is that God knocks on the door of our hearts. This intimates a work of the Spirit upon her soul, by which she who was unwilling was made willing (Psa 110:3). The conversion of Lydia is represented by the *opening of her heart* (Acts 16:14).

Suddenly, she has a change of heart which is evidence that she belongs to him. If you don't belong to Christ, your heart's not going to be stirred. She is deeply stirred. She's moved. She realizes who she has rejected, what she has rejected, and she longs to be with him. She finally decides to leave her comfortable place of rest, put her robe on, get her feet dirty, open the door, and let him in. She says: "I arose to open to my beloved, and my hands dripped with myrrh, my fingers with liquid myrrh, on the handles of the bolt" (5:5). It seems that Solomon is frustrated here. He wants to commune with the one who has dove's eyes – his "perfect one." He leaves, but he leaves a calling card on the door. These were special ointments and fragrances. Christ always leaves his fragrance, the aroma of his love by his Holy Spirit. Remember, if you are being chastened by the Lord, it is because he loves you.

Even if it seems you have grieved his Holy Spirit, the fragrance of his love will never stop drawing you to him!

The bride was expecting her beloved husband to be right there as soon as she opened the door and everything to immediately get back to normal. But that doesn't happen, does it? She was slow to respond to his initiative, and now she loses the conscious awareness of his presence. It's so important when we sense a call from the Lord in our hearts to come to communion with him, to come serve with him, whether in the middle of the night or the middle of the day. It's so important that we're quick to respond and say, "Yes, Lord." As Isaiah 55:6 says, "Seek the Lord while he may be found; call upon him while he is near." The queen didn't answer right away, and missed him! She cries out to her beloved.

Song of Solomon 5:6b | I sought him, but found him not; I called him, but he gave no answer.

Richard Sibbes, the beloved Puritan and Anglican theologian of the seventeenth century, in his series on the Song of Solomon, tells us how God's chastening can draw us closer and give us a fuller fellowship with Christ.

> RICHARD SIBBES (1577-1635), "Why does the bride testify: 'he gave me no answer'? She seems to be forsaken. Christ also, seems to forsake us, to test the realities of his graces and affections in us, whether they be true or not. His withdrawal causes us to seek after him. When he seems to forsake us, we shall undoubtedly seek after him, and this proves that his grace is truly planted in our heart. The temporary withdrawal of his presence helps us in our relationships with others. We grow in heavenly wisdom, and learn how to encourage those in affliction (2 Cor 1:4). God's chastening makes us wise, tender, and successful in dealing with others, when we have felt the same particular grievance ourselves. 'Brothers, if anyone is caught in any transgression, you who are spiritual should restore him in a spirit of gentleness. Keep watch on yourself, lest you too be tempted.' (Gal 6:1). Experience of spiritual grief in this kind, will make us fit, able, and wise in how we minister to others. Spiritual chastening also serves to wean us from the world, in the plenty and abundance of all earthly things. Consider a Christian that has no cross in the

world. Let him find some estrangement of Christ from his spirit.
Take away the comforts of the Holy Spirit, and that fullness of
joy he enjoyed in times past, and all the wealth he has. He cannot
enjoy any of the earthly contentments. They no longer please
him, nor can they content that soul that has ever felt sweet communion with Christ." [121]

There are such severe consequences of delayed responsiveness. If
you want to see that fleshed out, consider Proverbs 1:24-25 – "Because
I have called and you refused to listen, have stretched out my hand and
no one has heeded, because you have ignored all my counsel and would
have none of my reproof." Then that passage goes on to list serious consequences that will come about in our lives when we don't quickly respond to the Lord's call in our lives. Harry Ironside was the pastor of
the Moody Church from 1929-1948, and he speaks as to why the Lord
sometimes withdraws his presence.

> HARRY IRONSIDE (1876-1951): "If you do not respond to his
> voice when he comes in tender grace, you may seek him for a
> long time before you will enjoy fellowship with him again. Such
> is the sensitiveness of love. He wants to make you feel that his
> love is worthwhile, and he wants to test you as to whether you
> are really in earnest when you profess to desire fellowship with
> him."[122]

Moses said to God in Exodus 33:15, "If thy presence go not with
me, carry us not up hence" (KJV). That ought to be our attitude. I will
not go forward without God's presence.

A man and a woman speak radically different languages. The wife's
response is very telling. The wife observes, "I arose to open to my beloved, and my hands dripped with myrrh, my fingers with liquid myrrh,
on the handles of the bolt" (5:5a). The husband wanted to express his
love to his wife with closeness. Myrrh is a beautiful fragrance used in
the Temple. Solomon's intention was to express love, affection, and security for his wife.

---

[121] Sibbes. *The Love of Christ*, Kindle Locations 2574-2583.
[122] Harry Ironside. *Addresses on the Song of Solomon* (Chicago: Moody, 1933), 63.

The wife spoke a different language. She thought he should express his love by respecting her need for sleep! But it seems here that the wife changes her mind, and decides to let her beloved husband in.

Song of Solomon 5:4 | My beloved put his hand to the latch, and my heart was thrilled within me.

But it is too late.

Song of Solomon 5:6a | I opened to my beloved, but my beloved had turned and gone.

The man wanted to express his love, and all he got were excuses. "I'm already in bed! I'm sleeping. I don't want to get my feet dirty." The husband feels disrespected. He feels dishonored. He feels shot down.

The wife feels unloved because she thinks, "If he really loves me, he'll want me to sleep." What is the problem here? Husbands and wives speak different languages. Until you realize this, and you learn to communicate and actually help your spouse to understand you, then you are going to be in for a lot of pain, offense, hurt, misunderstanding, and confusion. According to 1 Peter 3:7, it is the husband's responsibility to learn the wife's language first. "Likewise, husbands, live with your wives in an understanding way, showing honor to the woman as the weaker vessel, since they are heirs with you of the grace of life, so that your prayers may not be hindered."

Men can usually get over conflict fairly easily and quickly, but we have to remember that our wife is a "weaker vessel," literally a "fragile vase," and though conflict can be forgiven by the wife immediately, she may struggle with insecurity until trust is rebuilt by the husband. This can last for months or years if the husband isn't careful.

Often newly married couples have not learned a planned, godly response but a spontaneous negative reaction to the hurt. Many times in a marriage a man will at first not want to fight with his wife. He will give up. Why? Because he knows he cannot win. If he ends up winning, he loses. If he ends up losing, he loses. So a man tends to want to escape. He will just not say anything and clam up. He will give the silent treatment. He's been shot down; he's hurt and he wants to run.

It seems that Solomon is frustrated here. He leaves, but he leaves a calling card on the door. The wife notices his calling card.

Song of Solomon 5:5 | I arose to open to my beloved, and my hands dripped with myrrh, my fingers with liquid myrrh, on the handles of the bolt.

Solomon respected her rejection and went away, but he left a reminder of his love for her – liquid myrrh. Solomon was saying, "I know you need your rest, but don't forget how much I love you."

THE CURE FOR CONFLICT (5:6-8)

Respond with Remorse

Solomon's bride feels the remorse for this seeming conflict. Listen to her sadness and desperation.

Song of Solomon 5:6 | I opened to my beloved, but my beloved had turned and gone. My soul failed me when he spoke. I sought him, but found him not; I called him, but he gave no answer.

Her soul failed. This is a very strong Hebrew phrase. Her heart burned with remorse or dropped with regret and pain is the idea. A paraphrase was, "I nearly died when I found out he had gone."

We see that the new queen of Israel has a great wave of regret overcome her. I believe this regret has godly repentance at the foundation. We can always trust God to shepherd our spouse. He can show us when we sin and the pathway to repentance. We the good queen's regret and remorse for her selfishness.

Conflict late at night is *bad*. Be careful not to get into difficult or intense discussion very late at night. That's the time when many marital conflicts begin. Our burdens are heavier, our strength is less, and we can often feel discouraged or weak at the end of a day.

Look at some consequences for handling conflict in a selfish way. Solomon's leaving makes the new bride feel unbelievably insecure. We will find the man meant nothing by it, but a woman's security is messed with, and she is beside herself. When a man leaves, though he may just need to "take a walk" and "calm down", the woman is prone to feel abandoned. We may just need some time alone, but we may be communicating abandonment.

Respond with Pursuit

The bride does not know where Solomon is, so she goes back to sleep, but her search for her beloved carries on even in her dreams. She doses off and has a kind of nightmarish sequence. Conflict is such that it brings unrest in the marriage and in *life* itself. When things are going great in marriage, everything is great. When marriage is going bad, everything is really, really bad. The dream of Solomon's bride reveals the toll that this conflict is having on her. Listen to this strange dream.

Song of Solomon 5:7 | The watchmen found me as they went about in the city; they beat me, they bruised me, they took away my veil, those watchmen of the walls.

She apparently has a nightmare where she gets no help finding her beloved. She's half-dressed so she looks like a woman of the night. She's got a veil that makes her look like a prostitute. At this hour, all respectable women are in their own beds sleeping.

The watchmen of Israel were the spiritual caretakers. It seems they misunderstood her. They assumed that a woman of good moral character would not be out in the street in the middle of the night. The watchmen punish her and beat her. They seem to mistake her for a prostitute. It shows that in marriage, our friendship and communion are easily lost, but not easily recovered.

Just as the bride goes searching for her beloved (albeit in a dream), so we ought to pursue Christ when we find ourselves backsliding or drifting away from him. "You will seek me and find me, when you seek me with all your heart" (Jer 29:13).

Respond with Love Sickness

The newlywed wife in our story wakes up from her dream, and she is sick with love and desperate to reconcile with her husband. She turns to the daughters of Jerusalem, her friends, and enlists their help in finding him. She says to them, "Can you please give him a message for me?"

Song of Solomon 5:8 | I adjure you, O daughters of Jerusalem, if you find my beloved, that you tell him I am sick with love.

The love sickness spoken of here is so strong, the same word is used for a woman travailing in childbirth (Isa 26:17, "pangs"). She has deep pain at the loss of her beloved. There is a vehement desire to find her lover and king. The bride feels like dying because of her intense longings for the presence of her husband.

Often our Beloved is trying to get our attention. This is where the Bride finally refocuses. When our love falters, we need to take our gaze off of our comfort and off of ourselves. It's dangerous to have your gaze fixed on yourself. We weren't paying attention, so he's getting our attention. And sometimes he can use calamity and crisis to do that. All our trials and difficulties make us turn to the one who never changes. When all our most exciting earthly plans are crumbling, Christ remains "the same yesterday and today and forever" (Heb 13:8).

> CHARLES HADDON SPURGEON (1834-1892), "Such is the character of this love-sickness. We may say of it, however, that it is a sickness which has a blessing attending it: 'Blessed are they that do hunger and thirst after righteousness;' and therefore, supremely blessed are they who thirst after the Righteous One—after him, who in the highest perfection embodies pure, immaculate, spotless righteousness. Blessed is that hunger, for it comes from God. It bears a blessing within it; for if I may not have the blessedness in full bloom of being filled, the next best thing is the same blessedness in sweet bud of being empty till I am filled with Christ. If I may not feed on Jesus, it shall be next door to heaven to be allowed to hunger and thirst after him. There is a hallowedness about that hunger, since it sparkles among the beatitudes of our Lord. Yet it is a sickness, dear friends, which, despite the blessing, causes much pain. The man who is sick after Jesus, will be dissatisfied with everything else; he will find that dainties have lost their sweetness, and music its melody, and light its brightness, and life itself will be darkened with the shadow of death to him, till he finds his Lord, and can rejoice in him."[123]

The bride is so sick with love, that she is determined to be reunited with her husband at all costs. When godly love is reignited, the offences we were so upset about disappear. When conflict comes, there needs to be a refocusing on what is most important: your love for one another.

---

[123] Spurgeon. *Pulpit,* Vol 42, Sermon 2469, "The Incomparable Bridegroom and His Bride" (1896), 285.

St. Paul writes to the Ephesians instructing them about resolving personal conflict. "Let no corrupting talk come out of your mouths, but only such as is good for building up, as fits the occasion, that it may give grace to those who hear. And do not grieve the Holy Spirit of God, by whom you were sealed for the day of redemption. Let all bitterness and wrath and anger and clamor and slander be put away from you, along with all malice. Be kind to one another, tenderhearted, forgiving one another, as God in Christ forgave you" (Eph 4:29-32). Notice, by refocusing on Christ's forgiveness, we can turn bitterness, rage and slander into tenderness, forgiveness and kindness. Such is the power of Christ's love. If you do not have this for your spouse, sincerely ask Christ, and he will give this love to you (Mt 7:7). Conflict in marriage is inevitable. Similarly, though our covenant with Christ can never be broken, yet our relationship with him can languish.

Life on this earth is filled with storms. Marriage has so many ups and downs. Our relationship with the Lord is the same way. One moment we feel "sick with love" for our Savior, and the next we are distant from him.

> RICHARD SIBBES (1577-1635), "Thus we may see that the way to heaven is full of changes in our walk with the Lord. The strength of corruption overclouds many times, and dampens our joys. How many various emotional states have any one of us been in! Sometimes the Lord's church is all compounded of joy, vehemently desiring kisses of her best beloved. She holds her beloved fast, and will not let him go; and sometimes, again, she is gone, having lost her beloved, is in a sea of troubles, seeks and cannot find him, becomes sluggish, negligent, and overtaken with self-love. After this when she has suffered for her omissions, as here again, she is all afire after Christ. As we say, no ground will hold her, away she flies after him, and is restless until she find him. We can clearly see that consistency and stability is for the life to come. In this life our portion is to expect changes, storms, and tempests. It is the portion of the whole church, who by sufferings and conformity to our Head shall enter into glory (2 Cor 4:17-18). God makes his power perfect in our weakness (2 Cor 12:9) overcomes Satan by unlikely means, and so gets himself the glory, even out of our greatest infirmities, temptations, and abasements. But God makes all things work for good unto his

children (Rom 8:28), even the devil, sin, and death, desertions, afflictions and all cannot separate us from his love." [124]

Conclusion

We all want fuller fellowship with the Lord. Whether you are married or single, if you have unresolved conflict in your life, it is affecting your fellowship with the Lover of your soul. You need to be tender-hearted and seek to be the first to reconcile. You cannot worship God if you have not dealt with sin and misunderstandings in your life. Set your gift down, that is before the next worship service, and get things right (Mt 5:24). Settle the conflict in a godly way. There is great joy and long-term stability if you will seek selfless giving instead of selfishness. Following God's path to restoration in conflict is one of God's primary tools to make us like Christ.

---

[124] Sibbes. *The Love of Christ*, Kindle Locations 107-111.

8 | SONG 5:9-16

THE GODLY HUSBAND

What is your beloved more than another beloved?
SONG 5:9

In March of 1923, my grandfather arrived from Scotland on Ellis Island where he could see the statue of liberty up close. The figure he had seen in photos was much more stunning in person. He could see the weathered exterior that had welcomed tens of thousands of immigrants into America. He noticed something especially encouraging at the feet of Lady Liberty: a broken chain. The hope welled up in my grandfather as he saw the symbol of liberty, as it were, face to face.

So it is as the new queen gazes upon her king. She is enthralled and thrilled with the vision of her beloved. All the faltering emotions she just experienced are vanished with one glimpse of her husband.

THE BELOVED'S FAVOR (5:9-10)

The bride thinks in her imagination of a question that the daughters of Jerusalem might ask. This common device is called soliloquy, where an imaginary conversation takes place in her mind.

Song of Solomon 5:9 | What is your beloved more than another beloved, O most beautiful among women? What is your beloved more than another beloved, that you thus adjure us?

In other words, what's so great about your beloved? Or as the NIV says there, "How is your beloved better than others?" "What's so special about him? There are lots of other men around here. If you've lost him, go find another one." Find another? There is no one like her beloved!

And for the Christian there is no one that compares to Jesus! In response, the bride begins to think about what makes her beloved so special. What makes him stand out from all other men? She sets out to explain to the daughters of Jerusalem what it is that makes him unique from all others.

J. Hudson Taylor, missionary to China says of Song 5:9, "This question, implying that her Beloved was no more than any other, stirs her soul to its deepest depths; and, forgetting herself, she pours out from the fullness of her heart a soul-ravishing description of the glory and beauty of her Lord."[125] She is truly "sick with love" (5:8). To be sick with love for Christ is the only way to kill and cure sin in your life. She says, "I am sick with love" (5:8), and she gives the reasons why (5:11-16). Are you love sick for Christ? He says to us as he said to Peter: "Do you love me more than these?" (Jn 21:15). Do you love Christ more than this world? More than your sin? More than any earthly relationship? You say, I want to, but my sin is so great. If you have sinned greatly, you should love Christ more, not less! Are you love sick for Christ? This is the way to kill and cure sin in your life.

Solomon's bride starts thinking about her beloved in a godly way. She esteems his character. She respects him above ten thousand. The bride begins: "My beloved is radiant and ruddy, distinguished among ten thousand" (5:10). As we see this Old Testament description of the Beloved One, I can't help but think of the revelation of the ascended Christ that the apostle John saw on the Isle of Patmos. We read it in Revelation 1:13-17, "And in the midst of the lampstands one like a son of man, clothed with a long robe and with a golden sash around his chest. The hairs of his head were white, like white wool, like snow. His

---

[125] Taylor, James Hudson. *Union and Communion or Thoughts on the Song of Solomon* (p. 26). Kindle Edition.

eyes were like a flame of fire, his feet were like burnished bronze, refined in a furnace, and his voice was like the roar of many waters. In his
right hand he held seven stars, from his mouth came a sharp two-edged
sword, and his face was like the sun shining in full strength. When I
saw him, I fell at his feet as though dead. But he laid his right hand on
me, saying, 'Fear not, I am the first and the last, and the living one. I
died, and behold I am alive forevermore, and I have the keys of Death
and Hades.'"

"You make known to me the path of life; in your presence there is
fullness of joy; at your right hand are pleasures forevermore" (Psa
16:11). Here David teaches us we are going to be learning more and
more about our Savior for all of eternity. In this chapter, we're just
barely scratching the surface.

In responding to the question of the daughters of Jerusalem,
"What's so special about your beloved?" she begins to remember what's
so special about him. Both in this Old Testament picture, and in this
New Testament description of Christ, we see that everything about him
surpasses and excels everyone else. Every detail is magnificent, and
overall, he is magnificent. He is magnificent in the parts; he is magnificent in the whole.

Song of Solomon 5:10a | My beloved is radiant and ruddy.

The word "radiant" speaks of a brilliant, blinding white. It reminds
me of the picture of Jesus in the gospels, when he's on the mount of
transfiguration, as his clothes were changed to dazzling white as his
glory and his deity shone through. What a description! It's brilliant. It's
dazzling. It's a picture of the deity of Christ, the glory of Christ.

Then she also says he is ruddy. That has to do with a healthy complexion, a wholesome, manly appearance. We could say he has a "rosy"
face. That often happens to us when we work hard or make a long journey by foot. Christ was ruddy in his humanity. He took a long journey
and did all the work for our salvation. He substituted himself. He took
our full punishment upon himself for our sins. He propitiated the wrath
of God for us. To have fellowship with him is better than life. "To have
fellowship with God is to be in heaven. He that has communion with

God is in heaven while he is on earth. This is the gate of paradise and puts us into the suburbs of heaven."[126]

Song of Solomon 5:10b | My beloved is... distinguished among ten thousand.

In marriage, you are to forsake all others and be dedicated to your spouse alone. Human marital love is a mysterious thing. In a proper marriage, the love between the couple enables them to prefer their spouse above all others. The wife of fifty is not the wife of twenty, yet the husband loves the wife all she is all the more – her mind, her heart, her body – above all others. Though perhaps the years have brought great changes to her, yet the husband prefers her because of true godly love. Love enables the heart, the mind and the eyes of both the husband and wife to prefer the one another above all others, "distinguished among ten thousand." But a mystery lies behind this verse about the bride's beloved – the mystery of Christ and his Bride. There is a love that we all must have if we are to be happy in marriage and in life. My happiness does not depend on my spouse, my job, my finances, my health or my circumstances. There is a love I must have above all others to bring me happiness even if all else is taken away. I prefer Christ above ten thousand, yea above all others.

> CHARLES HADDON SPURGEON (1834-1892), "Christ is higher, better, lovelier, more excellent than any who are round about him. If you shall bring ten thousand angels, He is the most exalted Angel, the Messenger of the covenant. If you shall bring ten thousand friends, he is the dearest Friend, the "friend that sticks closer than a brother" (Pro 18:24). Christ is the chiefest, the best, the highest of all beings; whatever excellences there may be in others, they are all eclipsed by the surpassing excellences that are found in him. Christ is the chiefest among ten thousand; that is to say, he is the Head, the Ruler, the Prince, the King, the Lord over all. Let Christ, and Christ alone, wear the

---

[126] David Clarkson. *Works of David Clarkson*, Vol 3 (Edinburgh: James Nichol, 1865), 174.

crown he bought with his own blood; he alone is King, and let him ever be so proclaimed-and acknowledged."[127]

THE BELOVED'S FORM (5:11-16B)

His Glorious Head

You look upon yourself and it's easy to be depressed. I want to look upon Jesus and be cured of my sin. Look upon his glorious head. By the head of Jesus, we may understand his deity, "for the head of Christ is God" (1 Cor 11:3). Jesus is a glorious bridegroom that will cure us of our sin. Look to Him.

Song of Solomon 5:11a | His head is the finest gold.

He is the Head of the Church. It was his wisdom that set his love upon you before the worlds began in spite of your sin. With his head of finest gold, he chose to set his love upon you. Before the counsels of all the worlds our glorious Head chose to display a mercy that is so astounding it cannot be comprehended.

Look upon his glorious head of gold, and you will realize that one-day sin will be forever wiped away from your nature, as it is right now from your record. You are justified, but one day you will be glorified. You will share in the glory that God gave Jesus. The Lord will not have you continue in sin forever. One day you will be glorified with him. You will share in the glory that was given to him.

As our High Priest, our Head who represents us before God, Jesus prayed for you in the garden of Gethsemane. Hear him pray for you: "Father, glorify me in your own presence with the glory that I had with you before the world existed" (Jn 17:5). He prayed this for you as you will see. You may be weary of your sin child of God, but you must know that the glorious One loves you, and that one day you will be glorified with him.

Look again at the words of his high priestly prayer: "I do not ask for these only, but also for those who will believe in me through their word, that they may all be one, just as you, Father, are in me, and I in you, that they also may be in us, so that the world may believe that you have sent me. The glory that you have given me I have given to them,

---

[127] Spurgeon. *Pulpit*, Vol 42, Sermon 2478, "Christ's Perfection and Precedence" (1896), 385.

that they may be one even as we are one, I in them and you in me, that they may become perfectly one, so that the world may know that you sent me and loved them even as you loved me. Father, I desire that they also, whom you have given me, may be with me where I am, to see my glory that you have given me because you loved me before the foundation of the world" (Jn 17:20-24).

You are best ruled when you are ruled by him. Look at his head of finest gold, and you will realize that His counsels are trustworthy! He's never steered anything wrong. Stop being ruled by your sin and desires. Stop being ruled by your suspicions of him. He is faithful and true. He's trustworthy. His head is of finest gold. His record is perfect. "Trust in the Lord with all your heart, and do not lean on your own understanding. In all your ways acknowledge him, and he will make straight your paths" (Pro 3:5-6). "All things work after the counsel of his will" (Eph. 1:11). You may be struggling with evil that has been done to you. God is not the author of evil. "He is not tempted with evil, neither does he tempt any of us" (Jas 1:13).

You can trust that though God does not create evil, he uses it to accomplish his purposes. This is because God is working out a greater glory with his mercy than he ever could with His mere justice. Mercy is outside of justice. In order to have mercy, God must forgive sin. Look upon his head of finest gold and realize that this is a Head that governs you in his mercy. Christ is our treasure, and "in him the whole fullness of deity dwells bodily" (Col. 2:9).

His Youthful Hair

Song of Solomon 5:11b | His locks are wavy, black as a raven.

Most of us have hair that is either turning gray or turning lose! Christ's hair is youthful.

> MATTHEW HENRY (1662-1714): "Sometimes Christ's hair is represented as white (Rev 1:14), denoting his eternity, that he is the ancient of days; but here as black and bushy, showing that he is always new and young and that there is in him no decay, nothing that grows old."[128]

---

[128] Matthew Henry. *Commentary,* 1069.

His mercies are new, like his youthful hair. He is strong and able to save you from your sins. He never grows weary or worn of relentlessly pursuing you and me. He is never tired of saving you from your sins. Like a young man in his prime, so God has the zeal and enthusiasm to save his Bride. You do not weary him, even in your sin. He sees you struggle. But look to him with his youthful hair, and "your youth will be renewed like the eagle's" (Psa 103:5).

The black hair indicates youthful vigor and strength. Others grow lethargic with age, but Jesus is "a priest forever after the order of Melchizedek" (Heb 7:17). He never grows old or weary – "he is the same yesterday and today and forever" (Heb 13:8). "Others come and go, but Christ abides as God upon his throne, world without end."[129]

Look at Christ's youthful hair. It reminds us that he never grew weary of chasing after you. He is our relentless Redeemer. He never grows weary. He has chased you down. No one will pluck you out of his hand (Jn 10:28). He never grows weary of you. Christ's love for you never wears out.

His Peaceful Eyes

Song of Solomon 5:12 | His eyes are like doves beside streams of water, bathed in milk, sitting beside a full pool.

He has dove's eyes of peace – he is not angry with you any way. His anger no longer flashes at you. The brightness of his eyes are so filled with peace that they are described as "bathed in milk." In his eyes, she sees depicted gentleness, compassion, tenderness and grace.

How does God see you? You may think he is against you. But no, he is for you. Sometimes we get confused at our cruel circumstances and think God is cruel. Romans 8 is the remedy for this. Don't mistake your pain for God's displeasure. For those who love God "he is working together all things for good" to conform you to Christ (Rom 8:28-30). Don't confuse separation from earthly comfort for a separation from God's love. Nothing in all creation can separate us from the love of God in Christ. "Who shall separate us from the love of Christ? Shall tribulation, or distress, or persecution, or famine, or nakedness, or danger, or

---

[129] Charles Haddon Spurgeon. *C.H. Spurgeon Devotions from the Song of Solomon: Derived from Morning and Evening* (Kindle Locations 401-403). AudioInk Publishing. Kindle Edition.

sword?" (Rom 8:35). Is this God's displeasure? Am I separated from his love? No! "[Nothing] in all creation, will be able to separate us from the love of God in Christ Jesus our Lord" (Rom 8:39). He loves you. He looks upon you with dove's eyes.

Let me help you grasp this with a story of my Uncle Lew Ahner. My Uncle Lew was a great hero. His fighter plane crashed into a mountain over France. They took my Uncle Lew to a barn in a small village in France where the doctors were able to save his leg. Now on the way over there, I'm sure he was in great pain! I'm sure being in a wheelbarrow with a severely injured leg is no fun. But the French villagers were not looking at my uncle with eyes of evil or eyes of war. They had dove's eyes. They wanted to help him. Many years later, my uncle got to go back and meet those people who saved him. One day we are going to see our Savior face to face. And he will still have dove's eyes for us.

His Cheerful Cheeks

Song of Solomon 5:13a | His cheeks are like beds of spices, mounds of sweet-smelling herbs.

Here we see that God is not frowning upon you, but he is smiling. The cheeks display the soul. Christ's love is so great for you his cheeks turn red. In his cheeks there's the fragrance of his passion and his suffering and his death. Look upon him. He is love is so fragrant, he will go through death for you!

That cheek once so rudely smacked with a rod, and often wetted with tears of sympathy and then defiled with soldier's spit – Behold that cheek as it smiles with mercy upon you! His cheeks that reveal his smile upon you smell so good, "like beds of spices, mounds of sweet-smelling herbs like beds of spices, mounds of sweet-smelling herbs" (5:13a).

As the Levitical blessing in Numbers says, "The Lord bless you and keep you; the Lord make his face to shine upon you and be gracious to you; the Lord lift up his countenance upon you and give you peace" (Num 6:25-26). God sees you through the Cross of Jesus. Before you were born, God chose you. He knew you would be a rebel and a sinner, yet he chose to lavish His love upon you.

Even then in eternity past, his cheerful cheeks were smiling upon you. His final pronouncement is recorded by St. Paul: "[God] has blessed us in Christ with every spiritual blessing in the heavenly places, even as he chose us in him before the foundation of the world, that we should be holy and blameless before him. In love he predestined us for adoption as sons through Jesus Christ, according to the purpose of his will, to the praise of his glorious grace, with which he has blessed us in the Beloved. In him we have redemption through his blood, the forgiveness of our trespasses, according to the riches of his grace, which he lavished upon us, in all wisdom and insight making known to us the mystery of his will, according to his purpose, which he set forth in Christ" (Eph 1:3-9).

His Loving Lips

Song of Solomon 5:13b | His lips are lilies, dripping liquid myrrh.

Myrrh is a fragrance of passion. With his lips he tells you, "you are my perfect one." "I have loved you with an everlasting love." Don't those words just drip with liquid myrrh? In his lips we see the truth, the power, the beauty of his words that counteract the ugliness of the deceptive words of our own heart.

You must meditate on the Word to counteract the poison of your own heart. You feel condemned. God says there is "no condemnation" (Rom 8:1). You feel alone. God says "I will never leave you" (Heb 13:5). You feel his hatred. God says, "I chasten only those who I love." You may feel defeated and undone, a person of unclean lips, but God says, "You are my perfect one." "Man shall not live by bread alone, but by every word that proceeds out of the mouth of God" (Deut 8:3; *cf* Mt 4:4).

His Secure Arms

Song of Solomon 5:14a | His arms are rods of gold, set with jewels.

We see his strong arms, and with those arms He holds us safe and secure. His arms are like "rods of gold." This could be referring to a warrior's amulet with jewels set in. Not just anyone gets to wear this gold amulet or "arm ring." Only the most important one wore it. The king! The general.

The most important Being in all the universe is guiding you. He is with you. He will never leave you stranded in your problems. He's working it all out for good. "There is none like God...who rides through the heavens to your help, through the skies in his majesty. The eternal

God is your dwelling place, and underneath are the everlasting arms" (Deut 33:26-27). Dear saint, the most important One with the bejeweled arm ring is the One who is guiding you, walking with you, and carrying you!

His Strong Chest

Song of Solomon 5:14b | His body is polished ivory, bedecked with sapphires.

The word "body" has been translated "bowels." It means the shaft of the body, the center part of our body that holds the vital organs. The Hebrews used this to mean the center of thought and emotions. The bowels, or the shaft of the body of Christ – his heart, his love, his compassion – is made of "polished ivory, bedecked with sapphires."

In other words, no one is going to put an end to Christ's love for you. It is like "polished ivory" – God sincerely loves you. His love for you is undefiled by pretense. It's not an act. He really, really loves you. His heart for you is bejeweled with dazzling blue sapphires! You wonder why he loves you? Yes, I do wonder that too! His love is like a dazzling sapphire in eternity. He should have judged us. Look at all our sin even since we've been saved. But his love stands out as extraordinary. It's unusual. Who loves like this? Only our Bridegroom!

His Foundational Legs

Song of Solomon 5:15a | His legs are alabaster columns, set on bases of gold.

In his legs, we see the kingly strength, the ability to support his people. His legs are strong and foundational. Alabaster is very strong, like ancient concrete. Gregory of Nyssa (335-394) said, "Christ is the truth upon whom are founded the legs, or pillars of the church." [130]

> AMBROSE (333-397), "Speaking of the shoes of his feet, to whom else but the Word of God incarnate can those words apply? 'His legs are pillars of marble, set upon bases of gold.' For Christ alone walks in the souls and makes his path in the minds of his saints, in which, as upon bases of gold and foundations of

---

[130] Saint Gregory of Nyssa. *Song of Songs*, 252.

precious stone the heavenly Word has left his footprints ineffaceably impressed."[131]

His Beautiful Appearance

Song of Solomon 5:15b | His appearance is like Lebanon, choice as the cedars.

Lebanon means pleasant and delightful. Lebanon was indeed a pleasant and fruitful place. Is there anyone that can compare to Jesus? We now see in a mirror dimly, but one day we will see him face to face. When we look upon him we ought to see not our judge, but our Savior.

Like the cedars of Lebanon, Solomon towered over his peers, for the Lord said to him, "I give you a wise and discerning mind, so that none like you has been before you and none like you shall arise after you" (1 Kings 3:10). Christ being the wisdom and and power of God (1 Cor 1:24) towers over all as the Head of the Church, as glorious and to be much esteemed, for he is higher than the mighty cedars of Lebanon.

> JOHN GILL (1697-1771): "His shape, form, personage, appearance, and look, like the goodly mountains on the north of Judea, high, pleasant, and set with fruitful and fragrant trees, made a very delightful appearance. Christ may be compared to the cedars of Lebanon for his height, being higher than the kings of the earth, than the angels of heaven, and than the heavens themselves. Christ is compared to Lebanon, which means pleasantness, being more glorious and excellent than that or any other mountain. Christ is compared to the fruitful and fragrant trees of righteousness that grow upon him, have their root in him, and their fruitfulness from him; and which diffuse a grateful aroma, by their graces and good works, to Christ and his saints. Christ himself, like the cedars of Lebanon, emits a fragrant smell, in his person, grace, righteousness, and sacrifice to all passers-by, and true believers in him. Christ indeed is excellent as the cedars; which grew on Lebanon; being the choicest, and preferable to

---

[131] St. Ambrose. *On the Christian Faith.* In *Fathers,* Vol 10, 253.

all others. In this way, Christ may be compared, for stature, stateliness, fragrancy, and durability."[132]

His Life-Giving Mouth

Song of Solomon 5:16a | His mouth is most sweet.

It is by the word of his mouth that Christ formed all things. He is called "the Word" because "he has made the Father known" (Jn 1:18) and is the "image of the invisible God" (Col 1:15). He is the Word of life incarnated whose word make the blind to see, the lame to walk, and the dead to live. It's so important that in seasons of spiritual dryness or separation from our Beloved, we take time to recall what he is like, to verbalize his features – by faith to praise him for what you've known to be true of him in the past, even when you're not feeling those things at the moment.

Martin Luther exclaimed, "His breath is not foul, but he breathes sweet things. That is, these fruits of the church which I have been reciting here please God and are acceptable to him."[133]

His Desirable Person

Song of Solomon 5:16b | He is altogether desirable.

Turn your eyes upon Jesus! As we get our eyes off of ourselves and on to him, in praise and worship, we find that God revives in our hearts an appreciation of Christ in the present. "To you who believe, [Christ] is precious" (1 Pet 2:7). As you focus on him, as you fix your eyes on him, as you describe him, as you praise him, you find him to be precious. Truly, "he is altogether lovely" (5:16a, KJV).

> JOHN FLAVEL (1627–1691), "He is altogether lovely in his offices: let us consider for a moment the suitability, fullness, and comforting nature of them. First, the offices of Christ are well suited to the miseries of men. We cannot but adore the infinite wisdom of his receiving them. We are, by nature, blind and ignorant, at best but groping in the dim light of nature after God

---

[132] John Gill. *An Exposition of the book of Solomon's Song,* Vol 2 (Edinburgh: Thomas Turnbull, 1805), 18.

[133] Luther, Martin. *Luther's Works, Vol. 15: Ecclesiastes, Song of Solomon, and the Last Words of David* (St. Louis: Concordia Publishing House, 1971), 242.

(Acts 17:27). Jesus Christ is a light to lighten the Gentiles (Isa 49:6). When this great prophet came into the world, then did the day-spring from on high visit us (Lk 1:78). By nature, we are alienated from, and at enmity against God; Christ comes into the world to be an atoning sacrifice, making peace by the blood of his cross (Col 1:20). All the world, by nature, is in bondage and captivity to Satan, a miserable slavery. Christ comes with kingly power, to rescue sinners, as a prey from the mouth of the terrible one. Secondly, let the fullness of his offices be also considered, which make him able "to save to the uttermost, all that come to God by him" (Heb 7:25). The three offices, comprising in them all that our souls do need, become a universal relief to all our distresses. Thirdly, unspeakably comforting must the offices of Christ be to the souls of sinners. If light be pleasant to our eyes, how pleasant is that light of life springing from the Sun of right-eousness (Mal 4:2). If a pardon be sweet to a condemned crimi-nal, how sweet must the sprinkling the blood of Jesus be to the trembling conscience of a law-condemned sinner? If a rescue from a cruel tyrant is sweet to a poor captive, how sweet must it be to the ears of enslaved sinners, to hear the voice of liberty and deliverance proclaimed by Jesus Christ? Out of the several of-fices of Christ, as out of so many fountains, all the promises of the new covenant flow, as so many soul-refreshing streams of peace and joy. All the promises of illumination, counsel and di-rection flow out of Christ's prophetic office. All the promises of reconciliation, peace, pardon, and acceptance flow out of his priestly office, with the sweet streams of joy and spiritual com-forts which accompany it. All the promises of converting, in-creasing, defending, directing, and supplying grace, flow out of the kingly office of Christ; indeed, all promises may be reduced to these three offices, so that Jesus Christ must be altogether lovely in his offices."[134]

Is there anyone lovelier than our blessed Savior? We have been chosen in him before the foundation of the world (Eph 1:4). He has chosen us according to the good pleasure of his glorious grace.

---

[134] John Flavel. *The Whole Works of Mr. John Flavel*, Vol 1 (Glasgow: John Orr, 1754), 213-214.

CHARLES HADDON SPURGEON (1834-1892), "All that is in Christ is lovely, perfectly lovely. There is no point in our Lord Jesus that you could improve. Each virtue in our Lord is there in a state of absolute perfection: it could not be more fully developed. In each one of his people you will find something that is lovely—in one there is faith, in another abounding love; in one tenderness, in another courage, but you do not find all good things in any one saint—at least not all of them in full perfection; but you find all virtues in Jesus, and each one of them at its best. If you would take the best quality of one saint, and the best quality of another—yea, the best out of each and all the myriads of his people, you would find no grace or goodness among them all which Jesus does not possess in the fullest degree and in the highest perfection. He combines all the virtues, and gives them all a sweetness over and beyond themselves."[135]

THE BELOVED'S FRIENDSHIP (5:16C)

The Bride exclaims her delight in her Bridegroom's friendship with her. To connect so deeply is greater than even physical intimacy.

Song of Solomon 5:16c | This is my beloved and this is my friend, O daughters of Jerusalem.

Our Bridegroom has not called us slaves or servants, but friends. We share the most intimate things with him, and he reveals the hidden things to us. Dear friend of Christ, dear lover of Christ, do you share the heavenly delights with him in his Word and in prayer?

JAMES DURHAM (1622–1658): "She says, 'this is my friend.' All that he is means much to me. He is all the world to me, unspeakably excellent in himself, and very dear and precious to me, my husband, and my friend. In sum, my friendly husband, and my loving friend. Truly, there are many sweet relations that Christ stands in to the believer, as husband, friend, brother, etc. Christ fills all the relations that he stands in to his people, and that exceedingly well. He is a singularly loving, faithful, kind and tender husband. He is a singularly kind, faithful and unchangeable

---

[135] Spurgeon. *Pulpit,* Vol 24, Sermon 1446, "The Best Beloved" (1878), 661.

friend, the best friend that ever a believer had. For, the expression, 'this is my friend' means Christ has no equal. He is a matchless husband and friend. Christ and the believer are upon one side. They are friends. There is a league of friendship between them. They have common friends and common adversaries. Those who are Christ's friends may expect much from him, for this is no bare title. Christ never neglects any sweet relation. Believers should lean much to Christ, trust him, and expect good from him, as their friend. It's also an advantageous and singular consolation for folks to have Christ as their friend. It's comfortable in life, death, and judgment, in prosperity and adversity. It implies these ways Christ acts toward his friends – constant kindness and faithfulness at all times. He is a friend who loves at all times (Pro 17:17). He is a friend who never fails – a friend who sticks closer than a brother (Pro 18:24)."[136]

What a friend we have in Jesus! We can say: "This is my beloved and this is my friend, O daughters of Jerusalem" (5:16c). What greater friend can we have? God could give us no greater.

JOHN FLAVEL (1627–1691), "In giving Christ to die for poor sinners, God gave the richest jewel in his cabinet; a mercy of the greatest worth, and most inestimable value. Heaven itself is not so valuable and precious as Christ is! Ten thousand, thousand worlds—as many worlds as angels can number, would not outweigh Christ's love, excellency and sweetness! O what a lovely One! What an excellent, beautiful, ravishing One—is Christ! Put the beauty of ten thousand paradises, like the garden of Eden, into one; put all flowers, all smells, all colors, all tastes, all joys, all sweetness, all loveliness into one; O what a lovely and excellent thing would that be! And yet it should be less to that loveliest and dearest well-beloved Christ—than one drop of rain to all the seas, rivers, lakes, and fountains of ten thousand earths! Now, for God to bestow the mercy of mercies, the most precious thing in heaven or earth, upon poor sinners; and, as great, as lovely, as excellent as his Son was—what kind of love is this!"[137]

---

[136] James Durham. *Clavis Cantici*, 320.
[137] John Flavel. *The Whole Works of Mr. John Flavel*, Vol 1 (Glasgow: John Orr, 1754), 22.

Conclusion

A godly husband should mirror the love that Christ has for his church (Eph 5:25). A husband's love, though it is strong, is imperfect. The husband is to love his wife in a profound way. He is to love her as Christ loved his church and gave his life for her. He is to love her in a way that will help her to grow in her relationship with God. The husband is called to provide for his wife and cherish her. There will be times when he will fall short. He is not perfect. But he is to be constantly "looking unto Jesus" who is the true Head and Husband of the church.

The married couple needs to remember to have patience with each other. Just as Christ as our true Husband laid down his life for his Bride, and his Bride submitted herself to him, so married couples should reflect that great love and sacrifice for each other. That is why if you are married, you must not withhold your love from each other when you disappoint and fail one another. You must pledge to give your love to each other unconditionally. You must never make your love something that must be earned. It should always be freely given to each other. In the same way, there is nothing any of us can do to earn God's love. The Bible says: "by grace you have been saved through faith. And this is not your own doing; it is the gift of God,[9] not a result of works, so that no one may boast" (Eph 2:8-9). Trying to be good enough never impresses God. We could never be good enough. God's love is a free gift that he gives you when you surrender your whole life to his Son Jesus Christ. "He saved us, not because of works done by us in righteousness, but according to his own mercy, by the washing of regeneration and renewal of the Holy Spirit" (Titus 3:5). Let us look to our perfect Bridegroom and consider that "Christ loved us and gave himself up for us, a fragrant offering and sacrifice to God" (Eph 5:2).

9 | SONG 6:1-13

GROWING IN LOVE TOGETHER

I am my beloved's and my beloved is mine;
he grazes among the lilies.
SONG 6:3

Charles Haddon Spurgeon confessed his amazement at God's love: "Nothing binds me to my Lord like a strong belief in his changeless love. Thank God you have got a Father that can be angry, but that loves you as much when he is angry as when he smiles upon you."[138] God doesn't just give us a spare corner of his heart. The vast, entire, infinite, unfathomably loving heart of God belongs to you as God's born-again child.

Chapter 6 of Solomon's song begins with the bride searching for her beloved. She longs to find him. We learn most how much we love someone when we seem to have lost them.

GROWING IN UNITY (6:1-3)

How the bride loves Solomon. She cannot find him. Yet he has never stopped loving her. He has not forgotten about her. So God never forgets about us, no matter how distant he may seem. God describes

---

[138] Spurgeon. *Pulpit, Volume 35*, Sermon 2120, "The Security of Believers; or, Sheep Who Shall Never Perish" (London: Passmore & Alabaster, 1889), 685.

his nature as love (1 Jn 4:8). He declares his eternal disposition toward his covenant people, and through Christ, that includes you (Gal 3:29). "The Lord your God has chosen you to be a people for his treasured possession, out of all the peoples who are on the face of the earth. It was not because you were more in number than any other people that the Lord set his love on you and chose you, for you were the fewest of all peoples, but it is because the Lord loves you and is keeping the oath that he swore to your fathers.... Know therefore that the Lord your God is God, the faithful God who keeps covenant and steadfast love with those who love him" (Deut 7:6-9).

Searching for the Beloved

The bride is searching for her beloved. When the daughters of Jerusalem hear the description of her beloved, there's a desire in their hearts to help her find him. They express their desire to help her find her beloved.

Song of Solomon 6:1 | Where has your beloved gone, O fairest among women? Where has your beloved turned aside, that we may seek him with you?

They're saying, "He's so amazing, we want to know him, too. How can we find him?" There's such an impact on others around us when we speak of the loveliness of Christ and what he means to us. That impact may be on those who don't know Christ at all and those who are lost.

Christ has made you so beautiful and fair that others want to know him. You don't have to be a Bible scholar to be a good evangelist. You just need to know him. More and more you will know his Word. How much better it is to know him than just cold facts about him! But it's not just talking to lost people that makes an impact—it's the value and importance of talking with other believers about Christ. What happens when we do that? It strengthens our own faith, but it also stirs up in others their affection and their passion for him, and most important of all, it blesses the Lord when we praise him.

Finding the Beloved

Remember, the bride could not find Solomon earlier in chapter 5? But where is he? He is in their special place, their garden of love that he has prepared. She wants to be together with him!

Song of Solomon 6:2-3 | My beloved has gone down to his garden to the beds of spices, to graze in the gardens and to gather lilies. I am my beloved's and my beloved is mine; he grazes among the lilies.

She has found what her soul desires. What a joy to realize we can say, "I am his and he is mine!" She's acknowledging his presence! She's no longer enjoying him just because he's satisfying her and blessing her. She's now loving him, not for what he is to her, but for how she can bless him. There's a difference there. The Lord says to us, "You will seek me and find me, when you seek me with all your heart" (Jer 29:13).

Of course, God does give us good and gracious gifts that he wants us to enjoy: the sense of his presence, his peace, his joy—but he wants us to treasure him above what we merely *feel* about him. He is faithful and worthy to be praise, whether we feel his presence or not. What about the whole issue of feelings and emotions in our relationship with the Lord? Can I just remind us that feelings have very little to do with reality? Feelings aren't bad, necessarily. Now, if we let them run our lives, that's another thing. But we have to learn to walk by faith when we cannot feel him, and to trust when we cannot sense his presence. There will be spiritually dry seasons in our lives, times when we don't have these warm, great, tender feelings toward the Lord. Sometimes it's maybe because of our lack of responsiveness in the past, and he's wanting to woo our hearts, to realize how precious he is.

The bride finds her husband in their special garden, and she shouts, "I am my beloved's and my beloved is mine; he grazes among the lilies" (6:3). We can shout as well with the old hymn "Satisfied" –

> *Hallelujah! I have found him*
> *Whom my soul so long has craved!*
> *Jesus satisfies my longings;*
> *Through his life I now am saved.*[139]

GROWING IN IDENTITY (6:4-10)

Solomon is delighted to see his bride. He has never stopped loving her. Like Christ, he will never leave or forsake his bride. Solomon's description of his bride in 6:4-10 is an exercise in identity. A husband is

---

[139] Clara Tear Williams. "Satisfied", *Sacred Hymns and Tunes* (Syracuse, New York: A.W. Hall, 1897).

called to love and cherish his wife by reminding her of who she is in
God's eyes, and Solomon is a good example of this. She may feel unlovable or unworthy, but the way he describes her helps her to see who
she truly is in his eyes.

God helps us as well understand who we as believers are in the Bible. Theologians call this the indicative – what we are in Christ. We may
have remaining sin within us, but that is not our identity. Sometimes
the Bible's genre's

Christ loves you by working in you at least nine things. These things
are what make you who you are in him. He gives you your identity. This
is who you are in Christ. This is how he loves you. He loves you by iden-
tifying you with himself. The nine attributes that make up our identity
in Christ in this chapter are not found in ourselves, but found in Christ
through the Spirit.

In Christ You are Beautiful

Listen to how Solomon describes his bride upon their reunion.

Song of Solomon 6:4a | You are beautiful as Tirzah, my love, lovely
as Jerusalem.

You are God's delight. That's what Tirzah means – "delightful." Tirzah is the most naturally beautiful and delightful city of northern Israel,
an ancient garden city with natural beauty that would later briefly become the capital of the Northern Kingdom. Jerusalem is the capital of
all of Israel. In other words, no one can compare to this Bride. She is
beautiful. There is no one like the Bride of Christ. She is delightful to
God because he has fortified and established her in the grace and righteousness of his beloved Son.

> MARTIN LUTHER (1483-1546), "Tirzah was the seat of the
> kings of Israel. It is as if he were saying: 'My bride, you are as
> beautiful as Tirzah, a well-fortified city. And you are formed and
> established like Jerusalem with its excellent laws.' It is nothing
> less than a description of the complete confidence that the
> church, or the people, feels that all its works are exceedingly
> pleasing to God." [140]

---

[140] Luther, Martin. *Luther's Works, Vol. 15: Ecclesiastes, Song of Solomon, and the
Last Words of David* (St. Louis: Concordia Publishing House, 1971), 244.

In Christ, we are like Tirzah, naturally, inwardly beautiful. We have a new nature. We are Christ's masterpiece (Eph 2:10). We have everything we need to live godly in Christ – the Spirit indwelling us, a new nature, the Word of God, the church of Jesus. Everything we need! Christ has made us beautiful inside like Tirzah.

You might say, "I don't feel delightful to God!" That's because you might be looking upon your flesh. The Bible says, in our flesh there is "no good thing" (Rom 7:18). So you'll be looking in vain for something delightful there. What makes you beautiful is your union with Christ. You are a new creation in Christ. In and of ourselves we are not delightful. We are dead in sins (Eph 2:1-3). But in Christ, who loved you for eternal ages before you were born, you are beautiful as Tirzah, the delightful city. Christ's love cannot be discounted. Your beauty is great in the eyes of God the Father. To see the delight and beauty you are to God, you must look at Christ the craftsman. He has paid for you and has sent His Spirit within you to make you beautiful and delightful in the sight of God.

Jerusalem was a city which Solomon had built and beautified. It was the joy of the whole earth. He built within the Jerusalem walls the Holy Temple where God dwells. In this New Covenant time, you are beautiful because you are God's Temple (1 Cor 3:16). Your heart is the city, the dwelling place of our great King Jesus. Your heart is like a burning bush, like Jacob's ladder, for Jesus, the Way, the Truth and the Life dwells in you. Your heart is his dwelling place. This is why you are so beautiful to him.

And so it is, like Jerusalem, God is building us, and we are outwardly beautiful. Of course, we are not completed yet. We are like a construction site with many things still left undone. But dearly beloved, you are in Christ and becoming more and more like him every day! You are part of Christ's gospel-church which Paul says is the Jerusalem that is above (Gal 4:26), the heavenly Jerusalem. When you come to your forever family, this assembly of saints, "you have come to Mount Zion and to the city of the living God, the heavenly Jerusalem" (Heb 12:22-24).

You can't do anything to make him love you less. You can't do anything to make him love you more. You cannot be more darling to him. You are his bride. He doesn't simply love you. You are darling to him, and you will always be darling to him, always, because he has done a work so that it will always be so. He has made you his darling. His own work is solid and strong and permanent and eternal, immutable. It will not change. He is always there loving you. He has always loved you. "I have loved you with an everlasting love" (Jer. 31:3). He is always there watching over you, desiring you, loving you. It will never change, never.

Why is the bride so beautiful? Remember the previous praise of Solomon to his bride: "You have captivated my heart, my sister, my bride; you have captivated my heart with one glance of your eyes, with one jewel of your necklace. How beautiful is your love, my sister, my bride" (4:9). The bride is so intensely beautiful – she makes Solomon's heart beat faster. Who gave her those jewels? Who made her beautiful love to flourish? "We love him because he first loved us" (1 Jn 4:19, KJV).

You say, "I don't feel beautiful!" What did Solomon say in Ecclesiastes 3:11? – "He has made everything beautiful in its time." In God's time, you'll grow into the beauty of Christ-like maturity. But now, consider that Ephesians says, you are seated with Christ in the heavenly places (Eph. 2:6). When God regenerated you, he raised you up and seated you with Christ. Right now, if you are in Christ, you are seated enthroned next to Jesus. Now Christ is not going to have a hag for a queen. You are beautiful in his sight.

But you say, "I still don't feel beautiful. The old life is such a temptation." To that you can say, "I have been crucified with Christ. It is no longer I who live, but Christ who lives in me" (Gal 2:20). And Christ is beautiful, isn't he? You say, I don't look like Christ. I'm not beautiful like he is. Ah, but there is a day coming when we shall be transformed completely. "Beloved, we are God's children now, and what we will be has not yet appeared; but we know that when he appears, we shall be like him, because we shall see him as he is. when he appears, we shall be like him, for we shall see him as he is" (1 Jn 3:2). You see your sanctification is not yet completed (Phil 1:6). You are in process. You are not there yet. But that great day is coming when how Christ sees you and how you see yourself will match. What you see is an unfinished masterpiece. In his eyes, because he sees outside of time, you are already "as beautiful as Tirzah, as lovely as Jerusalem" (6:4a).

In Christ You are Awesome

Solomon begins to speak to his bride in military terms: awesome like an army. Why would he do that?

Song of Solomon 6:4b | You are... awesome as an army with banners.

This girl inspires admiration mixed with dread. The idea is that the bride is splendid to look upon. Her beauty is so to be admired that it is dangerous. She can destroy the enemy's power with a glance. Do you realize you are dangerous? Just as you would see an army with banner coming to cease you and run away, so powerful is this bride.

The beauty of the Bride of Christ is dreadfully wonderful. The love of Christ constrains or grips us (2 Cor 5:14). The love of Christ is our armor. If you think of the armor of God in Ephesians 6, it is all girded by the presence of God: the shield of faith, the breastplate of righteousness, the belt of truth, the helmet of salvation, the shoes of the Gospel of peace, and the sword of the Spirit. If you think about it, we could just as easily say, be clothed with the Lord Jesus Christ (Rom 13:14). You are arrayed with power, "awesome as an army with banners" (6:4). One commentator paraphrased this:

> *Avert your tantalizing eyes,*
> *Your gaze which threatens danger.*
> *Your awesome beauty has the power*
> *To charm the depths of deep desire,*
> *To light the fire of yearning strong*
> *That drains me of all strength.*
> *A helpless victim I am left,*
> *A slave of beauty's mercy,*
> *Weak captive of magnificence.*[141]

The saints of God have awesome power. Like Jacob, we are re-named Israel. We are no longer deceivers (as Jacob's name means) but we are now called Israel, which means "prevailer with God." You have awesome power. Christ's banner over us is love. What army uses love as a weapon? God's heavenly army. It is the power of Christ's love that melts the hearts of rebel sinners.

In Christ You are Desired

The king cannot take the amazing beauty of his bride. Listen to him trying to expressed how he is overwhelmed at her attractiveness.

---

[141] Tom Gledhill. *The Message of the Song of Songs* (Downers Grove, IL: InterVarsity, 1994), 192.

Song of Solomon 6:5a | Turn away your eyes from me, for they overwhelm me.

In an even greater way, your King Jesus has made you beautiful and desired. You are accepted in the Beloved One (Eph 1:6). He is not a God who merely tolerates you. I pray you never hear that peached by any Gospel preacher. God is the God who tolerates you because he has to, the God who tolerates you because of the blood. No. We preach of the God who loves you, the God who desires you, the God who yearns for you. He is overwhelmed by you. This is why we can approach him with gladness and boldness in prayer. "The Lord rejoices over you with gladness, he quiets you with his love, and he delights in you with shouts of loud singing" (Zeph 3:17).

In Christ You are Covered

Solomon continues and speaks of his beloved's covering.

Song of Solomon 6:5b | Your hair is like a flock of goats leaping down the slopes of Gilead.

St. Paul says that a woman's glory is her hair because it covers her. Can I remind you of your beauty as the Church of Jesus Christ? You are covered in the beautiful life and righteousness of Christ. There is no shame or guilt that can be used against you (Rom 8:1). You are justified. You are covered with Christ's righteousness. His holy life is applied to your account. Luther called this an "alien righteousness." The passage from Romans 1 began the Protestant Reformation.

> For I am not ashamed of the gospel, for it is the power of God for salvation to everyone who believes, to the Jew first and also to the Greek. For in it the righteousness of God is revealed from faith for faith, as it is written, 'The righteous shall live by faith. —Romans 1:16-17

These verses confounded Martin Luther in 1517. Luther began to understand that what Paul was speaking of here was a righteousness that God in his grace was making available to those who would receive it passively, for no one could achieve "the righteousness of God" actively. They would receive it by faith, by which a person could be reconciled to a holy and righteous God.

The word *righteousness* which could also be translated "justification". It means to "count as righteous." In other words, the righteousness that makes me just before God is not my own. To Luther it was the righteousness of another applied to a rebel – an "alien righteousness" indeed. I need it. It is the righteousness that God counts toward me when I place my faith in Christ.

Aren't you glad that you are counted righteous in Christ? Paul says it so clearly in his testimony to the Philippian church.

> Indeed, I count everything as loss because of the surpassing worth of knowing Christ Jesus my Lord. For his sake I have suffered the loss of all things and count them as rubbish, in order that I may gain Christ and be found in him, not having a righteousness of my own that comes from the law, but that which comes through faith in Christ, the righteousness from God that depends on faith— that I may know him and the power of his resurrection, and may share his sufferings, becoming like him in his death. —Philippians 3:8-10

In Christ You are Hungry

In Christ you have a new hunger – and Jesus says your teeth are beautiful!

Song of Solomon 6:6 | Your teeth are like a flock of ewes that have come up from the washing; all of them bear twins; not one among them has lost its young.

Because we have a new heart, we have a new appetite (Eze 36:25-27). We hunger and thirst for righteousness (Mt 5:6). People with crooked, rotten teeth cannot digest food – they can't chew it. When you were lost you had spiritually messed up teeth! You choked on the Gospel of Jesus. Now you devour good, spiritual meat. You have a new nature. You are now hungry for the Word of God. You have a new appetite because you have a transformed heart that hungers for God. Your spiritual teeth are clean and pure and even. They are all in order – none of them are lost. The Spirit of God has given you a new appetite. You now desire the sincere and "pure milk of the Word" like a newborn baby (1 Pet 2:2).

In Christ You are Happy

Song of Solomon 6:7 | Your cheeks are like halves of a pomegranate behind your veil.

Your joy is fulfilled in Christ. He wants to fill you with all the fullness of God. It is in Christ we find true wholeness and happiness. Paul says, "Rejoice in the Lord…" Sometimes? When things go well for you? No! "Rejoice in the Lord always," and in case you forget, he says, "again I say: Rejoice!" Christ gives us joyful cheeks that find contentment in him! Your name is written in the Lamb's book of life! You are not yet what you shall be, but you will soon be completely whole

We are much like Jesus' disciples. They loved having the power to do miracles. Jesus said – don't be delighted that you can call down fire from heaven or raise the dead. Rejoice because your names are written down in the Book of Life. We have a tendency to rejoice in the Bridegroom's gifts, instead of in the Bridegroom himself.

God gives us plenty of gifts that are joyful. But our gifts are not our gods. We must never make them gods. They weren't meant to be a final means of happiness. God's gifts cannot save us, redeem us, or transform us into Christlikeness. Only Jesus by his Spirit can do that. Be happy! Let your joy be full in Christ. Let those "cheeks…. like… pomegranate" be high in a bursting smile!

In Christ You are Unique

Song of Solomon 6:8 | There are sixty queens and eighty concubines, and virgins without number.

But he calls you "my dove, my perfect one, is the only one" (6:9a). There is no one that is loved more than the Bride of Christ. She has her place above all others in this world. We all have different gifts and abilities to complete the Bride of Christ, but more important than the sixty queens or concubines that a pagan king might have – the Bride of Christ is far more important and unique than 10,000 others because of the gifts Christ gives to his church.

Did you know you are a gift that Christ has given to his Church? You are unique. You are loved. You are carefully placed in the Body of Christ to serve all. "Now you are the body of Christ and individually members of it" (1 Cor 12:27). Ephesians 4:11-12 says that you are each given a ministry to do in the Body of Christ. God has gifted you specially to fulfill it.

In Christ You are Prized

Song of Solomon 6:9 | My dove, my perfect one, is the only one, the only one of her mother, pure to her who bore her. The young women saw her and called her blessed; the queens and concubines also, and they praised her.

In Christ's eyes, you are his dove, his perfect one. In Christ's eyes, you are prized, as if you were the only one of your mother. What more could you ask for? You are prized in God's eyes!

The pagan kings had hundreds of queens and concubines, and yet Mrs. Solomon outshined them all. Compared to all the young women of Jerusalem, yea of the world, this Bride is blessed! What greater blessing than to be unified with Christ? "He who did not spare his own Son, but delivered him over for us all, how will he not also with him freely give us all things?" (Rom 8:32). You have every spiritual blessing in Christ in the heavenly places (Eph 1:3). God spares nothing for you. He holds nothing back. You are the apple of his eye. He says literally you are the "little maiden" of his eye (Zech 2:8). That means you are so close to God you see your own reflection.

In Christ You are Radiant

Song of Solomon 6:10 | Who is this who looks down like the dawn, beautiful as the moon, bright as the sun, awesome as an army with banners?

We have the radiance of the dawn, bright as the sun, but the secret is that we shine with the beauty of the moon. Our radiant beauty is like the moon who reflects the glory of the sun. Our radiance is the radiance of Christ. That radiance is so fierce, it's awesome, like an army on a mission. The beauty of Christ is so fearsome that it slays men and women of wanting anything but Christ. His beauty is so fierce that people give up all they have to know him.

GROWING IN CHARITY (6:11-13)

Sometimes we wander away from the Lord thinking he has left us. But he never will leave you or forsake you (Heb 13:5). We find here that

Solomon has been waiting for his bride the whole time in the extravagant nut garden that the queen designed herself. How surprised she is to find her dear husband in their special meeting place.

Song of Solomon 6:11 | I went down to the nut orchard to look at the blossoms of the valley, to see whether the vines had budded, whether the pomegranates were in bloom.

Like the vines in her special garden, her marriage was bearing fruit from following God's way of handling conflict. Though for a night her marriage was a cold, dark winter, it is springtime again. And Solomon has a some very encouraging words for her.

Grow in Love by Giving Honor

The Shulamite queen testifies that she feels cherished by the king.

Song of Solomon 6:12 | Before I was aware, my desire [*Solomon*] set me among the chariots of my kinsman, a prince.

She's caught up in joy—she's been treated like the queen she is, and she feels cherished and honored. "All of a sudden, she is placed in the king's royal chariot, doubtless the first of his fleet, and she finds herself racing along at his side before all the people. It is a public display of total reconciliation. They are together again, and a new spring has begun."[142] Life is too short to focus on the negatives. This couple is squarely focused on the joys of marriage! So it is that though we Christians at times wander from our Lord, he has never stopped loving us.

Before she knew it, she went as fast as a flying chariot to her beloved's garden. She is no longer burned out and scorched. She is now a woman who is growing as a woman and growing and maturing in her marriage. She has an eagerness to grow in her love with her beloved.

Grow in Love by Glorying in God's Work

The women of the royal court look on in wonder and cry out to the new queen, remembering that she was not long ago a simple Shulamite farm girl. Yet now her glory as a queen is dazzling to look upon. The ladies of the court shout with joy.

---

[142] Carson, D. A. *New Bible Commentary: 21st Century Edition.* Rev. ed. of: The New Bible Commentary. 3rd ed. / edited by D. Guthrie, J.A. Motyer (4th ed.) (Downers Grove, IL: Inter-Varsity Press, 1970), So 6:11.

Song of Solomon 6:13a | Return, return, O Shulamite, return, return, that we may look upon you.

The palace women call after her as she flies by in the chariot, wanting to see again the look on her face that speaks volumes about the joy of a restored relationship. But she so busy with her King she cannot stop. Yet her transformation is so breathtaking, the king's court desires the queen to return so they may glance upon her one more time. Though not directly mentioned in the text, we must notice the providence of God to put her in such a postion. We can all say "glory to God, great things he has done"!

Christ's display of affection for you is so great that others want to look upon you! John said in Revelation 21:2, "And I saw the holy city, new Jerusalem, coming down out of heaven from God, prepared as a bride adorned for her husband." The whole world at that time will want to see the Bride. All the angel armies. Those who will be judged, who fight against the Lamb will see and deeply admire the Bride of Christ. And when they see the glorious Church without spot or wrinkle, all will have to bow their knee to Christ and say, "All glory to the Father, Son and Holy Spirit!"

Grow in Love by Enjoying Oneness

King Solomon sees the excitement and responds.

Song of Solomon 6:13b | Why should you look upon the Shulamite, as upon a dance before two armies?

This is a comment from the king. Looking upon his wife is just like the excitement of watching a lively, exuberant victory dance where the war has been one between two armies. The two sides have signed the peace treaty, and now they should celebrate. They have been reconciled. They are no longer "two armies" against each other, but one. Solomon says, in essence, "She's mine for me to behold. She doesn't belong to the world, but to me."

Marriage is the bringing together of two very different people in to one. That is something that God "joins together." We ought always celebrate that God is the author of marriage. He creates each marriage to picture the love between Christ and his bride. So Christ died for our sins and reconciled us to God. We are now riding in our Lord's victory chariot. Christ has a victory parade for us. "But thanks be to God, who

in Christ always leads us in triumphal procession, and through us
spreads the fragrance of the knowledge of him everywhere. For we are
the aroma of Christ to God among those who are being saved and
among those who are perishing, to one a fragrance from death to death,
to the other a fragrance from life to life" (2 Cor 2:14-16).

And yet, salvation is of the Lord and for the Lord. Our redeemed
lives are by the glory of his grace and for his good pleasure. Salvation is
not mainly about me, but about God.

Conclusion

Whether you are married or single, if you have unresolved conflict
in your life, you are not right with God. You need to be tenderhearted
and seek to be the first to reconcile. You cannot worship God if you have
not dealt with sin and misunderstandings in your life. Set your gift
down, that is before the next worship service, get things right. Settle the
conflict in a godly way. There is great joy and long-term stability if you
will seek selfless giving instead of selfishness. Following God's path to
restoration in conflict is one of God's primary tools to make us like
Christ.

10 |SONG 7:1-13

GROWING OLD TOGETHER

I am my beloved's, and his desire is for me.
SONG 7:10

The world sees marriage kind of like "As the World Turns." You fall in love. You have a passionate honeymoon. And then you bear with or exist with one another. You put up with one another until Mr. or Ms. Perfect comes along, and then you "find happiness" with someone else. What a sad and selfish state marriage is in today. When you ask someone how long they have been married, it is rare to hear 40, 50 or 60 years. But God designed marriage to endure to the end. If you are married, he wants you to grow old together in true, deep happiness centered around him. Till death do you part. "What God has joined together, let not man separate."

God's design for marriage is very happy, thrilling pathway. Dissatisfaction in marriage is not God's plan. God designed marriage be deeply satisfying and to last a lifetime. If we follow God's way, we will find that marriages need to mature and deepen. The harvest of a godly marriage is unimaginably amazing.

God designed marriage to get deeper and happier as each day goes by. Your marriage is exactly what you put into it. If you are dissatisfied with your marriage, you need to look in the mirror. We reap what we sow. Can I ask you, what are you putting into your marriage?

Married people, if you want to grow old together with your spouse, listen up. Single people, you might be married one day soon. You might not believe me, but you need to pay attention to the wisdom of Solomon. The love and security that King Solomon gives his wife is an example that all married men ought to attain to.

MATURING IN BEAUTY (7:1-6)

Solomon looks at his bride, and the text seems to indicate it is several years after the honeymoon. He notices every part of her, from head to feet. "How beautiful and pleasant you are," he says (7:6). He admires every part of his bride.

Her Royal Feet

He says to her something he might not have noticed when he was courting her. He admires her feet.

Song of Solomon 7:1a | How beautiful are your feet in sandals.

The commentators picture King Solomon upon his knees before his wife, humbly unlatching her sandals. Several times a day I tell my wife I love her. It's a way for me to get bow down in my spirit and say, "God has favored me with you." I tell my wife constantly, "I'm not worthy to have you. I don't deserve you. Thanks for putting up with me—I know I'm hard to live with." She needs to hear this. She needs to know that you appreciate every part of her—even her feet! You are favored by the least things about her. Most women are not going to boast about their feet. But Solomon notices this farm girl's feet.

On the honeymoon in chapter three he noticed her face, her eyes, her cheeks, and her lips. Now he notices everything about her. Even the little things. Solomon's intimate knowledge of his wife has deepened. He cares about every part of her. He loves her from the crown of her head to the sole of her feet, and he tells her.

Married men, your wife wants you to notice her. Ladies long for that special attention. They long for appreciation. If you are not appreciating your wife, then it's not wonder she's lost that twinkle in her eye. If you've stopped pursuing her and telling her how sweet and beautiful she is, then you are not planting what you ought to plant in marriage. If you plant seeds of selfless admiration in your marriage, you will reap a harvest of holy happiness in your marriage. Do you appreciate something in your spouse? When's the last time you told her? I want to grow old together with my wife appreciating every little thing about her!

Though the others regard her as a mere "camp dancer" (6:13b), Solomon considers her his royal princess. She is like a prince's daughter. Certainly she didn't "feel" like a prince's daughter. Her family was messed up. She said, "My own vineyard I have not kept." And so it is that we do not "feel" like the children of God always. "and if children, then heirs—heirs of God and fellow heirs with Christ..." Our sandals are royal, are they not? You are to be doing the King's business. You are to go where he sends you! Once we were degenerate, "from the sole of the foot even unto the head" (Isa. 1:6), but now we are transformed from our feet to our head – we are "complete in Christ" (Col. 2:10). We are new creations! We are no longer what we once were!

The peasant princess's feet are dignified and royal. She is beautiful inside and out. Her feet tell that story. Where do your feet take you? Dear child of God, there is so much trouble in this world. Do your feet take you to the attractions of the "vanity fair" in this world? Or perhaps they take you to far away to isolate yourself in fear or depression of raging anger. Where do your feet take you? Or do your feet take you to serve the saints? Do you serve Christ's Bride? Or perhaps your feet take you to spread the good news to the lost. "How beautiful upon the mountains are the feet of him who brings good news, who publishes peace, who brings good news of happiness, who publishes salvation, who says to Zion, 'Your God reigns'" (Isa 52:7). Perhaps your feet take you to a prayer closet where you bow before the God of glory and bring the sweet incense of prayer and petition and supplication.

We are called to "keep in step with the Spirit" (Gal 5:25). If you are growing in Christ, you will be keeping in step with the Spirit of God. Are you open to his moving and leading? Are you willing to pray right now – "Lord show me the dark pathways I've been on. Clean me up. I need to see." "Your word is a lamp to my feet and a light to my path" (Psa 119:105). "Thy word have I hid [or, *treasured*] in my heart that I might not sin against thee" (Psa 119:11). Will you pray, "God give me royal feet?"

Her Noble Name

Solomon calls his wife, years after the honeymoon by a name of deep honor.

Song of Solomon 7:1b | O noble daughter!

She was not a daughter of nobility, and yet Solomon calls her that. He makes her feel special.

- If you read in chapters 1 and 2, early on he speaks of her as:
- "most beautiful among women" (1:8)
- "my love" (1:15)
- "a lily among brambles" (2:2)
- "my beautiful one" (2:10)
- "my dove" (2:14)
- By chapters 5 and 6, his favorite name for her is: "my perfect one" (5:2, 6:9)

And now in chapter 7 Solomon calls this farm girl, "noble daughter"—he's calling her the daughter of a king. Was she a daughter of a king? No, but he made her feel like one! This woman gets great esteem from the way King Solomon sees her. Remember in chapter 1, she was greatly concerned about her looks. Now she's secure in them. She's not royal. She's not the right stock. But Solomon makes her feel like she is: "O noble daughter" (7:1b).

Is there "good name calling" going on in your house. Maybe you call her "sweetheart" or "honey." Maybe you have a special name that only your spouse knows. Be careful to call each other sweet names. That will deepen your commitment in marriage. I want to grow old together with my wife recognizing how precious she is to me. What is described next is the bride's body. This is marital romance. It is holy and beautiful in marriage. It is forbidden and ultimately unsatisfying if trampled on outside marriage. It is so dignified and mysterious how the Lord presents this love relationship in the Word of God. We must always speak discretely and respectfully on these subjects, for they ultimately point to our relationship with Christ.

Her Jeweled Joints

Solomon looks upon his bride, admiring her form.

Song of Solomon 7:1c | Your rounded thighs are like jewels, the work of a master hand.

The idea here is that her joints are like jewels. The joints of her thighs and legs are like those hammered out by a master jewel crafter.

Today we have laser cut diamonds in order for them to be perfect. The joints of the church are "fitly joined together" (Eph. 4:16). We are fitted like jewels in the Body of Christ. We are to be edifying each other by being in the right place – with our "jeweled joints." It's so vital to be where God wants you to be. Are you serving where God wants you to serve? Are you right where he wants you to be? Are you born again? Are you saved? Pray with me, "Spirit of God, move me to here you want me to be in the Body of Christ. I'm willing! I'll do whatever you want me to do. I want to be a 'jeweled joint' in the Body of Christ."

Her Healthy Navel

Song of Solomon 7:2a | Your navel is a rounded bowl that never lacks mixed wine.

This woman brings great joy to her husband, a joy that is compared to drinking mixed wine. The Bible condemns drunkenness but most people in the ancient world drank wine on a daily basis. The joy of the Lord in a godly marriage is better than wine, even than mixed wine, which has more strength. This was a healthy woman who lacked for nothing. Her navel was like a rounded glass or goblet that never lacked wine.

This wife was to her husband like a cup of rich wine, filled with flavor and prosperity, just like David's cup that ran over (Psa 23:5). Her navel was rounded and well-shaped, which is a sign of the best medical care in the ancient world. This is a woman that has had the blessing of God upon her since before she was born.

The navel is what connected us to the supply of our mother when we were in the womb. The fear of the Lord is said to be health to the navel (Pro 3:8). The Christian's soul is filled with the fear of the Lord, like a navel filled with strong and rich wine.

In a healthy marriage, you must drink the rich wine of the Spirit through the Word of God. "Do not get drunk with wine, for that is debauchery, but be filled with the Spirit, addressing one another in psalms and hymns and spiritual songs, singing and making melody to the Lord with your heart, giving thanks always and for everything to God the Father in the name of our Lord Jesus Christ, submitting to one another out of reverence for Christ" (Eph 5:18-21).

Her Child-Bearing Belly

Solomon extols his bride in a most peculiar way to modern hearers.

Song of Solomon 7:2b | Your belly is a heap of wheat, encircled with lilies.

Today, if you say that to your wife, that's enough to get the cold shoulder for a while! The comparison of her belly to wheat may allude to the color of her skin, but it also implies that she is awaiting the birth of a child.[143] She is now big, bearing Solomon a little one. Lilies represent life. By the metaphoric description, she clearly has a baby on the way!

Realize that she's not as young anymore. Children are coming. Solomon tells his wife that she is a work of art, like she's been made by a master craftsman. The queen's form has certainly changed since her honeymoon, but Solomon is sincerely satisfied with his wife's changing figure.

What is beautiful has changed in the modern era. Many of the women posing for magazines today are dying of anorexia. They are malnourished. The look of starvation and malnutrition is sadly in vogue today. Married men, your wife needs to know you love her just the way she is. She is God's gift to you. All women are different, but God crafted her just for you. Solomon tells his wife that she is a work of art. She looks like she's been made by a master craftsman. Now realize that she's not as young. By the description, she may have had a baby or two.

Married men, do not ever insult your wife's appearance. Don't' be immature. Men, you try having three kids, maintain the house, care for your needs—and you're never allowed to get sick. You ought to be attracted to your wife's appearance and let her know how secure you are in her love. By the way, women are very sensitive about their appearance. Her goal in life is not to compete with the Hollywood divas. Her goal is to raise children for Christ and to be a helper for you. God made your wife just for you. Appreciate God's masterpiece!

Solomon is sincerely excited by his wife's new form, and he's not looking elsewhere. A married woman is not going to look like she stepped out of a swimsuit magazine. Why? Because—God has a totally different measure for beauty. I hope you get your value of beauty from

---

[143] Song of Solomon 7:1-13 (Proverbs, Ecclesiastes, Song of Songs (NAC)

the Bible and not from the trash in Sports Illustrated. Having lots of babies and raising them in godliness is attractive to God. Caring for the home and for her husband is attractive to God. Why are so many who profess Christ getting their values from Sodom and Gomorrah? Married men, are you sincerely satisfied with your wife's beauty? Do you tell her often how beautiful your wife is? She needs to hear it. Romance is a 24/7 engagement.

Everything changes when little one's come. First of all, life gets messy! Diapers. You gotta feed 'em. You gotta cloth them. They are work. Did I mention diapers. Oh, those diapers! They're messy. Do you want little ones? Are you ready for little ones in Christ? They are high maintenance. Solomon compares his beautiful bride to the harvest of wine and wheat.

"Your navel... never lacks mixed wine...Your belly is a heap of wheat" (7:2). Wheat was the Spring harvest (early June) and grapes were the Autumn harvest (late September).[144] Solomon says, I am encouraged and enriched by my wife's form. Her body is changing, and this harvest of children in our home is a gift from God, like wine and wheat. If you are a married man, thank the Lord for your wife. "House and wealth are inherited from fathers, but a prudent wife is from the LORD" (Pro 19:14).

Her Child-Feeding Breasts

The queen is now a mother, and she's not just interested in getting what she needs, but also in giving to her children, in giving benefit to others. That's a sign of spiritual maturity. Solomon admires her form again.

Song of Solomon 7:3 | Your two breasts are like two fawns, twins of a gazelle.

This is exactly what he said to her their wedding night. He's as happy with her as he was on their wedding day. He is still excited and happy with her, though her body and her schedule has changed. She is likely exhausted at times because of her duty to nurture the children, but her husband loves her just the same.

Do you know that little ones get hungry? So it is with babes in Christ. They desire the "sincere milk of the word that they may grow

---

[144] ISBE, "harvest".

thereby" (1 Pet 2:2, KJV). Are you ready to feed those new believers in Christ?

Solomon's wife is now capable of supplying and satisfying the hunger of others. It's not "gimme, gimme, gimme." A baby does that, right? "Waaah, feed me!" That's a sign of immaturity. It's okay to be immature if you're a baby, but the problem is, so many of our churches are at times just like big grown-up nurseries.

"Waaah, feed me! Tend to me, change me, fix me, touch me, help me." It's all me, me, me. The sign that we're seeing a mature love here is that here is a bride who is capable of giving, blessing, supporting others, encouraging others. As Christ fills and satisfies us with himself, then he wants to flow through us to minister grace and supply and satisfaction to others. As believers, we are all to grow up to be spiritual mothers. We are to get fully equipped by the ministry of the Word and Spirit to do the work of ministry (Eph 4:11-12).

Her Priceless Neck

Song of Solomon 7:4a | Your neck is like an ivory tower.

The groom had before compared the neck of his bride to the tower of David (4:4), but now compares her to a tower of ivory. There is no such thing as an ivory tower. It does not exist. It would be beyond what could be paid for. He is saying "You are priceless to me!" I could lose my home, my job, everything. But I could not imagine ever living without my wife. The thing about the neck is that you can't see it without a mirror. It is also true that you cannot see your position in Christ without the mirror of God's Word. We must always be reminding ourselves who we are in Christ.

> JOHN COTTON (1585-1652), "The neck is the faith of the church, joining Christ and his church together, as the neck joins the head and the body."[145]

The ivory in the tower pictures the bride's purity and brightness. Consider the glorious beauty of graces that are ours in Christ. The neck connects the head to the body. We are connected to Christ legally

---

[145] John Cotton. *A Brief Exposition of the Whole Book of Canticles, or Song of Solomon* (London, Philip Nevil, 1642), 211.

through justification and spiritually through regeneration. Justification means that because of Christ, we as sinners are declared to be righteous persons before a holy God. He's paid it all! You are priceless.

The grace of regeneration – the spiritual re-birth of the sinner to become a child of God – is all yours. You have received the Spirit of God – the same Spirit that raised Jesus from the dead, and now you are seated in the heavenly places, higher than any tower that could ever be built.

Her Peaceful Eyes

Song of Solomon 7:4b | Your eyes are pools in Heshbon, by the gate of Bath-rabbim.

The pools of Heshbon were an oasis. It is like saying, "Your eyes are like the oceans that surround Hawaii." Your eyes are a window to the soul. You are no longer at war with God in your soul. You are at peace. Christ has torn down the walls of hostility in your heart. He has united you and reconciled you with himself.

Her Loyal Nose

Song of Solomon 7:4c | Your nose is like a tower of Lebanon, which looks toward Damascus.

There was a tower in Lebanon that protected Israel from Syria (1 Kings 9:19). Solomon felt secure with his wife. Wherever her nose pointed, whoever she was talking to, she defended her husband's honor. She had a very loyal nose!

Christians have a loyal nose. Wherever they are, they boldly proclaim that Jesus Christ is Lord. Do you defend the honor of the Lord? Do you praise him? Do you extol him? When was the last time you boldly proclaimed the Lord's glory to an unbeliever? Do you have a desire to be on the lookout for those who are God's enemies, that he might transform them and bring them into his Kingdom?

Her Fruitful Head

Song of Solomon 7:5a | Your head crowns you like Carmel.

Carmel means "garden." It's the ridge above Jerusalem, and it is beautiful and fruitful. It is your head that gives you strength. We are more than conquerors (Rom 8:37). A believer's head is always lifted up over his enemies (Psa 27:6). We always overcome (Rev 21:7). "Have you not known? Have you not heard? The Lord is the everlasting God, the Creator of the ends of the earth. He does not faint or grow weary; his understanding is unsearchable. He gives power to the faint, and to him who has no might he increases strength. Even youths shall faint and be weary, and young men shall fall exhausted; but they who wait for the Lord shall renew their strength; they shall mount up with wings like eagles; they shall run and not be weary; they shall walk and not faint" (Isa 40:28-31).

It is in Christ that you are a garden! In Christ, you are fruitful. You cannot bear fruit without him. "I am the true vine, and my Father is the vinedresser. Every branch in me that does not bear fruit he takes away, and every branch that does bear fruit he prunes, that it may bear more fruit. Already you are clean because of the word that I have spoken to you. Abide in me, and I in you. As the branch cannot bear fruit by itself, unless it abides in the vine, neither can you, unless you abide in me. I am the vine; you are the branches. Whoever abides in me and I in him, he it is that bears much fruit, for apart from me you can do nothing (Jn 15:1-5).

Her Captivating Hair

Song of Solomon 7:5b | Your flowing locks are like purple; a king
is held captive in the tresses.

Solomon was the sovereign of Israel, but he was a slave to his wife's beauty, held captive by the tresses of her hair. The Lord is sovereign, but he chooses to use us in the advancement of his Kingdom. He chooses to become like a slave, a servant, a mere human to rescue us. He is God who became low because of his great love for his bride. We can say the Lord is held captive in the tresses of the church. He loves her. He uses her to carry his kingdom forward. He is using you. He is held captive by your tresses. He doesn't have to, but he wants to. He is your sovereign, but he chooses to use you.

My wife Jill is my crown. I can say that I would not be where I am today without her. I am held captive by her tresses, socially, emotionally, and spiritually. Men, if your wife is not your crown, you are missing out.

Her Pleasant Delights

Song of Solomon 7:6 | How beautiful and pleasant you are, O loved one, with all your delights.

For Solomon, the once worn and weary farm girl from the tribe of Dan is now all delightful to him. Her looks and life ravish his heart. Whatever ugliness she felt when she was alone and single is now washed away with the affirming love of her Beloved. She had neglected herself in times past. Without father or mother, she was destitute, alone, and forsaken with no pleasantness or delights. She said of her brothers, "they made me keeper of the vineyards, but my own vineyard I have not kept" (1:6b). But now she is Solomon's queen. Now she is delightful and pleasant. No longer is she worn and weary, but beautiful and loved beyond measure. She now brings infinite delights to her king.

We too were once destitute and ugly, dead in trespasses and sins (Eph 2:1-3). But now we ravish the heart of God and bring him infinite delights. Every delight that proceeds from us comes from our union with Christ. We are his "new creation," "God's workmanship created in Christ Jesus unto good works" (2 Cor 5:17; Eph 2:10). We were "brought forth" by Word of truth, by the Father of lights (Jas 1:17-18; *cf* Rom 10:17). There are so many delights. Every spiritual blessing in God's heavenly realm are ours (Eph 1:3). We are renewed and birthed by the Spirit. Now, can it be? We bring delight to the heart of our heavenly Father. "The steps of a good man are ordered by the Lord, and he delights in his way. Though he fall, he shall not be utterly cast down; for the Lord upholds him with his hand (Psa 37:23-24). God now delights in you. Even when you fall, God guarantees it will not be permanent, because the Lord upholds you with his power.

Dear ones in Christ, you want the kind of beauty that can last and increase as you age, unlike mere physical beauty. For physical beauty, the only way is down. There are only so many surgeries; there is only so much you can do. We are all deteriorating. As we get older, that outward person is decaying; it's deteriorating. But Paul says, "though the outward man perish, the inward man is being renewed day by day" (2 Cor 4:16).

MATURING IN STRENGTH (7:7-9A)

Song of Solomon 7:7-9a | Your stature is like a palm tree, and your breasts are like its clusters. I say I will climb the palm tree and lay hold of its fruit. Oh may your breasts be like clusters of the vine, and the scent of your breath like apples, and your mouth like the best wine.

Solomon says to queen, "This stature of yours is like a palm tree." This description of her speaks of maturity, beauty, and fruitfulness. There is freedom in holy matrimony. Paul tells us that the woman's body belongs to her husband and the man's body belongs to his wife. "For the wife does not have authority over her own body, but the husband does. Likewise the husband does not have authority over his own body, but the wife does" (1 Cor 7:4). This, of course, does not mean either spouse can demand whatever or whenever they want. There are at several guidelines to consider in what is allowed in the marriage bed. Anything that is prohibited in the Bible would be wrong (i.e. a third party, pornography, etc.). Intimacy must also be natural. It also cannot be anything that is harmful. Probably the most important consideration is that intimacy must be kind. There may be many intimate ways that are lawful but may not be pleasing to your spouse. In this, married people need to heed the desires and wishes of their spouse and not be unkind by pressuring them for something they are uncomfortable with. With that in mind, you see that when there is agreement, there is great freedom in the marriage bed. Solomon likens his wife's body to a palm tree. Most of us are quite unfamiliar with the power of this metaphor. For many reasons, Solomon is demonstrating that when a person has a strong marriage, their love life reflects this strength. He has freedom to "lay hold" of his bride's body, like the fruit of the palm tree.

Palm Trees Thrive Under Attack

Palm trees are quite amazing trees. For starters, you can cut it, but you cannot kill it. The nutrients that most trees need to survive are found just below the bark, so when you cut them, they die, but not the palm tree. Its life comes from its heart, so it thrives even under attack.

This reminds me of Psalm 92:12, "The righteous flourish like the palm tree and grow like the cedar in Lebanon." The bridegroom affirms the bride's growing maturity, her growing fruitfulness. We're reminded that our goal is that we would all arrive at "the measure of the stature of the fullness of Christ" (Eph 4:13). That's the goal. The evidence of maturity is when we look like Jesus, when his fruits are produced in us and through us in abundance.

Palm Trees Survive the Dry Times

Palm trees not only thrive in the tropics, they can also thrive in the desert, where very little thrives. You may be living in a spiritual desert—maybe in your family, maybe in a church where people don't seem to have a hunger for the things of God. If you are in Christ, you will survive those dry times. When you think about it, this whole world—apart from Christ—is a desert. But God can give His children the grace, the ability, to flourish—to grow, to be strong, to be fruitful, to be beautiful, even in a desert place. God can make "rivers in the desert" (Isa 43:19). He says, "I will pour water on the thirsty land, and streams on the dry ground; I will pour my Spirit upon your offspring" (Isa 44:3). Jesus said, "Whoever believes in me, as the Scripture has said, 'Out of his heart will flow rivers of living water.' Now this he said about the Spirit, whom those who believed in him were to receive" (Jn 7:38-39).

Palm Trees Have an Amazing Root System

If you took a cross section of a palm tree, you would find a number of brownish spots instead of the growth rings like you'd find in most trees. These are bundles of vascular strands that carry nutrients up and down the tree. It's like a thick steel cable-woven from a lot of smaller steel wires that go all the way down to the roots. Each strand in these vascular bundles is connected to the root system.

Other trees have woody roots, and in most trees, 80 percent of the root system is within the top two feet of soil. But not so with the palm tree. Anyone who has ever tried to dig up a palm can tell you it has fibrous roots that not only fan out to great distances but also go down deep. A palm trees roots sometimes go down around the tectonic plates.

As we keep our roots connected to Jesus, as we abide in him, as we let him abide in us, we will produce much fruit for his glory. The Bible tells us in so many places that we need to be rooted in our Lord. Jesus said, "I am the vine; you are the branches. Whoever abides in me and I in him, he it is that bears much fruit, for apart from me you can do nothing" (Jn 15:5). St. Paul says we need to have Christ make himself at home in our heart, that's when we are well-rooted in him. "That Christ may dwell in your hearts through faith—that you, being rooted and grounded in love, may have strength to comprehend with all the saints what is the breadth and length and height and depth, and to know the love of Christ that surpasses knowledge, that you may be filled with all the fullness of God" (Eph 3:17-19). And again, Paul says to the church at Colosae – "Therefore, as you received Christ Jesus the Lord, so walk in him, rooted and built up in him and established in the faith, just as you were taught" (Col 2:6-7).

Palm Trees Bend But Do Not Break

The palm tree bends, but it won't break. Hurricanes can blow most trees away, but not the palm tree. It can bend almost all the way to the ground, and when the storm is over, it straightens up again and is actually stronger. The root system of the palm tree combines to give a palm tree a very solid base in the ground and a very supple trunk that will bend in the wind without breaking.

How about you, did you know that it's trials that make us strong and help our faith to grow? "Count it all joy, my brothers, when you meet trials of various kinds, for you know that the testing of your faith produces steadfastness. And let steadfastness have its full effect, that you may be perfect and complete, lacking in nothing" (Jas 1:3-4).

MATURING IN COMMUNION (7:9B-13)

I want to grow old with my wife. No matter what, I commit to live with her until death. I know what will grow my marriage. I cannot be a true friend to my wife unless I am a friend of the Lord Jesus. Solomon had a relationship with his life that was enlivening to him. They had close communion with God and with each other.

Communion with Jesus Awakens Us

The bride responds to Solomon.

Song of Solomon 7:9b | It goes down smoothly for my beloved, gliding over lips and teeth.

I like the Authorized Version here: "And the roof of thy mouth like the best wine for my beloved, that goeth down sweetly, causing the lips of those that are asleep to speak." She's now awakened. If she was sleeping, she is now alerted by the love they have for one another. Their communion together was like sweet wine that awakens the senses. So many couples go by sleep walking in their marriages. They are like ships passing in the night. Communion means investing time together. This brings the wine that causes one to be jolted with joy and alert.

I think this can easily picture those who are spiritually asleep. There are those who maybe have never been converted or maybe believers who've been lulled to sleep by the world. As a result of Christ's bride – her devotion, her beauty, her fragrance, her fruitfulness – these sleepers are awakened. Their hearts are stirred; their hearts are revived, as they witness the intense joys experienced by this bride and her beloved.

Our lives should not be lulling others to sleep. Our lives should be awakening sleepers. As they see the beauty and the power and the life of Christ within us, they want to wake up and get in on what's happening in that relationship with him. The bride is awakened by the fullness of her communion with Solomon. She rejoices in his love.

Song of Solomon 7:10 | I am my beloved's, and his desire is for me.

A healthy marriage is place of refuge and revival of soul. All can be falling apart around you, but if your marriage is healthy two lovers can drink deeply of a place of acceptance even if all the world rejects them. And yet even the healthiest of marriages are imperfect shelters. Christ alone can shelter and revive the weary soul. We run to Christ that "times of refreshing may come from the presence of the Lord" (Acts 3:20).

> HARRY IRONSIDE (1876-1951): "Three times in this little book we have similar expressions to this, 'I am my beloved's, and his desire is toward me.' In 2:16 we read, 'My beloved is mine, and I am his.' That is very precious. Are you able to say, 'My beloved is mine, and I am his?' In other words, have you given yourself to him? Have you trusted him as your Savior? If you have, he has given himself to you. Just the very moment you give yourself to him in faith, that moment he gives himself to you and comes to dwell in your heart. This is the assurance of salvation: Christ is mine, and I am his. And then in 6:3, she says, 'I am my beloved's, and my beloved is mine.' That is communion. I belong to him and he belongs to me, that we may enjoy one another together.

And then in 7:10 we read, 'I am my beloved's, and his desire is toward me.' Every doubt and every fear is gone. She has found her satisfaction in him and he finds his in her. What a wonderful picture of the communion between the Christian and his Savior."[146]

We are dead in sin until Jesus awakens us and we can say: "I am my beloved's." Then the Lord awakens us. "wake, awake, put on your strength, O Zion; put on your beautiful garments, O Jerusalem, the holy city; for there shall no more come into you the uncircumcised and the unclean" (Isa 52:1). I belong to Jesus. I am his, and his desire is for me. As the bride looked into Solomon's eyes, so let every Christian be "looking to Jesus, the founder and perfecter of our faith, who for the joy that was set before him endured the cross, despising the shame, and is seated at the right hand of the throne of God" (Heb 12:2).

Communion with Jesus in Private Should be Sought

The bride speaks to Solomon with a wonderful invitation.

Song of Solomon 7:11-12a | Come, my beloved, let us go out into the fields and lodge in the villages; let us go out early to the vineyards and see whether the vines have budded, whether the grape blossoms have opened and the pomegranates are in bloom.

Look at this invitation from the queen to her beloved. It's an invitation for companionship and communion. She's never going to be alone again. "Now, for the first time, the Shulamite takes the initiative in the relationship and suggests that they spend a further day and night in the country."[147] Away from the palace they grow their friendship and romance, and the bride looks forward to it with great anticipation.

Song of Solomon 7:12b | There I will give you my love.

It is appropriate that they explore the vineyards and gardens that are in bloom. It is also appropriate that she gives herself to him in private. A healthy marriage needs these regular getaways. The imagery of

---

[146] Harry Ironside. *Addresses on Song,* 66.

[147] J. A. Balchin. *The Song of Songs.* D. A. Carson, R. T. France, J. A. Motyer, & G. J. Wenham (eds.), *New Bible commentary,* 4th ed. (Downers Grove, IL: Inter-Varsity Press, 1995), 626–627.

springtime is present to indicate the well-being of their relationship. Though they are well on into their marriage, they make time for each other away from the hustle and bustle and busyness of life. Just as the buds of springtime are blooming, so is their relationship.

Is your marriage blooming? Just as the tender buds of spring must be cared for, so gentleness must be the theme of the healthy marriage. Paul tells us that bitterness, rage, shouting and slander do not make for a happy marriage, but instead we are to put on tenderness and kindness and forgiveness (Eph 4:31-32). Gentleness is a key part of the Spirit's fruit. Spending time together with the intent to serve and give (and not to have any expectations of getting something for yourself) is the most powerful way to build up your marriage for lasting fruitfulness and health.

It is the same in our relationship with Christ. As we are abiding in Christ, one in him, communing with him, we will bear fruit. We are filled to overflowing. There's fruitfulness (Jn 15:5). We must take time to get alone with Christ and commune with him. This was Christ's practice. "And rising very early in the morning, while it was still dark, he [Jesus] departed and went out to a desolate place, and there he prayed" (Mk 1:35). Our Lord plainly taught us to seek him constantly in private. "But you, when you pray, go into your room, and when you have shut your door, pray to your Father who is in the secret place; and your Father who sees in secret will reward you openly" (Mt 6:6, NKJV). Jonathan Edwards said it well: "It is the nature of true grace, that however it loves Christian society in its place, yet it in a peculiar manner delights in retirement, and secret converse with God. So that if persons appear greatly engaged in social religion, and but little in the religion of the closet, and are often highly affected when with others, and but little moved when they have none but God and Christ to converse with, it looks very darkly upon their religion."[148]

Communion with Jesus Restores our Passion
The peasant queen is stirred up with love.

Song of Solomon 7:13 | The mandrakes give forth fragrance, and beside our doors are all choice fruits, new as well as old, which I have laid up for you, O my beloved.

---

[148] Jonathan Edwards. *Religious Affections* (Philadelphia: Goodman, 1821), 335.

Mandrakes which were an aphrodisiac supposedly eaten to stir up passion. She is proactive in stirring herself up with her husband. Let us not think that this passage is merely about their physical relationship. We err if we put all the emphasis there. The physical union is important, but the mandrakes were just one of "all choice fruits." There are new and old fruits that the bride lays up for her beloved. It is love that is the lifegiving fountain of all these fruits. We are to love as Christ loved. We cannot know love outside of knowing God who is love. The greatest of all virtues is love, for it never ends (1 Cor 13:8).

We cannot love our spouse if we don't love Jesus first. Perhaps your marriage is dry and dying. What are you to do? First, be patient. You didn't get here overnight. "He has made everything beautiful in its time" (Eccl 3:11). It's not going to happen overnight. It takes time to make your marriage beautiful in Christ. You are going to need to serve your spouse. Put off your critical spirit and accept your spouse as they are. If they are to be changed, it will be Jesus and not any human being that will do the changing.

The choice fruits are to be planted, cared for and harvested before they can be given as a gift to one another. Perhaps you are dry and no longer spiritually fruitful. As you commune with Jesus, the Spirit of God will stir you up to plant the seeds of a great harvest. Plant the spices of the living Word in your heart. Dig deep in your soul with the old fruits of foundational truths like God's love for you, Christ's work on the cross, and God's acceptance of you based on faith, not works. Plant the new fruits of prayer and daily power. Then water those seeds with rest and trust, gratitude and praise. Trust the Lord for the harvest. If you abide in Christ, you will bring forth much fruit, but without him you can do nothing (Jn 15:5). If we are in Christ and in his communion through the new birth, we are going to be growing and changing in Christ. It is only then that you can harvest those fruits, both new and old and give them to your spouse through humble prayer for each other, serving each other in the background of your lives, not looking for a return or any acknowledgement. As you live a life of service to each other, then the mandrakes of romance will be a bonus amidst all the other choice fruits you enjoy. Dig deep and plant those choice fruits in your walk with Christ not to improve your marriage, but because you need Christ. It is not your circumstances but Christ that should be your focus. He wants to bless you. He says, "Test me now in this, says the

LORD of hosts, if I will not open for you the windows of heaven and pour out for you a blessing until it overflows" (Mal 3:10). David testifies: "How great is your goodness, which you have stored up for those who fear you, which you have wrought for those who take refuge in you, before the sons of men" (Psa 31:19).

Expressions of love both express old, familiar and well proven ways, and explore the, as yet, unknown. Secondly, true love always includes a considerate looking ahead. This reflects the heart of a God who has laid up in store such good things (a lavish inheritance guarded in heaven) for those who love him (Jn 14:3; 1 Pet 1:4).[149]

Conclusion

In 1990, after 22 years as president of Columbia International University, Robertson McQuilkin announced that he would resign to devote full time to Muriel, his wife of 40 years, who was suffering from Alzheimer's disease. In March 1990, Dr. McQuilkin announced his resignation in a letter with these words:

"My dear wife, Muriel, has been in failing mental health for about eight years. So far I have been able to carry both her ever-growing needs and my leadership responsibilities at CBC. But recently it has become apparent that Muriel is contented most of the time she is with me and almost none of the time I am away from her. It is not just "discontent." She is filled with fear—even terror—that she has lost me and always goes in search of me when I leave home. Then she may be full of anger when she cannot get to me. So it is clear to me that she needs me now, full-time.

Perhaps it would help you to understand if I shared with you what I shared at the time of the announcement of my resignation in chapel. The decision was made, in a way, 42 years ago when I promised to care for Muriel "in sickness and in health...till death do us part." So, as I told the students and faculty, as a man of my word, integrity has something to do with it. But so does fairness. She has cared for me fully and sacrificially all these years; if I cared for her for the next 40 years I would not be out of debt. Duty, however, can be grim and stoic. But there is more; I love Muriel. She is a delight to me—her childlike dependence and confidence in me, her warm love, occasional flashes of that wit I used to relish so, her happy spirit and tough resilience in the face of her

---

[149] Balchin. *The Song of Songs: New Bible Commentary*, 627.

continual distressing frustration. I do not have to care for her. I get to! It is a high honor to care for so wonderful a person."[150]

Our Christian life is on a pathway of progressive growing and changing in Christ. A healthy marriage will also be growing in beauty, strength, and communion with one another and with the Lord.

---

[150] For more, see "Muriel's Blessing" from Christianity Today. http://www.christi-anitytoday.com/ct/2004/februaryweb-only/2-9-12.0.html. Accessed 11-28-2010.

11 | Song 8:1-14

GROWING A GODLY MARRIAGE

Love is strong as death, jealousy is fierce as the grave.
Its flashes are flashes of fire, the very flame of the LORD.
SONG 8:6

If you are like me, you feel that you have failed much in the Christian life. I have not been the father I'd hoped to be. I've not been the husband I'd hoped to be. I've not been the Christian I'd hoped to be. But God's not through with me yet. He's growing me. There's a lot of work still left to do.

Song of Solomon is a love song. As we close out the book, we find out Solomon and his wife share a growing love. The essential message of this love poem is that mature love doesn't stay static. We don't stay static in our relationship with the Lord or in marriage. True, mature love is always pressing onward and upward to higher ground. The secret to growing a godly marriage is not found in you or your spouse. Fix your eyes on Jesus, and you will have so much energy and power to grow your marriage. He's the perfect Spouse, isn't he?

Christians are to relate to marriage—whether married, unmarried, soon to be married, or formerly married. The Song of Solomon is not just speaking to married people. It is written to all Christians as the profitable, sufficient Word of God helping us know how we should relate to marriage on this earth. God's Word calls us to come together as one Bride that is to be married to Christ, not to divide the church into various special groups. All of us are promised to be married; all believers are betrothed to Christ (2 Cor 11:2). We listen for the trumpet. "It will happen in a moment, in the blink of an eye, when the last trumpet is blown. For when the trumpet sounds, those who have died will be raised to live forever. And we who are living will also be transformed" 1 Cor 15:52, NLT).

We come to the final chapter of this biblical love poem, and we find a woman who is happily married. She loves her husband, but she wants to love him more. How many married people would say the same thing – I love my spouse, but I want to love them more. How do we grow in our love in marriage, and also with the Lord?

GROW IN AFFECTION (8:1-4)

This wife was so thankful to be with her husband. She wanted to display public affection for her husband, even though it was not culturally appropriate for husband and wife to display public affection. Her identity was wrapped up in him. She loved being Mrs. Solomon.

She Wants No Limits

She wants to show public affection for her husband. She wants everyone to know she belongs to him.

Song of Solomon 8:1 | Oh that you were like a brother to me who nursed at my mother's breasts! If I found you outside, I would kiss you, and none would despise me.

Those in ancient Israel did not allow public displays of intimate affection unless you were a near relative. It is that way even today in Israel. Brothers, family members, cousins can display affection, but not husband and wife. It is considered immodest. It was for this reason that the queen wished that Solomon was her brother. She wanted to openly display her love for Solomon. She wanted to lift him up and show him off in public. She longs for the fullest possible expression of intimacy with her beloved. She feels restrained—unable to adequately display her affection for him.

Do you ever feel limited in your relationship with the Lord? God is a Spirit. How can we worship him in spirit and in truth when we live in the flesh? Do you feel limited in how you can express your love to him – limited by your flesh, limited by your sinfulness, limited by your weakness, limited by your failures or your failed promises to the Lord? We are all so weak here and now, but saints, there is coming a day when there will be no limitations. There is coming a day "when the perishable puts on the imperishable, and the mortal puts on immortality" (1 Cor. 15:54).

Jonathan Edwards in his miscellanies on this verse, makes the point that Christ indeed became a brother to us in order to seek us and rescue his bride, so that she may have full possession and enjoyment of him.

> JONATHAN EDWARDS (1703-1758): "Christ, descending so low in uniting himself to our nature, tends to invite and encourage us to ascend to the most intimate converse with him, and encourages us that we shall be accepted and not despised therein. For we have this to consider of, that let us be never so bold in this kind of ascending, for Christ to allow us and accept us in it won't be a greater humbling himself than to take upon him our nature. Christ was made flesh and dwelt among us in a nature infinitely below his original nature, for this end, that we might have as it were the full possession and enjoyment of him."[151]

She Needs No Fancy New Ideas

Song of Solomon 8:2a | I would lead you and bring you into the house of my mother— she who used to teach me.

Here is a lady who grew up on a farm in the tribe of Dan. She didn't have any noble graces that would attract royalty. She knew the wisdom she needed was not from this world. The kind of woman that attracts a godly man is one who avoids the world's wisdom. This very blessed lady had a mother who she could learn from. She saw her mother loving her father. This is something mothers must teach their daughters by example.

---

[151] Jonathan Edwards. *Miscellanies 501-382*, Vol. 18 of *Works*, 366-367. (From Edwards' Miscell. no. 741, "The Happiness of Heaven")

So many girls run from the wisdom of the godly mother. Young ladies, please I beg you, do what this humble bride did. Follow your godly mother. Listen to her teaching. Don't stray from her.

This humble lady didn't have the fancy fads of the world, but she had what really lasts: she has a mother who had the grace of God in her heart. This maturing bride has learned to be an attractive, godly woman from her mother. She doesn't act like a know it all. She's humble. She says, "I'm so grateful for my mother. I learned so much from her."

There are many who struggle in marriage or child rearing because they have not had a godly example. Don't use that as an excuse. The church provides you with dozens of godly examples. You who have learned contentment and godliness in marriage, teach the young wives to be content. Be a godly mother to them (Titus 2:3-5).

The queen learned so much from her mom. I can say I thank God for my wife who learned from a godly mother. If we are going to grow in marriage and in our walk with Christ, we can't do it alone.

She Wants No Distractions

Song of Solomon 8:2b-3 | I would give you spiced wine to drink,
the juice of my pomegranate. His left hand is under my head,
and his right hand embraces me.

Spiced wine – this is very strong drink. Her love and affection is powerful. She wants to spend time with him. Notice children and career are not mentioned. Couples need to turn the mobile phones off, say no to the office, turn off the TV, put the kids to bed and spend time together.

It is this way in our life with Christ. Do you know how many universes God controls? And yet we think we need to control our own lives. We need to slow down, tune in, and listen up to God. Spend time with him. He said, "Without me, you can do nothing" (Jn 15:5). Christ's presence is satisfying and encouraging. All time spent with him will be rewarded. Martin Luther who almost single-handedly turned the world upside down devoted much time to prayer. Luther's motto was "He that has prayed well has studied well."[152]

---

[152] E.M. Bounds. *The Classic Collection on Prayer* (Orlando: Bridge-Logos, 2001), 608.

MARTIN LUTHER (1483-1546), "If I fail to spend two hours in prayer each morning, the devil gets the victory through the day... I have so much business, I cannot get on without spending three hours daily in prayer." [153]

In the same way married couples, you need to spend time together. You are a living parable of Christ's love for his church. Talk with each other. Pour out the delicious pomegranate juice for each other. "The grains of the pomegranates were said by the Arabians to be from Paradise. Perhaps this reference to exchange of gifts may be taken as symbolizing the happy state of the Church when she pours out her treasures in response to the spiritual blessings which she is freely receiving."[154]

She Has No Regrets

Physical love is so precious that God reserves it for marriage alone. Godly men and women guard it as a picture of Christ and his Bride. If you have a great love life in marriage, that is a virtue, but outside of marriage it is a shame and a reproach and a stain. We must not soil that which is precious and pure.

Solomon's wife recalls that there is always a time and a place for physical affection. It is after the vows are made before God and others. It is specially reserved for marriage.

Song of Solomon 8:4 | I adjure you, O daughters of Jerusalem, that you not stir up or awaken love until it pleases.

The Shulamite bride now tells the "daughters of Jerusalem" to follow her example. She saved her love for her husband. She wife remembers the days before she was married and recalls how she reserved this for marriage. She has a healthy view of marital intimacy. She reserved herself for her husband so that she could give all that she was to him and him alone. The natural joy of sexual awakening is ruined by premature experimentation. Satisfying sexual passions outside of God's covenant of marriage is like a person who enjoys stolen money.

In contrast to "the woman Folly" (Pro 9:13) who says, "stolen water is sweet, and bread eaten in secret is pleasant" (Pro 9:17), here the

---

[153] Luther. *Documents from the History of Lutheranism*, 38.

[154] H. D. M. Spence-Jones, ed., *Song of Solomon, The Pulpit Commentary* (London; New York: Funk & Wagnalls Company, 1909), 180.

woman Wisdom gives her beloved "spiced wine" and "the juice of my pomegranate" (Song 8:2) in her mother's house, with total approval.

In Proverbs 9, there is a woman called Folly. It is said in verse 13 that "she is seductive and knows nothing. She sits at the door of her house; she takes a seat on the highest places of the town, calling to those who pass by, who are going straight on their way, 'Whoever is simple, let him turn in here!' And to him who lacks sense she says, 'Stolen water is sweet, and bread eaten in secret is pleasant.' But he does not know that the dead are there, that her guests are in the depths of Sheol."

In contrast, here is a woman in this love poem who has the total approval of her mother (and father). The marriage bed is approved by God. What a joyful safety is the marriage bed. There are no regrets when it comes to her honeymoon or any night that follows. Save yourself young people, for marriage. This woman reserved her affection for her husband. She wanted no limits and no distractions. She now has no regrets. Purpose in your heart to remain pure so that you can testify to your children that by God's grace, you kept yourself pure.

Are you lacking romance in your marriage? Do you have regrets about your own attitude of selfishness or neglect when it comes to romance with your spouse? There are some married couples who are rarely together physically. Outside of serious physical or health limitations, that kind of neglect of each other is sinful and selfish. Perhaps there is bitterness between you and your spouse. Do something about it before you lose your marriage. If you are not physically together as a married couple, your marriage is in danger. Hear me now. It's serious. In a healthy marriage, physical union can be a barometer of your marriage. It's not the main thing, but it tells you a lot about the state of communication, companionship and communion with each other.

GROW IN FRUIT-BEARING (8:5)

Again, we hear the voice of the bride.

Song of Solomon 8:5b | Under the apple tree I awakened you.

She's referring to the family tree. She speaks of the place where "your mother bore you." This now is clearly a reference to their family tree. She's having babies.

Solomon still has his queen leaning on him, intoxicated with love. They pass by an apple tree near Solomon's childhood home. It reminds them of their family tree and their children. She's saying, "Your mother bore you at this place. Now I am bearing you children and adding to the family line. Praise God!"

We Must Be Leaning to Bear Fruit

The first thing we hear is a comment from observers of the couple.

Song of Solomon 8:5a | Who is that coming up from the wilderness, leaning on her beloved?

Who is that girl? She's special. She's noticeable. The "wilderness" is a reminder of Israel's 40 years of trials to the Jewish mind. The couple had emerged from their trials successfully as well. They've had children, and their love is still strong. They are leaning on one another.

> AUGUSTINE (354-430), "Oh, bride of Christ, beautiful among women! Oh, you in white, coming up and leaning upon your beloved! For by his light you are illuminated that you may shine; by his help you are supported that you may not fall! Oh, how well it is sung to you in that Song of Songs, your wedding song, as it were, that 'there is love in your delights!'"[155]

This couple (and every couple) have to overcome the curse of disharmony that began at the fall of man into sin (Gen 3:16). They've come up out of the wilderness after going through so many minefields, but they are arm and arm. She is leaning on him. She comes out of years of marriage, and she is nourished, secure, safe, happy, and leaning on Solomon's arm. Men, our wives out to be closer to Christ because of us!

It's sometimes hard to be married. It's hard to adjust to marriage. But as hard as that is, children can be an even greater challenge. They demand so much. Yet after giving her all for her children, she is still "leaning on the arm of her beloved." Living the Christian life and bearing fruit for God is not easy either. Yet after all these years, you are still "leaning on your beloved," on Christ who will "never leave you nor forsake you" (Heb 13:5).

---

[155] Augustine of Hippo. *Tractates on the Gospel of John.* In *Fathers of the Church: A New Translation*, Vol 90 (Washington, D.C: Catholic University of America Press, 1947-2013), 53.

We Must Be Loving to Bear Fruit

Don't get so busy in ministry that you lose your love for the Lord. This girl is "**leaning on the arm of her beloved**" (8:5a). How is your love in marriage? Have you lost your love for the Lord? You can only love each other by the love you build in your walk with God.

In the ministry, there are many spiritual children. But don't get so busy in ministry that you lose your walk with the Lord. We need to grow in fruit-bearing. If you are so tired and dry from ministry, you are out of focus and out of balance. It's the same in marriage. Don't get so busy with your children that you lose your marriage. Slow down. Enjoy the fruit God gives, but don't enjoy it more than your walk with the Lover of your soul.

Remember this: you can't have a great family if you don't have a great marriage. You are rarely going to have godly kids if you don't have godly parents who love each other. "Delight yourself in the Lord, and he will give you the desires of your heart. Commit your way to the Lord; trust in him, and he will act" (Psa 37:4-5). Our Lord, in the New Testament makes the same point. "Seek first the kingdom of God and his righteousness, and all these things will be added to you" (Mt 6:33).

We Must Be Willing to Bear Fruit

If it is possible we are to have children in marriage. We are called to raise up "a godly seed" for Christ (Mal 2:15). "Behold, children are a heritage from the Lord, the fruit of the womb a reward. Like arrows in the hand of a warrior are the children of one's youth. Blessed is the man who fills his quiver with them" (Psa 127:3-5). Don't take it for granted. Not all marriages are blessed with children, but if you are blessed with offspring, you need to see the high calling you have. It's not easy.

Mrs. Solomon walks with her husband by the king's childhood home where the king had fallen asleep. She says to him,

Song of Solomon 8:5b | Under the apple tree I awakened you. There your mother was in labor with you; there she who bore you was in labor.

We might say it like, "I woke you up where the stork had been." It's a reference to the joy of children in marriage. The implication of the apple tree is symbolic of the "family tree" that bears the fruit of marital love, namely children. The desire is to carry on the family by having children. Listen, a marriage is more than companionship. It's more than romance and intimacy and fun together. It can be all that. But it's about building a family tree.

This scene may refer to their first meeting. Apparently, their love was sparked under this tree. Solomon was sleeping there, and she awakened him. Solomon's mother Bathsheba seems to have spent some time under the tree when she was in labor. This may seem strange, but this is a reference to fruitfulness in marriage. The implication of the apple tree points to the importance of continuing the family tree. A serious responsibility in marriage is to commit to carrying on the legacy of Christ by having children and instructing them in the fear of the Lord.

Deuteronomy 6 is my roadmap for family life. Some people ask me "How do you do devotions with the children?" My wife and I do have formal devotions with the children. We share that responsibility. But whenever I am home, we are having devotions. All day at all times we are rehearsing God's Word, his goodness, his praise, answered prayer, etc. The children are to be taught in every situation. "These words that I command you today shall be on your heart. You shall teach them diligently to your children, and shall talk of them when you sit in your house, and when you walk by the way, and when you lie down, and when you rise" (Deut 6:5-7).

GROW IN LOVE (8:6-7)

Godly love is not mere emotion. Love, as God defines it, is not primarily an emotion. The world says, "when the feeling stops, the love is over." Love is not a tingly sensation. Love is not sentimentalism. Love has nothing to do with how you feel. God so loved the world that he gave his only Son. He didn't look at the world and say, "I just can't resist them; I've got to get them in heaven. They're terrific." There wasn't one thing in us that was deserving. We were enemies; we hated God; we were sinful and vile, but God loved us anyway. And he loved us so much, he gave himself.

Biblical love is not mere appreciation. It is not just saying nice words to someone. "Faithful are the wounds of a friend; profuse are the kisses of an enemy" (Pro 27:6). Love is more than empty words. Love is action. Love is an act of your will that chooses the best for the other person. We can say all kinds of nice things to a person and it not help them. Sometimes love is saying very hard words to a person.

God's love is not admiration. It is not simply liking or being fond of someone. Agape love goes far beyond admiration. It sacrifices for those that are not admirable. We read in our Bible that "God is love" (1 Jn 1:16). Jesus is the exact imprint of God's love. By looking at the cross we can say that agape love is a voluntary abandonment of self-preservation for the good of another. Husbands are to use their position of authority to sacrifice their life for their wife.

True biblical love is a God-centered, sacrificial love. Understand the New Testament makes a shocking statement like: "God is *agape* – sacrificial love." Take that in. He is sacrificial love. Consider 1 John 4:16: "So we have come to know and to believe the love that God has for us. God is love, and whoever abides in love abides in God, and God abides in him." Do you "believe the love that God has" for you?

You cannot truly love your wife as you ought without being born again into this love. This kind of selfless love is impossible to know simply through the human nature. You must have the divine nature dwelling in you. We must "become partakers of the divine nature" (2 Pet 1:4). God must dwell in you. This is the only way to experience God-centered love. This kind of God-centered love is displayed by the words of the Shulamite queen in Song of Solomon 8.

Godly Love is Permanent

I'm told that my ancestors, the Scots, were the "original barbarians." I'm told they invented the tribal tattoo. That tattoo was a permanent marking of identity. The Shulamite talks about how she wants to be a seal on Solomon's heart and arm. Listen to peasant queen.

Song of Solomon 8:6a | Set me as a seal upon your heart, as a seal upon your arm.

A seal is a permanent marking of identity, in pagan society it might have been a marking on the skin. In Israel it is likely referring to a signet ring that might be worn around one's neck. A seal makes a mark that doesn't go away. Seals in ancient times were used to show ownership and permanence. This bride is saying, "Attach me to yourself, bind me to your heart, so that nothing will ever separate me from your love."

MARTIN LUTHER (1483-1546), "'Come,' the Bridegroom says, 'let me be to you like a seal, like a ring by which you will recognize me and embrace me from your heart. Look at me! Fix your eyes and your heart on me…. Affix this seal on your heart, etc.' The fact that he wants to be set not only over the heart but also over the arm signifies faith and love together — that we should both believe and live according to the Word of God. When this is the case, then in truth we walk in divine clothing, and wear this seal fitly."[156]

Christ has graven us on his hands (Isa 49:16). Your love ought to be like Christ's – the permanent kind. You are going to be dedicated to your marriage until death itself removes you from your spouse. Love is not a feeling, but a choice to sacrifice yourself for another, whether they are worthy or not. The bride describes the permanence of a long-lasting marriage relationship.

Are you plugged in, totally committed to marriage? Husband, it means you forsake *all* others and love only your wife. It means you always answer her phone calls. One of the biggest insults you can give a wife is to make her talk to your voicemail. The only way that ought to happen is if you lose your phone. It ought to be so rare that if your wife has to talk to voicemail, the next thing she feels compelled to do is file a missing person's report.

Be plugged in. You ought to be like a seal on your wife's heart, like a permanent marking on her arm. You are one flesh. Know your wife. Talk to her. Listen to her. She needs you to be engaged. For men, it is easy to ignore their wife. Show her attention. Have a rule when you get home. A good idea is to give her a ten second kiss when you walk in the door. Don't ignore your wife. She probably feels ignored at times. Listen to her. Love her. She'll want to lean on you. If you want a long-lasting marriage, be friends. Care for her needs without expectations in return.

Godly Love is Powerful

Song of Solomon 8:6b | For love is strong as death.

---

[156] Luther, Martin. *Luther's Works, Vol. 15: Ecclesiastes, Song of Solomon, and the Last Words of David* (St. Louis: Concordia Publishing House, 1971), 257.

No one is "half-dead." You are either dead or you are not. Death is so strong that once you die you can never come back. That's the kind of commitment godly love gives. Men are to love their lives as Christ loved the church and gave himself for it through the *death* on the cross. The love of Christ is as strong as death. His love is so strong that it can break the hardest, most stubborn hearts. Not only is his love as strong as death, but his love is even stronger than death. We know that death met its match in the love of Christ. Death could not overcome him. Because of his great love for mankind, he came to this earth. He chose to die, to lay down his life to rescue his Bride. He stared death in the face. He ran into the jaws of death, and he overcame it. Christ put death to death! Hallelujah. Yes, He did. Love is as strong as death. The love of Christ is even stronger than death.

> JOHN OF APAMEA[157] (400AD-?), "Let the love of God be stronger than death in you. If death releases you from the desire for everything, how much more appropriate is it that the love of God should release you from the desire for everything."[158]

Godly Love is Persistent

Song of Solomon 8:6c | Jealousy is fierce as the grave.

The grave never gives up its people. It has an eternal strong hold on everyone who goes there. That's how strong godly jealous love is. It never let's go. The queen's love was jealous for Solomon's good. She was envious that he might succeed.

So Christ's love is jealous that we be redeemed. He will stop at nothing to bring us to God. The Lord's love for you is as gripping as the grave. He is our relentless Redeemer. He will never let you go. He will never give up his grip on you. He has a divine persistence. He never lets us go. That kind of godly, possessive guarding love when displayed truly blesses marriage. Husband and wife are jealous to serve one another sacrificially. 1 Corinthians 13 says, "love does not envy"—It's not jealous in a selfish way. This jealousy is the kind that mirrors God. "I the LORD your God am a jealous God" (Exo 20:5) – jealous for our good

---

[157] Due to conflicting data on the identity of John of Apamea, dates are approximate.

[158] John of Apamea. *Letter 45, To Hesychius*. In *Cistercian Studies*, Vol 101 (Kalamazoo, MI: Cistercian Publications, 1973–), 92.

and for his glory. The wrath of God's jealousy for righteousness and goodness is only for those who bypass his mercy and love.

Godly Love Proceeds from the Lord

The queen continues to describe the power of love.

Song of Solomon 8:6d | Its flashes are flashes of fire, the very flame of the LORD.

This is the only place in the entire Song of Solomon that the Lord's covenant name "Yahweh" is used. This reference to fire reminds us of the presence of God. God often reveals himself in fire: the burning bush, the pillar of fire of his manifest presence, the tongues of fire at Pentecost. O God, bring your fire anew in my heart! This kind of love is possible only through the LORD. It is called "the very flame of the LORD." You can love like this only if you are walking with Christ. It finds it's very origin in God.

Godly Love is Perseverance

Song of Solomon 8:7a | Many waters cannot quench love, neither can floods drown it.

Many tests will come to your love, but love from God will overcome it all. Your love must not be based on fleeting emotion, but on covenant commitment to God. Many waters cannot put it out. It keeps on burning!

> HARRY IRONSIDE (1876-1951): "You cannot buy love, but oh, God's love to us creates love in us. It is not the wonderful things that he has done for us, it is not the fact that he has enriched us for eternity, but it is because of what he is. 'We love him because he first loved us' (1 Jn 4:19). 'His is an unchanging love, higher than the heights above; deeper than the depths beneath, free and faithful, strong as death.' What a blessed thing to know Him and love Him and be loved by Him! Oh, to be kept from wounding such a Lover, from grieving his Holy Spirit! For we read, 'the love of God is shed abroad in our hearts by the Holy Ghost which is given unto us (Rom 5:5)."[159]

---

[159] Harry Ironside. *Addresses on Song*, 79.

Godly Love is Priceless

Song of Solomon 8:7b | If a man offered for love all the wealth
of his house, he would be utterly despised.

This kind of love is so priceless. We often play with the worthless
toilet water when God has a beautiful ocean for us. His love is priceless.
MATTHEW HENRY (1662-1714): "Life, and all its comforts, will
not entice a believer from loving Christ: If a man could hire him
with all the substance of his house, to take his love off from
Christ and set it upon the world and the flesh again, he would
reject the proposal with the utmost disdain."[160]

GROW IN YOUR CONVICTIONS (8:8-10)

Be a Secure Wall

Keep the fires of marriage within marriage. God says they are pure
and holy in the marriage union! The Shulamite queen now tells the
story of her life long integrity from the time she was a little girl. The
brothers were taking the responsibility of the father. The father is not
on the scene. Listen to them.

Song of Solomon 8:8-9 | We have a little sister, and she has no
breasts. What shall we do for our sister on the day when she
is spoken for? If she is a wall, we will build on her a battlement
of silver, but if she is a door, we will enclose her with boards
of cedar.

She says she was a wall, not a door. She was not an easy woman
that men could walk through like a door. She was a secure wall. She
recalls her brothers wanting to protect her before she was a woman.
They were looking out for her—they were guarding her for her wedding
day. Do you see the imagery? Basically, if she seemed to want to be pro-
miscuous, they were going to protect her from herself. If she seemed to
be pure they would trust her. She looked at her body as a place of peace
and security. She was not a violated castle. She was not compromised.
Her body was like a wall. She did not give away her purity to win a man.
She would never have been with Solomon had she been like a "door."

[160] Matthew Henry. *Commentary,* 1074.

Be a Celebrated Wall

She no longer needs to defend her virginity against the male aggressor who would storm the walls. She, the female, and her lover, the male, are at peace. Instead of battle towers to defend her, she has breasts that adorn her beauty in his eyes. She testifies:

Song of Solomon 8:10 | I was a wall, and my breasts were like towers; then I was in his eyes as one who finds peace.

Love may be celebrated and awakened in marriage. That is the only place the fire is safe. As we've said before, fire inside a hearth is fine. Fire outside the hearth is disastrous. If you are married, determine that your physical union is reserved for your spouse alone.

10 Steps to Protecting Your Marriage

1. Resolve in your heart to honor the sacredness of your and others' marriage vows
2. Remember the picture that marriage is supposed to be illustrating a picture of God's covenant-keeping love.
3. Rejoice in the mate that God has given you.
4. Rely on the grace of God and the power of His Spirit to meet needs that your mate cannot meet.
5. Ask God to rekindle your love for your own mate.
6. Run from potentially compromising situations. Social networking, Facebook, some of these things have become a huge catalyst in divorces today.
7. Reject anything that could fuel impure desires. What goes into our minds is so important. The potential for impurity is so enormous today through movies, DVDs, magazines, romance novels.
8. Resist temptation to isolate yourself. When you're being tempted, when you're in a difficult marriage or compromising situation, sin's power is strengthened by secrecy.
9. Rehearse the consequences of sexual sin.
   - It eats away at the soul.
   - It defiles the marriage.
   - It defiles the picture of redemption.
   - It's destructive.
   - It's deadly.

10. Rehearse the blessings of faithful love, of being a covenant keeper, the blessings in your marriage, in your children, in your conscience, in your future.

A wise woman realizes that she can lead a man straight to hell by tempting him, and so she looks forward to marriage, and keeps herself pure. There is a reason that we speak of marital love as the most beautiful, free relationship that a human being can have. But something this sacred must be reserved for marriage. Regardless, this is a woman who is at home with her husband. She loves spending time with him. She feels safe. She knows him. She wants to display her affection publicly for him. She is his helper and speaks well of him!

GROW IN TRUSTING GOD'S PLAN (8:11-14)

Trust God's Plan

Song of Solomon 8:11a | Solomon had a vineyard at Baal-hamon; he let out the vineyard to keepers.

Solomon owned the vineyard. Who were these keepers? They were likely the Shulamite's brothers. They were to bring Solomon the profit of what they sold. "Each one was to bring for its fruit a thousand pieces of silver." But Solomon got something more than the price of the vineyard. He got these brother's little sister.

We can trust God for marriage. The Shulamite's eyes were not on marriage, but on being faithful.

Song of Solomon 8:12 | My vineyard, my very own, is before me; you, O Solomon, may have the thousand, and the keepers of the fruit two hundred.

Solomon can have the profit, and her brothers get some of the profit too, but Solomon got her! Her vineyard was hers to give. No one would invade her property at any cost. She gave herself away freely to Solomon. Solomon was interested in a business transaction, but God moved his heart to be interested in marriage. God's providence is that God will care for his people. He will provide a mate if we are to be married. We may be caring for our own business, but God cares for the whole of our lives, and that includes marriage. Christ indeed cares for us, for we are his vineyard.

ROBERT HAWKER (1753-1827): "The best comment perhaps on this verse is what the Lord Jesus himself has given in Matthew 21:33ff. The Church is Christ's vineyard, and he has servants in all ages ministering, and working – patriarchs, prophets, apostles, and pastors. The harvest of souls belongs to him, and to him will be all the fruit of it. He who now has his eye constantly upon his beloved church will come to bring in his harvest."[161]

Enjoy God's Plan

Solomon received more than the profit on a vineyard. He rejoices that he has his bride. He wants to hear her voice.

Song of Solomon 8:13 | O you who dwell in the gardens, with companions listening for your voice; let me hear it.

Solomon wants to hear his sweet love's voice. She is his dove, his perfect one, and he delights in hearing her voice. The bride's companions as well wanted to hear her voice. For Solomon, his businesses of vineyards and profits was a very small thing compared to the joy he had in hearing his bride's voice.

So it is that our Lord Jesus upholds all things by the word of his power (Col 1:17), but his great interest is not in the universes that he maintains, but the people that he died for. He hears the planets spinning and the most exotic animals yet undiscovered upon this earth. He knows and hears them all, but he wants your heart, and he wants to hear your voice. He said to Jeremiah, and he invites us today, "Call to me and I will answer you, and will tell you great and hidden things that you have not known" (Jer 33:3).

Maybe you would love to be married and have a lover as your companion, but for whatever reason you are still single or perhaps you are in a loveless marriage. This is often the case for so many of God's people. The greater truth of this verse is that God wants to hear your voice confessing your love for him. The greater marriage we all have is to Christ. He's calling to you listening for your voice and says, "Let me hear it" (8:13).

---

[161] Robert Hawker. *Poor Man's Commentary (Complete and Unabridged): A 9 Volume Commentary on the Whole Bible* (Harrington, DE: Delmarva Publications, 2013), Song 8:12.

APONIUS[162] (405-451): "By saying, 'let me hear your voice,'
Christ makes known the voice that he desires to hear. He wants
to hear his Bride confess that he alone on earth, alone among all
humankind (true man, but born in an ineffable manner), alone
found to be a foreigner and pilgrim, alone fleeing the sordid lifestyle of humanity, alone ascending upon the prophesied 'mountains of spices,' he alone in every way is made Lord of heaven
and earth. It shows that he alone fled both internal and external
sin. He alone, who would bind the devil, fugitive of heaven, is
himself a fugitive of the earth in the midst of a perverse and depraved nation. He alone is your Savior. May his Bride lift up her
voice and confess who he is."[163]

Let him hear your voice. He is all I need, whether I am married or
single. "The joy of the Lord is my strength" (Neh 8:12). Shout it out!
Don't wait to enjoy life until you get married or have a perfect marriage.
Even if you are alone, you need to enjoy God's plan. A spouse cannot
bring the happiness we long for. Christ alone promises us full satisfaction. "May you experience the love of Christ, though it is too great to
understand fully. Then you will be made complete with all the fullness
of life and power that comes from God" (Eph 3:19, NLT). "So you also
are complete through your union with Christ, who is the head over
every ruler and authority" (Col 2:10, NLT). A spouse does not complete
you. You are complete through your union with Christ.

Be Free in God's Plan

The peasant queen is delighted with the freedom she has with her
husband.

Song of Solomon 8:14 | Make haste, my beloved, and be like a
gazelle or a young stag on the mountains of spices.

The image of a gazelle or a young stag leaping through the mountains is a beautiful picture of our freedom in Christ.

---

[162] Due to conflicting data on the birth and death of Aponius, dates are approximate.

[163] Aponius. *Exposition of Song of Songs*. In *Corpus Christianorum. Series Latina*,
Vol 19 (Turnhout, Belgium: Brepols, 1953), 305.

AMBROSE (333-397), "She urges that her Bridegroom make haste, because already, although she is of earth, she can follow him in his flight. She says this so that it may be like the young deer that escapes the nets; for her desire is to flee and to fly away above the world."[164]

What a picture marriage is of Christ and his Bride. Yet the Scriptures tell us that marriage is but a faint and temporary reflection of an eternal communion we have with God. This is why Paul clearly instructs us that our ultimate identity is not bound up in whether we are single or married. "The appointed time has grown very short. From now on, let those who have wives live as though they had none, and those who mourn as though they were not mourning, and those who rejoice as though they were not rejoicing, and those who buy as though they had no goods, and those who deal with the world as though they had no dealings with it. For the present form of this world is passing away" (1 Cor 7:29-31). In other words, we ought not be identified by our state of marriage or singleness, by our present difficulties or joys, by our financial status or business dealings. None of those things should define us. We need to be free from being defined by those things. We are in Christ. That's all that matters. Don't concern yourself so much with earthly pursuits. Yes, plan for them. Be wise. Be ready for however God directs. Don't be negligent. But remember this above all things: none of these things define you. Your identity comes from Christ and Christ alone. Hallelujah.

In a healthy marriage, like the one portrayed in the Song of Solomon, certainly there is freedom with one another. Solomon may come like a young stag or a gazelle and have great freedom with his wife. Marriage can produce the greatest earthly joys, as if there were "mountains of spices." These are not just little piles of spices, but mountains! There are moments in a healthy marriage that are like that. But there is only one Lover of your soul that can give you joy that far exceeds the earthly spice mountains. Listen to the wisdom of Solomon's father, King David. "O God, you are my God; earnestly I seek you; my soul thirsts for you; my flesh faints for you, as in a dry and weary land where there is no water. So I have looked upon you in the sanctuary, beholding your power and glory. Because your steadfast love is better than life, my lips

---

[164] St. Ambrose. *Death as Good.* In *Fathers,* Vol 65, 84.

will praise you. So I will bless you as long as I live; in your name I will lift up my hands. My soul will be satisfied as with fat and rich food, and my mouth will praise you with joyful lips" (Psa 63:1-5).

This life never satisfies. Be freed from the addictions of this world, even legitimate ones. The very best marriage could not satisfy any one of us. Don't look for your spouse to satisfy you in a way only God can satisfy. David was thirsty for God. He says his experience of God is "better than life"—better than anything this world could hope to offer. This world offers a lot of counterfeit pleasures, but it can never deliver what it offers. Not even legitimate pleasures (like marriage) can offer what God offers. God alone is the only one who always delivers what he promises. He is ready to give you more than you can ever handle of him. This kind of experience filled David with overwhelming praise, to the point where he raised his hands to heaven. He is addicted to God, absolutely addicted. He is satisfied with God.

David Brainerd (1718-1747) died before the age of thirty, yet his influence goes on today. He said, "O how much better than life is the presence of God.... I never feel comfortably, but when I find my soul going forth after God: if I cannot be holy, I must necessarily be miserable forever." [165] Ed McCully (1927-1956), missionary martyr to the Waorani tribe of Equador: "I have one desire now, to live a life of reckless abandon for the Lord, putting all my energy and strength into it." [166]

David knew no one but God could satisfy him, and he could be satisfied even in the most barren times in his life. David was a man after God's own heart. My hope for you is that you would be a man or a woman after God's heart. Marriage is but a mere, faint picture of what every believer, single or married, already has: the love between Christ and his Church.

Conclusion

How do you build a lasting marriage? All this is vain if you only see the surface of marriage. This is not meant to be a "self-help" study. Moralism helps no one. This study of the Song of Solomon is a clarion call to know your God. The famous English professor (and author of *The Chronicles of Narnia* series) C. S. Lewis said it this way, "When I

---

[165] Jonathan Edwards. *Memoirs of the Rev. David Brainerd* (Oxford University Press: Oxford, UK, 1818), 207.

[166] Elisabeth Elliot. *Through Gates of Splendor* (Wheaton, IL: Tyndale House Publishers, 1986), 50-51.

have learnt to love God better than my earthly dearest, I shall love my earthly dearest better than I do now."[167]

Marriage is hard. As we have learned, marriage is really not about the romance or happiness or even your children or your legacy. The Bible calls marriage a "profound mystery" that is a picture of Christ and His bride (Eph 5:32). Indeed, marriage is not ultimately about marriage. Marriage is a tool God uses to sanctify and grow his people to maturity. Tim Keller in his book *The Meaning of Marriage* writes:

> "While marriage is many things, it is anything but sentimental. Marriage is glorious but hard. It's a burning joy and strength, and yet it is also blood, sweat, and tears, humbling defeats and exhausting victories. No marriage I know more than a few weeks old could be described as a fairy tale come true... Sometimes you fall into bed, after a long, hard day of trying to understand each other, and you can only sigh: 'This is all a profound mystery!' At times, your marriage seems to be an unsolvable puzzle, a maze in which you feel lost."[168]

Marriage humbles us. I remember before I got married, I thought: "Wow, I am growing in Christ. My wife-to-be is growing in the Lord. This is going to be an amazing marriage." Then we got married, and I realized how immature and selfish I really was. I know now that in some ways I will struggle against this indwelling selfishness until the day I see Jesus face to face. But I am so grateful that he promises to complete the work he has started (Phil 1:6). His mission will not be fulfilled until I am fully conformed into Jesus' image (Rom 8:29).

Marriage is a picture of Christ and the church. Christ is our oasis. Let Christ's flame burn in you, and your marriage will burn brightly. Draw near to him single and married people as we await our marriage to our sinless Bridegroom, Jesus Christ.

---

[167] C.S. Lewis, *Letters of C.S. Lewis* (Orlando: Harcourt Books, 1988), 429.

[168] Timothy Keller, *The Meaning of Marriage: Facing the Complexities of Commitment with the Wisdom of God* (Crawfordsville, IN: Penguin Publishing Group), 13.

Index of Ancient and Modern Commentators

ORIGEN (185-254): Bishop of Milan and teacher of Augustine who defended the divinity of the Holy Spirit and the perpetual virginity of Mary.

BASIL THE GREAT (330-379): One of the Cappadocian fathers, bishop of Caesarea and champion of the teaching on the Trinity propounded at Nicaea in 325. He was a great administrator and founded a monastic rule.

AMBROSE OF MILAN (333-397): Bishop of Milan and teacher of Augustine who defended the divinity of the Holy Spirit and the perpetual virginity of Mary.

GREGORY OF NYSSA (335-394): Bishop of Nyssa and brother of Basil the Great. A Cappadocian father and author of catechetical orations, he was a philosophical theologian of great originality.

JEROME (347-420): Gifted exegete and exponent of a classical Latin style, now best known as the translator of the Latin Vulgate. He defended the perpetual virginity of Mary, attacked Origen and Pelagius and supported extreme ascetic practices.

AUGUSTINE OF HIPPO (354-430): Bishop of Hippo and a voluminous writer on philosophical, exegetical, theological and ecclesiological topics. He formulated the Western doctrines of predestination and original sin in his writings against the Pelagians.

CYRIL OF ALEXANDRIA (375-444): Patriarch of Alexandria whose extensive exegesis, characterized especially by a strong espousal of the unity of Christ, led to the condemnation of Nestorius in 431.

THEODORET OF CYRUS (393-466): Bishop of Cyr (Cyrrhus), he was an opponent of Cyril who commented extensively on Old Testament texts as a lucid exponent of Antiochene exegesis.

APONIUS (405-451): Author of a remarkable commentary on Song of Solomon (c. 405–415), an important work in the history of exegesis. The work, which was influenced by the commentaries of Origen and Pseudo-Hippolytus, is of theological significance, especially in the area of Christology.

GREGORY THE GREAT (540-604): Pope from 590, the fourth and last of the Latin "Doctors of the Church." He was a prolific author and a powerful unifying force within the Latin Church, initiating the liturgical reform that brought about the Gregorian Sacramentary and Gregorian chant.

BEDE THE VENERABLE (672-735): Born in Northumbria, at the age of seven he was put under the care of the Benedictine monks of Saints Peter and Paul at Jarrow and given a broad classical education in the monastic tradition. Considered one of the most learned men of his age, he is the author of *An Ecclesiastical History of the English People*.

BERNARD OF CLAIRVAUX (1090-1153): Born in Burgundy to a family of lower nobility, he was called the "honey-tongued doctor" for his eloquent writings on the love of God. He wrote eloquently on humility and was an adviser to five popes. John Calvin considered him the major witness to truth between Gregory the Great and the 1500s. Wrote the famous hymn "O Sacred Head Now Wounded."

MARTIN LUTHER (1483-1546): Born 120 miles outside of Berlin, he became the most prominent sixteenth century reformer. He nailed the 95 theses to the Wittenberg castle door, which were mainly a denunciation against indulgences. Luther almost singlehandedly reintroduced the Gospel to the church, thereby splitting the church between the Roman Catholics and Protestants. Luther formulated the Gospel with five "solas" describing true salvation in Christ: Scripture alone (Sola Scriptura), Grace alone (Sola Gratia), Faith alone (Sola Fide), Christ alone (Solus Christus), to the Glory of God alone (Soli Deo Gloria). Martin Luther's life's work resulted in the greatest revival of that time, deposing many from the authority of the Catholic church and a return to the authority of the Bible and the preaching of the true Gospel of grace.

THOMAS WILCOX (1549-1608): Puritan divine, was a scholar in 1566 at St. John's College, Oxford. Upon leaving Oxford he became a minister of God's Word in Honey Lane, London. In 1572, he was charged under the Act of Uniformity (which forbade anyone from preaching formally in churches without ordination from the Church of England) and sentenced to a year's imprisonment and defrocked from his pastoral post. He preached where he could, and for the greatest part of ten years very frequently at Bovington in Hertfordshire. He was deposed in 1581 and again in 1591 before the church courts where he suffered another term of imprisonment. He encouraged and advised many who were troubled in conscience because of the Act of Uniformity.

RICHARD SIBBES (1577-1635): Born at Tostock, Suffolk, in 1577. His father wanted him to follow his own trade as a wheelwright, but his love for gooks led Sibbes to St John's College, Cambridge in 1595. He was converted around 1602-3 through the ministry of Paul Bayne, the successor of William Perkins in the pulpit of Great St Andrew's Church. After earning his B.D. in 1610, Sibbes was appointed a lecturer at Holy Trinity Church, Cambridge. Later, through the influence of friends, he was chosen to be the preacher at Gray's Inn, London, and he remained there until 1626. In that year he returned to Cambridge as Master of St Catherine's Hall, and later returned to Holy Trinity, this time as its vicar. He was granted a Doctorate in Divinity in 1627, and was thereafter frequently referred to as 'the heavenly Doctor Sibbes'. He continued to exercise his ministry at Gray's Inn, London, and Holy Trinity, Cambridge, until his death on 6 July 1635 at the age of 58.

ARTHUR JACKSON (1593-1666): English clergyman of strong Presbyterian and royalist views. He was imprisoned in 1651 for suspected complicity in the 'Presbyterian Plot' of Christopher Love, and ejected after the Act of Uniformity 1662. The last four years of his life, he devoted himself to exegetical writing on the Bible.

JAMES DURHAM (1622–1658): One of the most highly esteemed of Scotland's 17th-century ministers. Following on a short period of study at St Andrews University he was converted, and thereafter he devoted himself so ardently to theological study that before he was 25 years old 'he had the appearance of an old man' who rarely allowed himself to smile. During the Civil War of the 1640's he became a captain in the Scottish army. In 1650 he was appointed Professor of Divinity in Glasgow University, but before he could take up the post the General Assembly of the Kirk appointed him chaplain to the Stuart royal house, and of course especially to Charles, son of the King who had been executed in 1649. Meanwhile trouble between England and Scotland brought Oliver Cromwell to Scotland where he defeated the Scots at the Battle of Dunbar. Later he was chosen as minister of Glasgow's 'Inner Kirk', and became renowned for his preaching gift. In 1653, his first wife having died in 1648, he married the widow of a noted Glasgow minister, but lived only five years longer, preaching and writing to the end.

JOHN FLAVEL (1627–1691): English Puritan, born at Bromsgrove, studied at Oxford, was a Presbyterian, and settled at Dartmouth. He suffered much under the Act of Uniformity. The repressive legislation which followed 1662, while it broke the evangelical ministry of England in a public sense, scattered Gospel light into new areas and led not infrequently to the use of strange pulpits. We hear of Flavel preaching at midnight in the great hall of a house at South Molton; on another occasion in a forest three miles from Exeter; and – the most colorful site of all (though it could not have been a comfortable one) – at Saltstone Rock, an island in the Salcombe Estuary which is submerged at high tide. But wherever Flavel was forced to wander he was never far from Dartmouth: 'O that there were not a prayerless family in this town!' was one of many petitions he offered for Dartmouth.

MATTHEW HENRY (1662-1714): Gave up his legal studies for theology, and in 1687 became minister of a Presbyterian congregation at Chester, removing in 1712 to Hackney. Two years later (June 22, 1714), he died suddenly while on a journey from Chester to London. Henry's well-known and beloved *Exposition of the Old and New Testaments* (1708-1710) is a commentary of a practical and devotional rather than of a critical kind, covering the entire Bible.

JOHN GILL (1697-1771): English Baptist, Bible scholar, and staunch Calvinist. Gill received the degree of Doctor of Divinity from the University of Aberdeen in 1748. He was a profound scholar and a voluminous author. Pastored the church that would one day be led by Charles Haddon Spurgeon.

JONATHAN EDWARDS (1703-1758): Puritan theologian, pastor, and devout Calvinist and was the most significant American churchman of the 18th century. Said to be one of America's greatest preachers, he was a leading figure in the first Great Awakening.

JOHN WESLEY (1703-1791): Eighteenth century Anglican clergyman and Christian theologian who was an early leader in the Methodist movement.

JOHN NEWTON (1725-1807): Born in London to a Puritan mother who died two weeks before his seventh birthday, and a stern sea-captain father who took him to sea at age 11. After many voyages and a reckless youth of drinking, Newton was impressed into the British navy. Later he was the captain of the Pegasus, a slave ship. He transported over 20,000 slaves from West Africa to Britain. In order to keep the slaves in order he resorted at times to torture and even murder. Yet on March 10, 1748 he had his "day of great awakening," where during a storm that threatened his life for several days, he read Thomas à Kempis' book "Imitation of Christ." Immediately after, he began to read the Bible and was eventually converted. Later in his life, he helped end the slave trade and became a pastor and prolific hymn writer, his most famous of which is "Amazing Grace."

ROBERT HAWKER (1753-1827): Anglican priest in Devon vicar of Charles Church, Plymouth. Called "Star of the West" for his popular preaching, he was known as an evangelical and author. Most known for his "Poor Man's Commentary" on the Bible.

HENRY LAW (1797-1894): Dean of Gloucester in the eighteenth century and an influential figure in the evangelical party of the Church of England.

ROBERT MURRAY M'CHEYNE (1813-1843): Scottish pastor, theologian, poet, and wrote many letters. He was also a man of deep piety and a man of prayer. He studied at the University of Edinburgh where he distinguished himself by his poetical talent. In 1831 he took up the study of theology at the Divinity Hall of the university under Thomas Chalmers. In 1836 he was ordained to the pastorate of St. Peter's Church, Dundee, which he held till his death.

J. HUDSON TAYLOR (1832-1905): British missionary to China and founder of the China Inland Mission.

CHARLES HADDON SPURGEON (1834-1892): English Baptist preacher and author in the Calvinist tradition. He remains highly regarded by Reformed Christians and Baptists, among whom he is still known as the "Prince of Preachers."

HARRY IRONSIDE (1876-1951): Bible teacher, preacher, evangelist, and author in the late 19th century and early 20th century. For eighteen years of ministry (1930-1948), he was pastor of the Moody Memorial Church in Chicago.

NANCY DEMOSS WOLGEMUTH (1958–): Christian radio host and author, host of the radio show, "Revive Our Hearts," heard on nearly 1,000 radio stations. DeMoss is a graduate of the University of Southern California where she earned a degree in piano performance. Since 1980, she has served on the staff of Life Action Ministries.

You may obtain this and many other fine resources made available by
Proclaim Publishers by contacting us:

Web:
proclaimpublishers.com

Email:
contact@proclaimpublishers.com

Postal Mail:
Proclaim Publishers
PO Box 2082
Wenatchee, WA 98807

SOLI DEO GLORIA